you Gotta
Laugh to keep
from Cryin'

Other books by Sam Venable

An Island Unto Itself

A Handful of Thumbs and Two Left Feet

Two or Three Degrees Off Plumb

One Size Fits All and Other Holiday Myths

From Ridgetops to Riverbottoms:
A Celebration of the Outdoor Life in Tennessee

I'd Rather Be Ugly Than Stuppid

Mountain Hands: A Portrait of Southern Appalachia

Rock-Elephant: A Story of Friendship and Fishing

you Gotta Laugh to keep from Cryin'

**A Baby Boomer
Contemplates Life
beyond Fifty**

Sam Venable

Illustrations by
R. Daniel Proctor

THE UNIVERSITY OF TENNESSEE PRESS

Knoxville

Copyright © 2003 by The University of Tennessee Press / Knoxville.
All Rights Reserved. Manufactured in the United States of America.
First Edition.

Most of these essays originally appeared in the *Knoxville News-Sentinel.*
They have been edited for book use and may differ from their original form.
Used with permission.

This book is printed on acid-free paper.

LIBRARY OF CONGRESS CATALOGING-IN-PUBLICATION DATA

Venable, Sam.
You gotta laugh to keep from cryin': a baby boomer contemplates life
beyond fifty/Sam Venable; illustrations by R. Daniel Proctor.
        p. cm.
A collection of the author's columns from the Knoxville News-Sentinel.

ISBN 1-57233-250-6 (pbk.: alk. paper)

1. Aging—Humor. I. Title.

PN6231.A43 V46 2003
814'.54—dc21   2002152534

For my children—son Clay, daughter Megan, and son-in-law Tommy—who take great delight in laughing at the foibles of the old man. Just wait, kids; your time is coming.

Contents

Chapter 3 ~ A Redneck in High Tech

Chapter 4 ~ Less Gravy, More Fiber

Chapter 5 ~ The "Helpful" Hand of Uncle Sam

Chapter 6 ~ No Longer a Slave to Fashion

Chapter 7 ~ A Flat Tire on the Road to Riches

Chapter 8 ~ Misplaced in Modern Society

Chapter 9 ~ Home Is where the Heartburn Is

Talking 'bout My Generation

There are only two times men and women should reveal their age.

The first comes long before they are either "men" or "women." It's when they are known collectively as "children" and, with minor prompting from parents, uncles, aunts, and other relatives, will let everyone in the room know they are "fwee'n-a-haff" years old. The next time this revelation is acceptable occurs during adulthood—but only when the questioner and the questionee are of similar age. At this point, the inquiry is made strictly for detail purposes. As in, "I know we were both born in the spring of '47. Is your birthday in April or May?"

Beyond that, forget it. It's a hopeless, losing cause that has nothing whatsoever to do with vanity. Instead, it's strictly a matter of boring predictability. Upon hearing a person's age, everyone within earshot who is younger will groan and say something stupid, like, "My God! You're older than dirt!" The opposite also holds true. Everyone within earshot who is older will groan and say something equally stupid, like, "My God! You're a mere child!"

There is nothing original about this cycle of conversation. It has been exchanged for millions of years. Archaeologists believe its first utterance occurred when Ig, Og, Org, and Ugh were hanging around the tar pit one morning, and Ig revealed his age. Og wisecracked about dirt (which, truthfully, wasn't far off the mark, as dirt was only nineteen years old at the time). Org came up with the bit about "mere child" (which, again, wasn't too great a stretch because Ig's loincloth bore a striking resemblance to prehistoric Pampers).

Ugh was about to chime in, but a saber-toothed tiger happened along about then and ruined the gaiety by consuming Ig, Og, and Org. Ugh, who, not so coincidentally, was older and wiser than his three buddies, managed to escape during the melee and trudged back to his cave mumbling about how the neighborhood sure has gone to hell since he was a boy.

It's been that way ever since, and it'll be that way until the sun flickers out and Earth turns to ice—and even then, some smart-ass planet in a distant galaxy will probably muse, "Look at that ignorant kid, Earth. He thinks it's cold now. Bah! Why, I remember the time a few million years ago when. . . ."

It just so happens that during the course of human existence, there appeared in North America a generation of people—believed to be *Homo sapiens,* but the jury's still out—known as "Baby Boomers." I am one of them. Indeed, I'm one of the early members of this unique association. Not a charter member, perhaps, but they were still ironing out the details when I signed on.

My father, an infantry major in the United States Army during World War II, marched home in April 1946 and picked up where he'd left off with family life and his teaching-coaching career. Big Sam, a very practical man, didn't believe in fooling around. Not even when he was foolin' around. I arrived May 24, 1947, four weeks overdue. That exercise in procrastination has never been lost on my mother. Even today, she still chuckles that before I left the womb, I was goofing off and not getting down to business.

Between the years of 1946 and 1964, seventy-six million of us were born in the United States. We were without question the most pampered bunch of children this country has ever produced. In the wake of Depression doom and post-war boom, we reaped the best of everything. The best pediatric care. The best schools. The best food. The best economy. The best opportunities.

As we aged, we showed our gratitude by growing shaggy hair, wearing floppy clothes, and engaging in unlimited sex. Not bad work if you can get it.

I tease, of course. The sex wasn't all that unlimited back then. Despite what you might have heard and read about the life and times of those crazy kids during—huh? What's that? You mean abundant whoopee WAS available throughout this period? And nobody told me? Wait a minute! That's not faaaaa-yir!

Yeah, we were whiners. Still are. And the loudest is yet to come as Baby Boomers begin to deal with shrinking Social Security funds and expanding pains where there used to be taut flesh. We have spent a lifetime watching our parents slide into old age, and we're not about to go as peacefully and gracefully as they did. We have been the center of comfort since day one and, by gosh, we intend to be mollycoddled all the way to the grave!

OK, I'll be serious for just a minute. Although some of us were raised by the "board" of education (I speak with great experience in this regard), it wouldn't hurt our entire generation to have been trotted to the woodshed on a regular basis. There was an awful lot we took for granted. "Took" is the operative word here because our folks kept saying, "We want things to be better for you than we had it." We took 'em at their word and claimed everything—jobs, salaries, benefits, houses, recreation—as our birthright. This was not the result of training or perseverance. It was pure luck on our part. By the sheer whims of fate and timing, our generation escaped many of the hardships our parents and grandparents were forced to endure. For Pete's sake, we thought "doing without" meant owning only one car, or maybe a black-and-white TV when *eeeevvverybody else* had color.

But trying to paint all seventy-six million Baby Boomers with the broad brushes of criticism and praise is just as risky as doing the same to any other generation of people. You will find ample amounts of selfishness and generosity in my era. Also hatred and compassion, ignorance and intelligence, foolishness and wisdom, despair and joy. Despite our stereotypic idiosyncrasies, we were, and are, a most diverse group of individuals. Like our mamas used to tell us, "There's good and bad in just about everybody and everything. You'll find whatever you're looking for. It's up to you to decide."

I've spent much of my lifetime looking for humor. I can't help it. It's in my genes. My father and my uncles were natural-born storytellers. Often as not, they'd make themselves the butt of a joke. Thus, I grew up with the wonderful gift of being able to laugh at myself as well as others. And I've been lucky enough to spend most of my newspaper career exploring the lighter side of life.

Baby Boomer humor is as diverse as the millions of us who came of age in the '50s and '60s. Like humor universally, it needs to be taken with a few grains of salt. Just laugh and move on and don't try to analyze too deeply.

I loved reading the late Lewis Grizzard's columns in the *Atlanta Constitution,* for example. Yet I knew the nostalgia he portrayed with words was merely the Southern version of the warm fuzzies Norman Rockwell painted on canvas for Yankees. I've always laughed at the standup routines of Jeff ("You might be a redneck if—") Foxworthy, even though he neither lives in a trailer park nor punches a time clock down at the mill. Dave Barry's riotous columns in the *Miami Herald* leave me green with envy, and David Letterman's New York wit can bring me to my knees; yet I have about as much in common with those big city fellows as Farmer Brown. Then again, Farmer Brown—who checks the Internet daily for wheat futures and operates a computer-driven combine—is likely more cosmopolitan than any of us.

I could go on for twenty chapters about the positive and negative impacts of the Baby Boom generation. About how we changed the sound of music for better or for worse. About our involvement in, or rejection of, the war in Vietnam. About social and cultural changes we helped forge. About our alleged early indifference to material wealth and our insatiable greed that marked the '90s. But I won't. Volumes of books already address these issues, and many more wait to be written. It's easier for me to gloss over a serious discussion of my generation because, hey, I'm one of those shallow Baby Boomers. Whadaya expect?

In the pages that follow, you will find no deep thoughts, no scholarly undertones, no lofty purposes, no high-brow enlightenment. Rather, this is a reflection of the silly work I do on a daily basis. I poke fun at life from the eyes of a Baby Boomer. Most of the time, this fun-poking comes from the male point of view, as I am biologically prohibited from any other perspective.

Back when I was a teenager, you never would have convinced me otherwise, but I've become my parents. I daresay the vast majority of Baby Boomers have—and with any luck, this trend will continue with our children and grandchildren.

My father was surely laughing up there in the heavenly choir loft not long ago when I leaped out of my chair and angrily clicked off *Saturday Night Live*. A band—I use the term loosely—had been playing on the show. Oops, I used a term loosely again. Those sneering punks were not "playing." They were making painfully loud noises on musical instruments, as well as emitting screeching sounds from their mouths, and jumping about as if their ragged britches had been dumped full of fire ants. The audience loved it. So did I—until I realized this wasn't a skit that parodied the antics of unwashed grunges. Quite the contrary. This was a *real* performance by a *real* band.

"There is no way to call that spectacle 'music,'" I thought to myself as I stormed across the room to the television. "It's nothing but high-volume, unintelligible garbage. It's an abomination. It's. . . ." I stopped and began to chuckle. Forty-five years ago, my old man was railing the very same way about Elvis. I'd be willing to bet that forty-five years from now, my own son will be fuming about how music has changed for the worse.

Of course, music is only one tiny facet of my life that has changed. Seems like the entire world has been out of kilter since I got out of college, married, started a family, bought a home, and began equating the word "weed" to dandelions. I, the epitome of cool, have turned into a doddering nerd. I can't keep up with today's technology. I don't like the clothes. *Eeeeevvverybody else* is making tons of money, and I'm still broke. I'm too cheap, not to mention embarrassed, to visit a therapist—so, as the title of this book suggests, the only way I know how to cope is by laughing instead of crying.

And speaking of crying. Did you know the price of a single Viagra pill is up to *thirteen dollars?*

It's the story of my life. Then or now, there's no such thing as free love.

I Am Codger, Hear Me Roar

When I was a kid, I always wondered why old people were so cranky. Now, I'm beginning to understand.

As a rule, older people don't feel as good as they used to. Their knees creak when they go up and down stairs. Their ankles ache when they stand up. Their backs throb every morning when they roll out of bed. They can't see as well. Their hearing's fading. Even worse, they know their clocks are starting to run out of ticks. Unlike those innocent, carefree days of yore, they are now fully aware the term "bulletproof" is no longer valid.

What's more, they find it harder and harder to keep up with changes—technological, societal, and otherwise. "Dadburnit, it was easier to accomplish most chores in the good ol' days, back before all these 'labor-saving' (translation: eighteen extra steps someone else used to do for you) devices came along!" they rail. "People were a lot nicer back then, too. Youngsters today are rude, insensitive jerks, not the kind, caring cherubs, harrumph, from our childhoods!"

But perhaps the chief reason people get crankier as they age is because they're forgetful, and it scares the bejabbers out of them. Every time there's a break in the mental process, the question immediately arises: It is simple absentmindedness or (gulp) Alzheimer's? We've had a lifetime to build up millions of gray cells (discounting what we ruined during heavy drinking in college), but now they don't seem capable of handling the load. A case in point:

One day I read a story in *Modern Maturity,* the magazine published by the American Association of Retired People. It discussed forgetfulness and listed several exercises to stimulate the brain.

"A-ha!" I thought. "This is just the sort of piece I can spoof, now that I'm flirting with forgetfulness myself." So I ripped out the story and stuck it in my satchel and promptly forgot all about it. Every few weeks, the article would surface as I was digging in my satchel for something I'd lost or forgotten or was desperately trying to locate.

"Oh, yes—the AARP piece," I would say to myself—myself and I love to carry on conversations. "I *must* get around to writing about that thing." Meaning, of course, that it would be re-deposited into the satchel and forgotten once more.

Finally, the clipping, frayed and worn, came up for air at the right time. I plucked it out of the satchel and transferred it to my shirt pocket. This is an important step in my column-writing ritual. It meant the article had advanced to the on-deck circle. That night, I took it out of my shirt pocket and placed it on the dresser along with my money clip, change, and other pocket junk. "Tomorrow," I resolved, "I'll sit down at the office with this article and write the column making fun of forgetfulness and be done with it."

The next morning, so help me, I walked out of the house without the article. When I reached the office and realized my mistake—arrrgh!—I called my patient wife. She got the clipping off the dresser and dictated it, word-by-word, over the phone. I meant to thank her but, naturally, forgot all about it.

In any event, the story quoted a memory expert named Allen D. Bragdon. He said the brain was a lazy organ that had to be constantly re-conditioned. Bragdon recommended several mental exercises to pump new life into the ol' bean. Such as naming as many vegetables as possible in thirty seconds, counting backward from one hundred by sevens, and visualizing a route driven regularly, trying to recall how many turns and road signs there are along the way. He also stressed the importance of learning what he called the New Three R's: Record. Recall. Re-create.

I gave his vegetable test a try and realized my brain was a mental couch potato—saaay! potatoes! there's a veggie! Okra came immediately to mind. It was an encouraging start. But instead of continuing with green beans, pinto beans, broccoli, lettuce, cabbage, rice, and carrots, my lazy brain drifted into pleasant thoughts of fried okra, and I was forced to move on before I forgot what I was trying to accomplish in the first place.

I tried counting backward from one hundred by sevens. And stopped just as quickly. Is this guy serious? Writers are not numbers people. We can't count *forward* by sevens, let alone in reverse.

Bragdon's "visual route" exercise came next. It too showed promise. But then I realized that, thanks to the ever-changing face of road construction in and around

Knoxville, I never travel the same route to and from down-town and likely won't until the year 2010. Why bother?

In desperation, I thought about Bragdon's New Three R's. But I ditched 'em immediately for something better. Something more resourceful. Something we codgers-in-training learned long ago when writing English themes during finals exams—the Old Three B's: Baffle. Bumble. Bullshit.

When it gets down to crunch time, there are some things we brilliant Baby Boomers never forget.

Good Hair, Bad Place

A few days ago, my wife grabbed me by the right ear and looked closely. Then she busted out laughing. It is not uncommon for my wife to laugh at my appearance. This usually occurs shortly after I have dressed up in my finest, spiffiest, twenty-year-old fashions. But this time, her riotous mirth had nothing whatsoever to do with my clothes.

"You have officially entered old age," Mary Ann declared. "There is hair growing out of your ear."

I ran to the bathroom mirror—as fast as an old croak can run, you understand—and looked for myself. Sure enough, sprouting vertically out of the crest of my ear, right at the top of the curve, were two hairs, side-by-side. It was as if a teeny-tiny bean plant had taken root.

The instant I saw those hairs, my belt line shot up to my chest, I had an insatiable desire for cafeteria food, the turn signal on my car began flashing permanently, and I swerved into the inside lane of traffic on the interstate at the blinding speed of twenty-seven miles per hour.

I knew this day would come some day. I just didn't expect it would arrive so abruptly and cruelly because none of the other signs of "middle age" have mattered.

I have had gray hair on my head for more than a decade and have long-since grown used to it. Considering the fact that many of the lads I grew up with now comb their hair with a washcloth, I am happy to still own a lush forest of native vegetation.

I have had a pot belly for quite a number of years, too. So? That's why they make that wondrous size known as XL.

Yes, I do have trouble reading newspaper print and telephone numbers. But who cares? All you gotta do is buy the next-strongest reading glasses at the drugstore.

I drink my daily ration of psyllium fiber and gulp my daily dose of cholesterol-lowering medicine. Big deal.

But hair sprouting out of my ears is a giant-sized step toward old age. I am seriously thinking about making preliminary investigations into retirement home options.

What I want to know is: Where does this stuff come from?

Men are supposed to *lose* their hair with advancing age, not *gain* it, for Pete's sake. And certainly not in vibrant tufts that come steel-wooling out of nowhere in places where hair had never grown before.

Why can't it emerge among the jungle in my mustache? Or somewhere out on my forehead, which seems to creep backward every few years? I wouldn't mind having it on my arms or chest or legs. Or even on my back, which already is hairy as an ape.

But the ears? Oh, the shame of it all!

Then again, perhaps I should look upon this as an opportunity instead of a problem. Maybe I should advertise my ears as a follicle farm and grow replacement hair for chrome-domed men. Could be an excellent source of supplementary income in my golden years. If anybody's interested in renting some of this deluxe real estate, give me a call.

And speak up, will ya? Geeze! Why does everybody mumble these days?

Why is there such a big stink these days about high school students who dye their hair blue? When I was in high school, many of the people I came in contact with every day had blue hair. They were called "teachers." ⏤

Now, where'd I put that thought?

Good morning. The subject of our discussion today is—

Hmmm. That's funny. It slipped my mind. Hang on. It'll come to me in just a second. . . .

Oh, yes. Now I remember. I wanted to talk to you about forgetfulness.

I'm very sensitive about this issue right now because I just failed at a simple task I've done hundreds of times. The situation made me realize I'm not as young as I used to be, and maybe my gray cells are starting to fall down on the job.

What I tried to do was change the ribbon on a manual typewriter. Please stop laughing.

Yes, I know I am a relic. I know typewriters are business antiques. I know people use computers to relay electronic messages back and forth. I, myownself, write on a computer, both at home and at the office, nearly every day. But I also have typewriters at each location and peck on them quite often.

The ribbon on my trusty Royal typewriter wore out a few days ago. The poor ol' frayed thing had been punched into a bazillion filaments. I happened to be at an office supply store where they sell parts for antique machinery and picked up a new ribbon. But when I tried to install the hateful thing, I couldn't get it to work.

I dropped it into place, but it wouldn't feed correctly. No matter how many times I jiggled all the right parts—jiggling is one of the fine arts of antique machinery maintenance—the cussed ribbon refused to move back and forth. Finally, in desperation, I turned it upside down.

Click! It worked.

How embarrassing. In thirty-five years of newspapering, I have changed enough typewriter ribbons to be able to perform the task blindfolded, wearing boxing gloves. And now, I can't even tell upside down from rightside up. Is this what advancing age does to a person?

There may be hope on the horizon. Recently, I received some information that might help forgetful fossils like me.

The first is a product called Brain Gum. It is being marketed by an outfit in Beverly Hills, California, called Kevis. According to the company, Brain Gum contains phosphatidyl serine, which "plays an important role in the function of the brain cells and the transmission of thought."

The people at Kevis recommend a stick of Brain Gum after meals. In addition to helping stimulate the noggin, they say, it has a "great minty flavor." Makes sense. If you've got the kind of breath that peels wallpaper at fifteen paces, you'd *want* to be forgetful.

Then there's the Lifetime Reminder Service, being offered by a company in Lancaster, Ohio. For a one-time fee of thirty-nine dollars, these folks will send post cards to remind you of important dates, birthdays, and holidays. There was no mention of reminders about how to install a new typewriter ribbon.

I am not joking about either of these two items. They're the real deal. Honest. But I've got my doubts about their effectiveness for us Baby Boom codgers. How are we gonna chew Brain Gum when we don't have any teeth? And what's the use of getting a post card about an important date when we'll just set the stupid thing down and forget where we put it?

I want my pudding.

The Ultimate Excuse

The next time some kid calls you a "pea brain," don't be offended. Instead, smile from ear to ear and say, "Why, thank you! That's the nicest thing anybody's said to me in years. Matter of fact, the last time someone was this kind to me was back about the time—"

That's all you'll have to say. For two reasons. In the first place, the person you were speaking to will already have walked away, rolling his or her eyes. In the second place, that's all you can think to say because you will have forgotten what you were talking about. This is especially true if you're of the aging male persuasion.

We men can't help it. Our brains are shrinking. We're just skipping merrily along on the road of life with a head full of gray matter when—zap!—there's nothing rolling around inside the ol' noggin but a BB.

Don't take my word for it. Hey, at my perilous age, you never know when downsizing might occur. Maybe it has already. Where was I? Oh, yes, brain shrinkage.

According to a recent study published in the *Archives of Neurology*, men's brains shrink faster than women's through the normal aging process. Up to thirty times faster in some instances. And none of the experts who worked on the study has a clue why it happens this way. Possibly because they are old men themselves.

Whatever the cause happens to be, I hope the scientists never discover it. And I dearly hope they never find a way to reverse the process.

Why? Because this is the most exciting news that ever came down the pike for married men, that's why. We now have a perfect response when the topic of discussion around home turns to chores that went undone, errands that went unrun, and birthdays and anniversaries that slipped by unnoticed.

After more than thirty years of marriage, I have seriously depleted my supply of excuses for missing important dates, times, places, and appointments. But now that this glorious scientific news has been revealed, I'm going to keep a copy of the report in my pocket. And then, whenever my wife asks why I haven't done this or that, I'll just reach into that pocket and whip out the article and say, "Not my fault. It's my normal brain shrinkage. Sorry."

Assuming I can remember where my pocket is.

New Skills for Old Age

I officially crossed the river into Codgerland the other morning, and it happened so quickly, I didn't even have time to shout, "Whippersnappers!" I got the senior citizen discount for breakfast at a fast-food joint —without asking for it.

I didn't even realize the cut-rate transaction had taken place until several minutes later when I was munching my sausage biscuit and sipping my coffee. I casually glanced at the cash register receipt. There it was, big as life, in blue ink—at least I think it was blue; you know how faintly they print things these days—"Senior Coffee."

I don't mind saving money. I'll take my drinks at a discounted price any time, any place. That goes for milk, bellywash, beer, or hooch, as well as coffee. Nor do I mind admitting my age. It's just that I've always been able to do it on my own terms.

No more. Now that some teen-aged clerk can take one glance at me and immediately hit the "senior" button on the cash register, I am marked for life.

In some respects, I'm relieved by this milestone.

Being an official codger means I can stand in a fast-food line and stare at the menu for two minutes without saying a word, and nobody behind me is allowed to grumble out loud. They can grumble under their breath as much as they choose. As an official codger, I can't hear 'em.

I also get to poke along on the highway and don't have to worry about returning The Finger from other motorists. We codgers are too old and slow to even know what The Finger means. Besides, we are too busy concentrating on the empty space in front of our car to relax our death grip on the steering wheel.

I won't have to listen to what other people are saying to me, either. All I have to do is look their way from time to time and say, "Huh?"

But it's not all going to be prunes and cream, by any means. I've got a lot of learning to do. For one thing, I'm going to have to brush up on my potty language. I don't mean cussing. I'm talking about *true* potty talk—the evils of constipation and incontinence, the pros and cons of various brands of laxatives, fiber versus chemical, that sort of thing. Codgers are allowed to launch into a discourse on bowel ailments right in the middle of supper, and nobody is supposed to get offended.

I also need to learn to chew with my gums. I don't wear dentures—not yet, anyway—and thus have not acquired this skill. Perhaps I should stand in front of a mirror for awhile, pursing my lips and moving them up and down, in and out, until I get the hang of it.

I've got to learn the Senior Shuffle, too. You know, that slow, sliding, six-inches-at-a-time movement of shoes across the floor. Right now I travel at far too brisk a pace for someone of my advanced age, so please bear with me as I adapt.

What's more, I need to start cinching my belt at chest level, about where waders would be if I were fly-fishing. This is going to be uncomfortable; I just know it. I am sway-backed as a mule to begin with. That factor, plus my beer gut, creates a natural, sub-navel belt crease I have proudly cultivated for years.

Then again, all of this may be easier than I think. If my belt is cinched good and tight under my chin, it means the seat of my pants is wedged, forcefully, in an exceedingly delicate region somewhat to the south. I have a suspicion the ensuing pain will cause me to slow my pace and purse my lips automatically.

W hatever happened to whitewall tires? I see very few of them on cars these days. Did it finally dawn on drivers that they were paying extra for a frill that added absolutely nothing to the performance and longevity of the product? Or have tastes merely changed? Then again, with today's cars selling for more than the price of a house thirty years ago, motorists may simply be cutting corners wherever they can. ⌣

Kin Anybidy Read, Spel, and Rite Anymoore?

If signs keep getting dumbed-down, I'm going to be the most confused person in America. And, quite possibly, the one with the wettest pants.

(This is further proof I am closing in on geezerdom at blinding speed. As people age, they begin to rant with increasing frequency about how things ain't as good as they used to be and the entire world is going to hell in a hand basket. When you are young and hear some old person sermonize this way, you roll your eyes and think silent thoughts about the benefits of euthanasia. As you grow older, these fulminations begin to make a lot more sense. That is because, by gosh, they're true. And by the way, what's a hand basket? But I digress.)

I have never gotten used to those cussed, newfangled "one-way" traffic signs—even though they have been around for years. You know the ones I'm talking about. Instead of pointing which way *to* go, they point which way *not to* go.

Back in those quaint and innocent days B.C. (Before Craziness), all it took was a quick glance to see if there was one-way traffic on a street. Besides a stampede of truck bumpers rumbling your way, you simply looked at the traffic sign. If it said "One Way," you steered your car in the direction the arrow was pointing and proceeded.

With these new abominations, however, there's a diagonal red line telling you not drive that way. This makes about as much sense as pointing a finger due north when a stranger asks for directions and saying, "Not south."

But the latest dumbed-down signs that irritate me to the point of moisture are those stupid, wordless symbols on the doors of public rest rooms.

Again, I hark back to those wonderful years B.C. (Before Cretins) when the doors simply said "Men" and "Women" or "Gentlemen" and "Ladies." Rhodes scholar that I am, I could even interpret those inane "Buoys" and "Gulls" signs at boat docks and seafood restaurants. But then some genius determined Americans can't read simple English. So they started adding the cut-out image of an alleged man and an alleged woman above the words.

Fine. If the illiterate or non-English speaking need a picture, far be it from me to object. But now—%$#@* it!—there are no words at all! A picture's all you get! And between the so-called "trousers" of the male image and the supposed "dress" of the female, you've got a fifty-fifty chance of making a *baaaaad* decision.

I stopped at a burger joint on the way home from Athens a few days ago. While my "fast" food was being microwaved into lava, I strolled down the hall to recycle my coffee. I swear I stood in front of the doors a good six or seven seconds, trying to figure out which was which. I was hoping someone would exit to give me a hint. But in these days of unisex clothes and hairstyles, even that's not always reliable.

finally, I peeked inside the door that looked more likely and saw a urinal on the wall.

Whew. What a relief. In more ways than one.

Push? Pull? Oh, Forget It

I have made forgetfulness a lifelong mission. Names, dates, appointments, important or otherwise—you name 'em; I've forgotten 'em.

I have shaped my forgetfulness, honed my forgetfulness, and polished my forgetfulness to a brilliant sheen. Many times I look at my reflection in the luster of my forgetfulness and say, "Venable, you numbskull, you can't remember *anything!*" That's as far as the self-scolding gets, of course, because by that time I will have forgotten what I was fussing about and move on to forget something else.

Yet there is one area of forgetfulness that really does irritate me. I'm talking about the routine stuff, the stuff you're never supposed to forget in the first place. Consider:

There is a door on the east side of the lobby of the *News-Sentinel* building. It swings to the east. On the west side of the door is a sign that says "PUSH." On the east side, a sign says "PULL." It doesn't matter what those signs say. They might as well shout, "Attention, everybody! Stop what you're doing and watch! He's about to do it again!" for I will push when I should pull and vice versa. I've done it nearly every day since March 5, 1970, when I started working for this newspaper.

Never fails, despite thousands of attempts. Even if I'm carrying papers in one hand and a cup of coffee in the other, I will stick the papers in my mouth and try to pull when all I have to do is push. Or if I'm on the other side of the door carrying the same items, I will lean against it only to have it refuse to budge. Either way, I spill a lot of coffee.

Consideration II: There was a light panel at our old house that toyed with me throughout the twenty-seven years we lived there. It was mounted on a wall that separated the den from my office. It contained two off-on switches. Every time I started to walk into my office, I hit the switch for the den. If I was going into the den, I'd light up the office. The neighbors learned to track my movements at night by watching signals flash from one room to the other.

Why did I always forget which switch to use? Beats me. Indeed, I am sitting here right now (at the newspaper, rubbing a hand I just jammed on the one-way door), trying to visualize the hateful light panel in my mind, and I still can't tell you which switch was connected to what room. Sure, I could have put labels that said "DEN" and "OFFICE" on top of each switch. But why bother? I won't have paid pay any more attention to them than the "PUSH" and "PULL" signs on the door.

Oh, well. If you're going to be forgetful, at least you should be consistent.

Consistent about what?

After an absence of over twenty years, it is officially cool for teenagers to use the word "cool" again. With certain modifications, of course. As any young person will tell you, you cannot borrow a word from your parents without changing it. That's why the pronunciation today isn't "kool." It's "kuhl." Sounds like they've got a fishbone stuck in their throat. Definitely uncool. ～

Newspapering Is No Longer a Sticky Situation

If there was any doubt I am a card-carrying relic, it was erased a few days ago when I turned the *News-Sentinel* building upside down looking for glue.

There once was a time when every desk in every newspaper in America had a "paste pot" sitting on top of it. It's what bound the entire operation together. Didn't matter if the pot contained rubber cement or old-timey white paste. Everybody used it. Otherwise, you couldn't publish a newspaper.

Reporters and copy editors used glue to bind long-running stories together. Assignment editors slapped it on the back of news clippings and stuck 'em in a date book for future reports. The people in the advertising department went through bucket loads of it to build display ads.

My favorite was rubber cement because it did a lot more than hold stories together. It was the source of boundless entertainment, especially as it began to dry into a semi-soft, gelatinous state.

Long before Nerf balls bounced into the workplace, newspaper people were pelting each other with giant balls of rubber cement. Or else they coated telephone receivers with the stuff and watched newly hired colleagues get an earful when they answered the next ring. Or they painted a disgusting yellow blob on a piece of copy paper, pretended to sneeze into it, and then flung the entire works at some unsuspecting soul. Ah, those were the days when newspapering was professional!

Then along came computers, and glue went out like manual typewriters. (You know the "cut and paste" commands on your computer's tool bar, children? I can remember when those tasks were performed with *real* scissors and *real* glue and *real* hands, not with digitized icons directed by a mousy piece of plastic.)

In any event, I was attempting to put together a flier the other day. It wasn't something that required a computer. All I needed to do was slap a couple of drawings onto a sheet of paper and run the thing through the copying machine.

But first, I needed glue. There was no glue to be found. None. I looked diligently and asked frequently. The youngsters around here looked at me blankly, like I'd asked for a leisure suit. The other old-timers simply shook their heads sadly.

After intense hunting, I located an old sports department paste pot. It was drier than Queen Elizabeth's humor. Someone mentioned the advertising department. It took a minute or two of quizzing, but there, on Bill Osborne's desk, was a sure-nuff jar of rubber cement, still in usable condition. I wanted to weep for joy.

Yes, my little task was successfully completed. And, yes, I returned the bottle to Bill. And, yes, I managed to . . . excuse me, *aaaa-CHUUUU!*

Tee-hee. Still fools 'em.

And you Can wipe That smirk Off your Face, Too!

"Drive a car to school? Bah! When I was your age, we walked barefoot through chestnut burrs, rocks, and snow!"

"I'll tell you what's wrong with America these days! The younger generation, that's what! They've been mollycoddled! Mollycoddling wasn't allowed when I was growing up! Why, I can remember—"

Oops. Excuse me. I didn't realize you were standing there. Why don't you tell somebody when you're sneaking up from behind, huh? Dadburn it, you liked to scared me to death. You never heard of knocking? Anyhow, if you must know, I'm practicing my codgereze. See how this one sounds:

"Taxes! Taxes! Taxes! Those people in Washington must think money just falls off trees! Back in my day, a dollar was worth something! The guv'mit didn't just fritter it away on every willy-nilly program that came along!"

Yeah, this stuff's a little weak, but I'm working on it. I'm relatively new to the codger game. Just give me some time, and I'll be preaching with the best of 'em.

The reason I'm practicing my codgereze is because I just joined the American Association of Retired Persons. Even though I'm a good decade away from retirement, there was a Senior Expo in town the other day, and I took advantage of the event to sign up at the AARP booth.

I can't wait for my membership card to arrive. I'm going to whip it out every time I see the words "AARP discount" listed on a menu or hotel registration form.

This means I get to complain loud and long about my health, too. When my knees hurt, everybody's going to know it. Ditto my back, feet, arms, fingers, toes, joints, stomach, and bowels.

What's more, I get to dress like a geek, mixing plaids, colors, stripes, and fabrics like some crazed cook stirring a pot of empty-the-pantry stew. True, I dress like a geek already. But now that I'm in AARP, I will no longer be the subject of ridicule. Instead, I will be performing my solemn sartorial duty.

I'll also have a lobbying voice in Washington. All us Baby Boomers will. That way, we get to raise hell any time a member of Congress breathes the words "Social Security" and "cuts" in the same sentence.

There is one thing that worries me about AARP membership, though. It's the magazine, *Modern Maturity*. I have never exhibited the slightest trace of maturity and have no intention of starting now.

Frustrated reader Jerry Lyons wants to know who coined the phrase "24/7" to indicate "twenty four hours a day, seven days a week."

"Last week, I even saw something that said '24/7/365,'" he told me. "I don't know why this is so irritating to me, but I would like to know where this trend started."

Beats me, Jerry. Perhaps I should stay on the case 9-5/5/52 until I find out. ~

Bank Cards and ATMs Oughta Just GIT!

As a charter member of GIT (Geezer In Training), I am pleased to make the following announcement: I do not own an automatic teller bank card. Never have. Never intend to, either, if there's any way to avoid it.

I have only used an ATM twice. The first was sometime in 1997, when I was traveling with my brother. He needed cash. I was driving. We pulled into a bank parking lot. The ATM was on my side. Rick gave me his card, told me what code numbers to punch in, and I transacted the deal. The second time, a year or two later, I was with my mother-in-law. She wasn't real sure how to operate the blasted machine, either, but between the two of us we finally got the contraption to cough up two hundred bucks. I assume it came from her account.

Ever since the concept of "automatic banking" hit the local scene, accompanied by direct deposit of checks and withdrawals via ATM, I've been asking my cutting edge friends, "What's the big deal?" And to the person, they tell me, "It's so much more convenient. With direct deposit, you don't have to go to the bank on pay day. You don't have to fool with all that paperwork."

"Then how do you get cash when you need it?" I ask.

"Easy," they respond. "You go to an ATM."

"Doesn't that constitute going to the bank? And don't you get 'paperwork' in the form of a receipt?"

"Well, you do get a receipt," they say, "but you don't have to go inside or anything like that. You don't even have to go to a bank, per se. There are ATMs all over town. You just duck in somewhere and get cash."

"How much does this service cost?"

"A dollar, if it's not your bank. Sometimes two."

"It doesn't cost me anything," I say. "Nor am I shackled with another plastic card to keep track of and another number to remember."

If you can slow the cutting edge people down long enough to let that message sink in, they sometimes will ask for more. That's when I tell them the GIT method of banking. It's a novel concept: I take my real, written-on-paper check and walk it one block from my office to the bank. I make my deposit, keeping out enough cash to tide me over till next time. Simple. Quick. Cardless.

"Yeah, but with direct deposit, you get your money sooner," my cutting edge friends invariably say.

"Depends on how you look at it," I reply. "True, your check goes in a day before mine. At least the first time. After that, there's the exact amount of time between deposits for each of us."

Then I go for the kicker: "What happens if you get short-changed at the ATM? I've been hearing a lot in the news about this problem. It amounts to millions of dollars in errors each year, and it's your word against the bank's. Not to mention the possibility that some crook is watching and copying down your number."

"So?" they shoot back. "Haven't you ever been short-changed at the bank?"

"Maybe once or twice. But at least there's a real, live human being sitting in front of me I can talk to. I don't have to kick a machine or beat it with my fist or fill out any additional documents.

"I am willing to concede two points," I continue. "Automatic banking is probably an asset for people who don't work in a downtown office located within walking distance of a bank. For them, it may be easier to have their check deposited directly. In addition, this service would be handy for people who travel frequently, which I don't. Other than that, automatic banking is a royal pain in the ass that saves time and money for the banking institution, not for the customer."

By this point in the conversation, I can usually tell my cutting edge friends are starting to see the light. Yet they can't admit it. They call me a goof and go merrily on their way, dodging in and out of ATM locations and paying through the nose for the privilege of getting their own money.

That's fine. We members of GIT have no intention of converting the masses. We're like the Marines. All we want is the few, the proud, the intelligent.

How to Look your Age

I nearly lost my dentures the other evening when I opened some junk mail and the following salutation leapt off the page:

"Dear Senior American...."

The letter sits on my desk as I type these words. I, forever-the-teenager, was officially being addressed as a old man. The letter was from an insurance company in Dallas. It was advertising long-term health care.

"Nursing home care costs currently average between $25,000 and $35,000 a year," the letter said, "which quickly exhausts the income and assets of most individuals."

(I reckon so. If anything cost between twenty-five and thirty-five *dollars*, I'm in deep doo-doo because I'm broker than a convict. Especially during hunting season, when there are more important things to buy. Like shotgun shells, decoys, knives, boots.)

I stood there in stunned silence. My mouth went dry. A gaping hole opened in the pit of my stomach. Or maybe it was just gas.

"I ain't no senior nothing!" I finally shouted. "Who do these #@%!-heads think they are?"

> **D**o you not find it ironic that only one generation ago, young people were angry at an old president, while today, old people are angry at a young president? ⌐

Mary Ann walked into the room just then. "I'm going to the grocery store," she announced. "I can't make out your writing on this shopping list. Do you want regular Metamucil or the kind without grit?"

I ignored her.

A bit later our son, Clay, telephoned and asked if I wanted to take a hike in the Great Smoky Mountains National Park during the upcoming Christmas vacation. Of course I did. But then I thought, "Uh-oh. I hope he picks some easy trails. If not, my knees will be ruined for the holidays."

Fortunately, Clay said his time was short and that we could only hit some of the quicker trails. Whew! Sure dodged that one.

About that time, our daughter, Megan, and her husband, Tommy, arrived from Georgia, demanding we go cut a Christmas tree and decorate it right away.

"So soon?" I wailed. "Didn't we just take it down last month?"

But lest you think it's time for the rocking chair, let me tell you what happened exactly five days after that hateful letter arrived. I got carded while buying beer. I promise on a stack of Bibles. I've got a buddy who witnessed the while thing.

I was honored, of course. Indeed, I was delighted. But I had to know—did the clerk *really* think I wasn't twenty-one?

"Lord, no!" he laughed. "The boss makes me do it for everyone. The law's really cracking down."

Big deal. Just the fact that he asked to see my driver's license was flattering enough. At my advancing age, I'll take a compliment whenever and wherever it's offered.

This will Be on the Final

OK, class. The big day is here. The government requires I give you a high school proficiency exam, so please sharpen your pencils and let's get to work. Don't feel intimidated. I'm sure you'll do just fine. You students are the recipients of the most expensive, state-of-the-art educational system in the history of your nation. You'll probably breeze through this quiz in a matter of minutes.

We'll start with a few questions from the geography section:

Draw a map of North America; outline the various countries; trace the Mississippi River system, including the Ohio, the Missouri, the Arkansas, and the Tennessee; indicate a commercial center for meat, grain, lumber, steel, and cotton.

Write an explanatory note on each of the following terms: trade winds, sea and land breezes, monsoon, gulf stream, isothermal lines, and heat belt.

Beg pardon? You say geography has always been a toughie for you? No sweat. Let's move to the penmanship portion and solve a few problems. Such as:

Write the following words, showing clearly the proper slant and connection of the letters: onion, young, right, pigmy, pippin, hurrah, kinked, hundredth.

State clearly the proper position of the forearm and hand, also the body and paper in relation to the desk, to secure legible, rapid writing.

Hmmmmmmm. You're right. The penmanship portion is wicked, too. So let's see what's cooking in composition:

Write a theme of about thirty lines on not more than one of the following subjects: autumn woods, a day in June, a day spent at a friend's, the story of Braddock's defeat, a butterfly's story of its own life.

Tell you what; let's try math. How hard can it be to add, subtract, multiply, and divide? Then we'll go back and finish the others.

A room is thirty-six feet long and twenty-seven feet wide. On the floor is a rug that leaves uncovered a border eighteen inches all around. What will it cost to paint the border two coats at eighteen cents per square yard for each coat? What will the rug cost at two dollars per square yard?

Yipes! This thing is a big-time brain bender! It's un-American to make high school students take an examination this difficult!

You better believe it is. But nearly one century ago, Canadian teenagers were asked these and many other questions *before* they entered high school. I am not pulling your leg. I got these problems from a high school entrance exam published in 1910 by the Ontario Department of Education. The person who sent it to me found it while rummaging through his late mother's papers.

I took the test myownself. Tried to, anyway. And I came away with the realization that the grandfathers of this world were right when they used to thunder, "College? Bah! In my day, an eighth-grade education was all a fellow needed!"

> **P**ity the poor school kids of today. They can't win. If they want extra credit in American history class, they can plunk down eighteen bucks for thirty-minute recordings of the secret tapes Richard Nixon made in the White House. But then if they write a report about the contents or—gasp!—actually bring the filthy things to class, they can be expelled for having X-rated materials in their possession. ∼

Time Flies when you're Changing Contacts

As members of every generation grow older, they undergo the "simply can't believes."

They simply can't believe the music that's popular. They simply can't believe the clothes kids wear. They simply can't believe the prices at grocery stores. They simply can't believe advancements in technology. Indeed, they simply can't believe how everyday life has changed—inevitably for the worse—since back in the Age of True Enlightenment when they were young.

I understand this phenomenon and accept my role in it. I grumble about today's music and fashions with the same contempt my father reserved for Elvis and blue jeans. All that notwithstanding, I simply can't believe that I just threw away another set of contact lenses.

(Yes, I know. This is a "simply can't believe" in and of itself. One generation ago, geezers simply couldn't believe youngsters would stick something foreign into their eyes to improve their vision. These days, geezers like me simply can't believe youngsters will lie down and let a doctor carve on their eyeballs to improve their vision. And the beat goes on.)

I started wearing contacts in college more than thirty-five years ago. In today's parlance, they were "hard" lenses because they were made of rigid plastic. They felt like it, too. No, that's not wholly correct. Hard contacts felt like a roofing shingle. They itched and burned and caused your eyes to blink and water like you'd just been exposed to Mojave Desert winds.

You only got one set of contacts back then. If a lens popped out of your eye, you had to get down on the ground and grope for it. If today's kids will consult their history books and thumb all the way back to the ancient 1960s, they will likely find a photograph of basketball players on their hands and knees, searching for an errant contact lens. No basketball game could be played back then without at least three timeouts for contact lens recovery.

Hardly anybody wears hard contacts anymore. They have been replaced by "soft" lenses so thin and so slick you honest-to-gosh cannot feel them in your eye. What's more, they're disposable. You wear 'em for a set amount of time (my wife changes hers every two weeks; mine last for two months), and then throw 'em away.

That's the part I find so unsettling. I can't help it. Even though I've done it dozens of times, I simply can't believe I'm actually chucking perfectly good contacts into the can.

Oh well. My father, a Gillette Blue Blades man, never could get used to the concept of disposable razors.

Buying That Special Card

I was perusing the goods at a local greeting card shop the other day and saw illustrated proof that we Americans have too much time on our hands and too much money in our pockets. Right there in the display rack, tucked amongst clever and touching sentiments about birthdays, anniversaries, illness, friendship, and sympathy, was a card about menopause.

I'm serious. For $1.85, you can buy a card that extends touchy-feely expressions of hope and cheer to women afflicted with hot flashes, mood swings, and other out-of-sorts aspects of The Change. Boorish oaf that I am, I did not buy one.

Valentines, yes. Mother's Day cards, yes. Birthday cards, Christmas cards, sympathy cards, yes, yes, yes. But menopause? As they say down on the farm, that beats the hens rootin' and the pigs peckin'.

Please understand. I feel sorry for women going through this period of physiological adjustment. It surely can't be a fun time in their lives. But must there be a card to honor it? If so, what's next? A card for sufferers of diarrhea? Circumcision? Zits? Dandruff? Heat rash? Boils? Athlete's foot? Kidney stones?

Maybe the card companies should go full bore and introduce an Ailment of the Month selection featuring soft, swirling colors and a one-size-fits-all text on the order of:

Into every life, a, little pain must come; I want you to know I'm always here to help you through the heartache of (insert medical condition here).

From paper cuts to head lice, sore throat and scabby crust, I'm a faithful, loyal friend that you can always trust.

When did "no problem" officially replace "you're welcome"? Listening to casual conversation anywhere in America these days, you'd swear "you're welcome" has been relegated to the same oratorical dustbin as "hep cat" and "twenty-three skidoo!"

When a waiter refills your tea and you say, "Thanks," he or she will invariably reply, "No problem." If you stop someone on the sidewalk to ask for directions and then express your gratitude for the assistance, you'll hear, "No problem." When a sales clerk in a store brings—Oops! Strike that example. Sales clerks have also gone the way of "you're welcome."

I suppose there's nothing wrong with this new term. Maybe it's further proof my undies wad faster and tighter by the day as I grow older. It's just that "no problem" seems more negative than "you're welcome." If you agree and want to thank me for pointing out this lapse of social grace—hey, no problem. ～

That'll only be the beginning, of course. Next thing you know, the greeting card companies, plus their colleagues in the flower shop business, will start lobbying Congress for a special holiday to commemorate the event.

In the case of menopause, for instance, I figure they'll be shooting for Hot Flash Day sometime around the middle of August. Cold and Flu Day will probably hit around the end of January. Allergy Day anytime during the spring.

There's even the chance these barons of commerce will try to piggyback new observances onto existing holidays. Such as Wallbanger Hangover Day on January 2. Toothache Day on February 15. Backache Tuesday immediately following Labor Day. Food Poisoning Day on July 5. And my personal favorite—Hemorrhoid Day on April 16.

The Kids will Thank Me for This

Dear High School Graduate:

Congratulations on completing your classes. I know you're relieved to be shed of books, tests, rules, and teachers. That's the best news you're going to hear for a long time.

The bad news is, life isn't going to get any easier. Just the opposite, in fact. You won't realize it for several more years, but fun time has officially ended for you and your classmates. You now belong to the league of adults. As a member of long-standing, I'm here to tell you it ain't all it's cracked up to be. So we might as well get right down to business.

Thought about a career yet? If not, listen up. You can trust me. I'm not one of your parents. Thus, I am blessed with wisdom, insight, and a degree of cool neither your mother nor your father is remotely capable of attaining.

The secret to picking a job is to look way down the road—twenty or more years away—and try to predict what's going to be hot then. I know this isn't easy. But in today's (and tomorrow's) ever-changing world, you're gonna have to stay ahead of the curve or be content with minimum wage.

That being the case, let me recommend two possibilities that have "long-term financial security" written all across them: dermatology and orthopedic surgery.

You can thank the fellow members of your generation for these two opportunities, kid. Choose one of these two careers, and by the time you have high schoolers of your own, your classmates from way back in high school will be lining your pockets with mega-dollars.

You know how everybody who's anybody these days has a tattoo? Guess what? A few years from now, those same guys and gals who thought a rosebud or a daisy on their shoulder or ankle was a beautiful form of art will suddenly emerge from their trance and scream, "Aaak! What in heaven's name was I thinking about back then? How can I get rid of this horrid thing?" That's when you, doctor of dermatology, will happily be at their service.

If skin isn't your idea of a good time, no problem. Think bones. Specifically, neck bones.

You know how everybody who's anybody these days has a cellular telephone? And you know how they all talk on their cellular phones when they drive? And you know how they all bend their necks to one side to hold the phone on their shoulder while they steer?

Guess what? A few years from now, all these people will suffer from a painful condition called "cellular phone neck." They will not be able to hold their heads up straight. Every nerve between their skull and shoulders will throb. They will pay anything for relief. And you, doctor of orthopedic surgery, will happily end their misery.

Trust me, kid. Forget what your parents and guidance counselors say about math and computer science. Stick with skin and bones. A few years from now, you'll be able to hire yourself an entire staff of computer geeks to keep track of your dough.

Politically Correct Cities

In an attempt to create a kinder, gentler nation, an animal rights group has asked the citizens of Fishkill, New York, to find a new name for their town. The group PETA recently sent a letter to Fishkill mayor George Carter requesting the change.

"Fish are able to feel pain," said Davey Shepherd of PETA headquarters in Norfolk, Virginia, "and therefore to use them for your enjoyment is wrong."

(Point of order. PETA in this case means People for the Ethical Treatment of Animals. It should not be confused with another group called PETA—People Eating Tasty Animals—that formed a few years ago to combat the animal-rights folks. Personally, I'm thinking about organizing PETA—People Enjoying The Antics. But just as sure as I do, a group of lawyers will form PETA—People Envying The Action—and sue the pants off me. So forget I mentioned it.)

No, the town is not going to drop the name it has had since being settled by the Dutch in the 1600s. As Mayor Carter pointed out, the "kill" portion of the word has nothing to do with ending life. Instead, it's Dutch for "stream."

Good. Put a stop to this idiocy before it goes any farther. Changing the names of cities, towns, communities, and geographical locations across this country to appease the animal extremists would be a major undertaking. If you don't believe it, stroll through a couple of atlases like I did. Right off the bat, these ghastly links to hunting, fishing, and related activities would have to go: Trappers Lake, Colorado; Killbuck, Ohio; Fishtrap, Kentucky; Gunsight, Montana; Gunpowder Falls Creek, Maryland; Winchester, Tennessee; Hunter, Missouri; Hooks, Texas; Knife River, Minnesota; Buckskin, Indiana; Shooting Creek, North Carolina; Shooters Hill, Indiana; Arrow Creek, Montana; and Arrowsmith, Illinois.

Naturally, the exploitation of animal body parts by humans is a travesty. So out with the likes of: Birdseye, Indiana; Rabbit Ears Peak, Colorado; Horseheads, New York; Beaverhead, New Mexico; Hogshead Mountain, Connecticut; Buckeye, West Virginia; Doe Ear Creek, South Dakota; Monkey's Eyebrow, Kentucky; Moosehead, Maine; Owls Head, Maine; and Gnaw Bone, Indiana. Not to mention the Calfkiller River in Virginia.

While PETA's at it, why not eliminate any hint of mayhem and destruction? Such as: Savage, Minnesota; Slaughter, Louisiana; Slaughters, Kentucky; Hanging Rock, West Virginia; Hanging Limb, Tennessee; Lynchburg, Tennessee; and Graves, Georgia. Particularly painful, and certainly in need of redemption, are Scalp Level, Pennsylvania, and Cut Off, (yeee-iiii!) Louisiana.

Indeed, one could go for a total environmental cleansing and get rid ecologically unpleasant locations. Including: Deadwood, South Dakota; Sulphur, Louisiana; Stinking Creek, Tennessee; and Dry Creek, Mississippi.

But if this foolishness does get out of hand and municipal names are changed from sea to sea, there's one that shouldn't be touched. In fact, we oughta make it the nation's capital.

I speak, of course, of Looneyville, West Virginia.

The Excruciating Sounds of "Music"

I reached a personal geezer milestone recently when a car with horrendously loud music blaring from within pulled alongside me, and I was smitten with an overwhelming desire to find a baseball bat and rearrange the headlights.

It occurred as my friend Charles and I were walking along Gay Street in downtown Knoxville. We were on our way to lunch. When we reached the corner, Charles turned to me and said, "Where do you want to go?"

I couldn't answer. In fact, I could barely hear what he was saying. Even though we were standing less than seven feet apart, the only sensation filling my ears was a thunderous, pulsating "THUNKKAA-CHUKKAA-THUNKKAA-CHUKKAA-THUNKKAA-CHUKKAA" emanating from a car that had just pulled up at the light.

"Huh?" I yelled.

"What?" Charles shouted back.

Fortunately the light changed about then, and Charles and I were able to make the transition to more intelligent conversation. The car proceeded down Gay Street, rattling windows and buckling pavement, until it turned into a side street and, thankfully, lowered the noise level in the immediate area by approximately four thousand decibels.

"Punks!" I groused in my best codger growl. "There oughta be a law!"

Come to find out there is. When I returned to my office, I called the Knoxville Police Department and discovered an anti-noise ordinance has been on the books for years. It's a misdemeanor that carries a fifty-dollar fine. Alas, nabbing the culprits isn't that easy, a department spokesman told me. Just as speeders and red light runners walk the straight and narrow when a squad car approaches, the ear-splitters reach for the volume knob during times of potential blue-light crisis. When the danger passes, up goes the noise once more.

I understand this concept. Long before I became a geezer in training, I regularly loosened my earwax with the car radio. Everybody my age did. It was expected of us. But it was a different experience.

M ac Wiseman, the famous old-time country musician, was leaning against a rail fence at the Museum of Appalachia, regaling a group of admirers. A buddy of mine happened to be among the fans. He noticed two teenagers in the background, anxiously pointing in Wiseman's direction, and was both amazed and impressed that today's youth would recognize this heralded performer.

"Turned out they weren't even lookin' at Mac Wiseman at all," he told me later. "They were pointing to a bush growing next to the fence. One of 'em said to the other, 'You reckon that's pot?'"

No, it wasn't. Just a gourd vine. ⌒

For one thing, the music back then contained words instead of that THUNKKAA-CHUKKAA madness. It wouldn't shake the meat off your bones. Most important, we didn't roll down the windows to share our joy with everyone in three adjoining counties. That's what astounds me more than anything else about the four-wheeled stratoblasters kids drive today. Seems to me they'd want to concentrate all that marvelous mayhem inside the car, not dilute it with quite air from outside. But what do I, a doddering old goat, know about modern music?

Just this: There's no way to stop it. Young people are going to crank their car radios up to the max and throw away the knob. The more codgers they can offend, the better they like it. No way conventional fines will ever stop them.

Ah, but there is a way to punish them, an alternative so callous and cruel it might run afoul of international laws on humanity. Just make a video tape of these pimply-faced jerks in action—goofy car, horrible music, blasting speakers, the works—and keep it in a safe-deposit box for forty years. Then, when they have passed through the portals of geezerdom themselves, force them to sit down and watch the tape. Trust me. The embarrassment factor will kill 'em.

Chapter 2

Clean Living Can Be Hazardous to your Health

I remember reading in my six-grade health book about the evils of smoking. It recommended against the practice for children because it might stunt their growth. One of the kids in our class smoked regularly. He stood over six feet tall and shaved every third or fourth day. I have been leery of health warnings ever since.

Naturally, that old book said nothing about smoking among adults, like it was no more serious than bad breath. Nor was there any mention about cancer, heart disease, stroke, or any of the other risks now associated with smoking. Back then, medical science hadn't proven the link between cigarettes and the undertaker. In addition, the tobacco-addicted culture of America was in denial and refused to wean itself.

For the most part, we're still in denial. Despite thirty years of public health warnings, smoking is still considered chic by many young people. If you doubt my words, see what's playing in the movies and then watch the kids on the street. They're stupidly smoking, just like we did. Now that I think about it, many of them are a lot taller than six feet, too.

So what else is new? Americans have a history of talking a better game of health than actually practicing it. We tend to wait until a cardiologist is standing over us, working frantically with wires and gizmos, before we get serious about our bodies. And in all honestly, you can't blame us. Ever since the surgeon general's famous report about the dangers of smoking, we have been bombarded, virtually on a daily basis, about what to eat and not eat, how to exercise and not exercise. About the time some landmark piece of research proves conclusively that one type of food is good for us, another study comes along proving just as conclusively that the very same food will kill us deader than Kelsey's mule. Where are we Baby Boomers supposed to turn?

My advice is to find the right kind of research. In other words, enjoyable, comfortable, non-controversial research. The kind of research that agrees with your particular lifestyle. Then you can keep plodding merrily down the same path, and to hell with all the worrywarts. Let them find their own path.

Just the other day, for instance, I wanted to leap to my pudgy feet and shout, "Yee-haw! It just doesn't get any better than this!" Indeed, that's exactly what I would have done, except I was eating a delicious doughnut at the time and didn't want to go to all the trouble of setting it aside and standing up. Besides, I get so winded when I jump up and holler like that.

What I discovered were some golden nuggets of medical research proving conclusively that the keys to a long and healthy life are, in no particular order, fishing, sex, and alcohol.

First, there was a report in the *Journal of the American Medical Association* about the benefits of eating fish. According to a study led by Dr. Christine Albert, an electro-physiologist at Brigham and Women's Hospital in Boston, even one meal a week of fish can drastically cut the chances of sudden cardiac arrest.

The study had been going on since 1982 and tracked the lives and eating habits of 20,551 subjects. Dr. Albert concluded that those who ate fish at least once a week had a fifty-two percent lower chance of sudden death than those who ate it less than once a month.

As anyone worth his weight in sinkers knows, not all fish are healthy. Especially those from polluted waters. The only way to be sure is to catch them yourself. Thus, for the sake of my health, I made a devout promise to go fishing at least once a week.

As for the matter of sex, I discovered a study conducted by Dr. George Davey Smith, a professor of epidemiology at England's University of Bristol, which was reported in the *British Medical Journal*. Dr. Smith surveyed the sexual habits of nine hundred men, ages forty-five to sixty-nine. I'll quote directly from his findings, and pardon me if I blush: "Those who reported having an orgasm at least twice a week were half as likely to die in the next ten years as those who had orgasms less than once a month."

I am not one to argue with this kind of science. My advice is to hit the sheets immediately and don't let up.

Now for the likker. I read a report by Dr. Mary Jane Ashley, a professor of public health services at the University of Toronto. It said that although red wine had long been touted as beneficial to the heart, "the important protective element is alcohol, which is also found in white wine, beer, and spirits."

Well, yes, now that you mention it, Dr. Ashley did say something about moderation. Her guidelines said men should have no more than two standard drinks a day, a total of no more than fourteen per week. For women, the upper limit was nine a week. Petty details, if you ask me. I always take everything in moderation—including moderation.

Please excuse me now. I must go. I need to gather my fishing gear, round up a bottle of Ol' Stump Blower, wink at the missus, and sigh peacefully to myself, "Is this a wonderful time to be alive or what?"

In downtown Knoxville a few nights ago, I saw two fashionable Gen-Xers, a he and a she, apparently on a date, walking arm-in-arm down the street. Each was puffing a huge, dark cigar. Probably one of those imported jobs that costs what we used to pay for dinner and a movie. And to think we once agonized whether a gentleman should light a lady's Tiparillo. ⌣

One Step Forward, Two Steps Back

Trying to maintain a healthy lifestyle is about to kill me. At this point in my life, I figure there are two choices remaining: Work harder than ever at physical fitness, or say to hell with it and go back to living like I did twenty-five years ago. Either way, I'll probably clock out at about the same time.

Twenty-five years ago, I had a cigarette or a pipe or a chew of tobacco stuck in my mouth nearly every waking hour. Hot dogs, fried eggs, Penrose smoked sausages, and raspberry Twinkies were daily dining rituals. No evening was complete without happy hour, and it usually stretched on for a lot longer than sixty minutes. I could stay up two or three nights a week fishing for bass, or go duck hunting in the snow, and never miss a beat at work the next day.

But in a moment of extreme weakness, I listened to medical experts, and my life ever since has been in a slow, downward tailspin.

The first thing they convinced me to do was quit smoking. Just to show them, I gained lots of weight. Next, I submitted my holy temple for a thorough physical examination, and they found the Big C. As in cholesterol.

Cholesterol is the black plague of our era. It was discovered after medical researchers conquered rickets, beriberi, croup, clap, TB, small-pox, chicken pox, polio, and ingrown toenails and had nothing to do to occupy their spare time. They dreamed up cholesterol and have managed to scare the oatmeal-eating, yogurt-slurping bejesus out of us ever since.

When I was first diagnosed as having a high level of cholesterol—I became known by the hierarchy of Tennessee's medical corps as the Human Crayola—I sought salvation through vigorous exercise. I started walking. I walked two miles every evening with a passion. I walked through thunderstorms, through blizzards, through gloom of night. I walked through packs of barking, biting dogs. I walked through convoys of crazy drivers. And—pass me another platter of those yummy bran muffins, please—it worked. I lost twenty pounds. My waistline shriv-eled. My cholesterol plummeted.

I also developed heel spurs.

Heel spurs, more teams of physicians told me, commonly affect people who walk for exercise. Science is not certain of the process, but it is believed aliens sneak into your bedroom at night and insert large, needle-pointed screws into the bottom of your feet. So when you get up the following morning and start toward the john, you have the dis-tinct impression that a .357 magnum has been fired, point-blank, into your heels.

So I quit walking.

My weight came back. My waistline billowed back. My choles-terol climbed back. My heel spurs, however, enjoyed their new home and voted to stay put.

Undaunted, I followed more medical advice—I sometimes won-der if physicians don't sit around over brandy and cigars and belly laugh about the top ten diagnostic tricks they played on their patients the preceding week—and begin taking anti-cholesterol medicine. Once again, it worked.

My cholesterol dropped immediately. It fell so hard and so quickly, in fact, that my gall bladder didn't have time to get out of the way and got smashed flatter than a roach. More teams of doctors inspected my body and said my gall bladder had OD'ed on all the anti-cholesterol medication I'd been taking. So they carved my guts apart and took it out.

To summarize: What started as a simple change in lifestyle to make me healthier has led to heel spurs and gall bladder surgery, and I don't mind telling you I'm getting pretty damn tired of the process. You got a Marlboro I could bum?

"Some Discomfort"

The latest news for the world of dentistry is so exciting, I am tempted to celebrate by eating two candy bars, drinking a chocolate milkshake, and rinsing my mouth out with maple syrup. The United States Food and Drug Administration has approved the use of lasers to treat cavities.

In case you are not familiar with dental instruments, let me phrase this another way: No more drills and the horrifying *wwwwrreeeeeee!* you hear when you step inside Dr. Molar's death chamber—office, I mean.

An FDA spokeswoman said this breakthrough "has the potential for changing the way dental practice is handled in this country." In more than six hundred studies, lasers proved to be just as effective as drills. The fillings tended to last just as long as before. There were no side effects, either. This is joyous news for the 99.999 percent of humanity—surely there is *someone* out there who doesn't mind getting a filling—who turn into human mush the instant they hear the words "cavity" and "drill" used in the same sentence.

Remember the 1976 movie, *Marathon Man?* Remember when Sir Laurence Olivier began boring into Dustin Hoffman's choppers, trying to make him talk? Remember your toenails growing straight through the ends of your shoes before you and the rest of the audience leaped to your collective feet and yelled at the screen, "Aaaaiiii! Stop it, you Nazi goon! He doesn't know the answer!"? I rest my case.

Ah, but before you drift off into complete oral ecstasy about this laser business, let me throw one small fly into the ointment. Even though researchers said the vast majority of patients who underwent the new treatment needed no local anesthetic, the coast is not *completely* clear. You see, the FDA also noted that a few of the others did report "some discomfort."

Gulp.

As anyone who has even been to a doctor or dentist knows, "some discomfort" is a patently bogus health-care term. What it really means is, "This is gonna hurt so bad, your eyeballs will melt."

I don't know why doctors and dentists persist in using this myth. It is not the least bit descriptive. To the rest of society, "some discomfort" is a slight irritation. It bears no resemblance to raw, unbridled pain. "Some discomfort" means chairs in the waiting room have lumps in them, the most recent magazine in the reading rack was published in 1985, and the temperature in the examination room is three degrees off what you consider ideal.

I'm all for advancements in any kind of dental treatment, and this one looks like it may have the potential for being a blessing. But if the

---

A friend recently described the sad state of American medicine by describing what happens when a mother calls the doctor about her child's fever.

"In 1956, the doc would have said, 'Give her a children's aspirin, and I'll see her at your house at 3:00 this afternoon.' In 1966, the doc would have said, 'Give her a children's aspirin and bring her to my office at 3:00 this afternoon.' In 1976, the doc's nurse would have said, 'Give her some Tylenol, and we'll try to work her into the doctor's schedule sometime this afternoon.' In 1986, the doc's nurse would have said, 'Give her some generic acetaminophen, and if she's still running a fever tomorrow morning, call again.' By 1996, however, the doc's answering service simply says, 'Here's the phone number for Dr. Kervorkian.'" ⌣

switch from drills to lasers merely means trading one form of "some discomfort" for another, I say we all pick up a hoe handle and administer "some discomfort" until there's a change in the language.

Time to Recharge

If you happen to peek into my office some day soon and find me head down on the desk and snoring peacefully, do not accuse me of napping on the job. Quite the contrary. I will be "recharging my system." There is a very important difference.

Napping is what goof-offs do when they think the boss isn't watching. The cartoon character Dagwood Bumstead is an accomplished napper who can nod off to dreamland at the drop of a paperclip. True, he does have a terrible sense of timing. Mr. Dithers always manages to catch him in the act and kicks him squarely in the buns. But Dagwood never quits trying to hone his skills. For more than fifty years, he has set an excellent and enviable example for goldbricking office workers throughout America.

On the other hand, people who "recharge their systems" are not goof-offs. They are highly energized, upwardly mobile business gurus whose bodies are as finely tuned as the engines in their Infinitis. If their boss happens to catch them in the midst of a recharging session, he does not plant a shoe in their butt and scream, "Bumstead, you're fired!" Instead, he whispers, "Sweet dreams," tucks in the corners of their blankey, turns off the light, and tiptoes out.

I am aware of this marked difference because I just got off the telephone with the experts at General Time Corp., in Norcross, Georgia. General Time has unveiled a couple of new, battery powered timepieces that are designed to help frazzled office workers sneak a nap—oops, I mean "recharge their systems"—during the course of their busy daily schedules. There's a desk model, plus a smaller, compact version for traveling.

All of which is a fancy way of saying they are alarm clocks.

They tell time just like a regular alarm clock. They are set just like a regular alarm clock. What's different from a regular alarm clock is a button that can be activated for a "recharging session" of fifteen to ninety minutes without having to adjust anything else on the clock.

These clocks come complete with a cardboard doorknob hanger—like the one you use in a motel to tell the maid you're hung over as hell so please stay away with that noisy vacuum cleaner—that announces, "I'm recharging my system! Please return in fifteen minutes!"

And yes, before you ask, there is a snooze button, just in case your system needs another ninety minutes to recharge. Plus ninety more on top of that.

"Our market research shows these two clocks should be very well received," a General Time spokesman told me. "There's a different attitude in corporate America today. People recognize the health benefits of taking a quick nap in the middle of the day. This is also a lifestyle attitude change, like flexible work schedules and fathers taking maternity leave. Taking a nap will improve the quality of life and work."

Excellent! This is the moment I've waited for my entire career! When it comes to rest and relaxation on the job, I consider myself first class executive material. Whatever name this new sleeping venture goes by, I'm ready *(yawn!)* for maximum exposure.

And tell Mr. Dithers that when I wake up, I expect a generous raise.

Hot Enough for you?

Scientists at the Smithsonian Astrophysical Observatory in Cambridge, Massachusetts, recently took the temperature of gaseous particles blasting off the sun. They pegged it at one hundred and eighty million degrees Fahrenheit, hotter than any temperature ever recorded.

Don't ask me how they reached this conclusion. All I know is, they used physics instead of a thermometer. Thermometers are relatively small, short devices. Even though a rectal thermometer appears to stretch fifty feet from end to end when it comes in contact with your body, this instrument is far too short to take an accurate reading from ninety-three million miles away. Suffice to say it's just plain hot Up Yonder.

But fortunately, we don't have to suffer Down Here any longer. Not since sunscreens were invented. These are among the true wonder products of this era. Properly applied, they will keep you from turning into a strip of bacon as you work or play under the summer sun.

We aging Baby Boomers are well-versed in matters of sunscreens. We swear by sunscreens. We wouldn't go anywhere without our sunscreens—except maybe to the dermatologist for removal of more skin cancers that started in the days of our silly youth when bronze skin was the sign of a "healthy glow."

Alas, there is a down side to sunscreens. By the time you finally make a selection from the dozens of brands and styles on the market today, the sun already will have set. The only thing you have to worry about then is stumbling in the dark while walking back to your car in the parking lot.

Don't take my word for it. Check out the sunscreen sales counter at your friendly local drugstore or supermarket.

First, which brand suits your fancy? To name just a few: Coppertone, Banana Boat, Panama Jack, Tropical Blend, Hawaiian Tropic, and Tropic Isle, plus a generous selection of generics. Next, do you want liquid, lotion, spray, stick, cream, or gel? With aloe vera, vitamin E, coconut oil, cocoa butter, lanolin, or collagen? Scented or fragrance-free?

And that's just for starters. You must also decide between "non-greasy", "oil-free", and "dry oil" formulas, making it seem like these products belong in the automotive section, not skin care. But we don't have time to ponder, for we must now make the truly *big* decision: How much "SPF" or sun protection factor?

SPF ranges from two to fifty. Best I can tell, SPF two is like a thin coating of Pam that will protect you from sunbeams for a good, oh, fourteen minutes—assuming it's a cloudy day. On the other end of the spectrum, SPF fifty provides a virtual body condom capable of deflecting ultraviolet rays, cosmic rays, X-rays, stingrays, and James Earl Rays until the turn of the next century. My suggestion is to pick something in between.

Hang on, sun worshipper. You're still not ready for the checkout aisle. Do you want rub-proof sunscreen? Waterproof? Sweat-proof? Sand-proof? Thanks to a brilliant blend of alchemy and marketing, you can even pick a sunscreen that is "waterproof" and provides "essential moisturizers" at the same time.

Decisions, decisions, decisions. Why not just stay inside, crank the central air down to sixty-eight, and watch some *Andy Griffith Show* reruns? Based on Barney Fife's pearly white skin, I'd say he's a big fan of SPF fifty.

The Ol' Brush-Off

I wandered into the dental care section of a supermarket the other day and very nearly lost my bearings. Between miles of dental floss, untold gallons of toothpaste, and vast plastic forests of toothbrushes, it was all I could do to eventually find my way back to the motor oil section, the video rental section, the hardware section, and other nutritional regions of today's modern food store.

I understand the importance of oral hygiene, and I realize American dental advertising has come a long way since that goober stood behind Colgate's Invisible *("knock-knock")* Protective Shield. But when did tooth stuff become so specialized? I swear the dental aisle of any modern supermarket has to be at least twice the size of the entire meat and bread aisles just a few years ago.

If you are thinking to yourself, "A toothbrush is made up of a handle and some bristles; how complicated can that be?" it is obvious you (1) chew with store-bought choppers or (2) have enough gaps in your smile to let a Peterbilt pass through. Either way, I guarantee you haven't spent much time polishing the pearlies.

First off, there ain't no such thing as a plain handle any more. They come long, short, straight, and bent. There are so many designs, in fact, I'm amazed sales reps don't have them on touch-and-feel display, like a car showroom.

Some of the handles have springs that flex as you scrub. Others are curved in such an arc that brushing with them surely requires a fifteen-minute, aerobic warm-up, lest your hands cramp under the strain of all those contortions. There's one that even offers an "anti-bacterial" handle. Presumably for people who have never heard of the novel concept of washing their hands first.

But handles are a piece of cake compared to the bristles. Is it just my imagination or was civilization more advanced when bristle selection was limited to "hard," "medium," and "soft"? These days, you can get "bi-level" bristles. Or "rippled" bristles. Or "inter-dental" bristles. Or "extender" bristles. Or "pro-care" bristles. Or "multi-clear" bristles. Or "micro-textured" bristles.

Lord help. I'll bet Picasso didn't have this much variety in his paintbrushes.

The scariest toothbrush I saw, though, had "indicator" bristles. They are supposed to change color when the brush is worn out. I don't know how it works. Maybe it's a disappearing ink that fades over time with water contact. Maybe there is a resin inside that reacts with repeated applications of toothpaste. Maybe it has a computer chip that measures wear and tear on the bristles. Or maybe this was the result of a fraternity prank at the University of Toothbrush Design, and manufacturers were crazy enough to fall for it.

Whatever the case, I'm worried. You know what's next, don't you? Yes, of course you do: A toothbrush that dings like the stupid dashboard bell in your car if you fail to buckle your seat belt.

Tell that goober behind the Invisible *("knock-knock")* Protective Shield to scoot over. I want in.

X-Ray Rules

Fortunately, my doctor wanted me to have an X-ray. I say "fortunately" because X-rays make it possible, painlessly, for doctors to see what is ailing their patients. Otherwise, they cut, carve, poke, and gouge, bringing innards, living peacefully in Innardville, to the surface.

I am not overly excited about having my sacred temple bombarded by X-ray cooties, especially after reading that sometimes men wind up singing in a very high voice, if you get my drift, after repeated X-rays—even if the X-rays aren't targeted Down There. I never have understood how an X-ray of, say, your elbow, can wind up causing trouble Down There, but what do I know about medicine?

That risk notwithstanding, I'm always happier to hear a doc say, "We need to take an X-ray," than, "We need a tissue sample," which sounds innocent but is medical parlance for, "Yee-ha! Watch this boy scream!"

In any event, I took the instructions the doc gave me and walked next door to the X-ray department. The folks in X-ray looked at the papers and said, "Hmmm."

I couldn't tell whether this was a "Hmmm," as in, "Ho-hum, a routine piece of cake," or a "Hmmm," as in, "Wow! We haven't done one of these since 1977! Hope this guy can still sing bass when we get through."

But I didn't have a chance to ponder the matter because at that very instant, the woman behind the counter gave me a strange command. She told me to remove my earrings.

"But I don't have any earrings," I replied. I even tugged on my ear lobes. "See?"

"I know," she said. "But I have to tell you that anyway."

Rules. Everywhere, rules. I'm sure we would have discussed it further, but the X-ray people were stoking a fire under their trusty X-rayometer and loading it with black and white film (you'd think somebody would've invented a color model by now), and I had to go.

And as I sat in the chair, being cootized from a variety of angles, I couldn't help but chuckle about the situation. Are so many men wearing earrings these days that X-ray technicians give the command routinely? Or is this yet another instance of cover-your-butt, thanks to the ready availability of medical malpractice lawsuits?

During lunch at my wife's office the other day, one of her colleagues remarked that her father had just undergone heart bypass surgery. He was in and out of the hospital in three days. Someone else chimed in and said she'd taken her cat to the vet for treatment of a seizure. That was two weeks ago, and kitty still had not been released.

Does this say something about the wonders of modern medicine? Or the fact that veterinary science isn't ruled by skinflint HMOs? ～

A little of both, I assume. I know a grandmother who, in her late seventies, underwent a hysterectomy. She was twenty-five-plus years beyond childbearing age. Her youngest child was past forty. That didn't matter. Before the surgeon would cut, she had to fill out an elaborate form acknowledging that the operation would render her physically unable to conceive and deliver any more children. Go figure.

Happily, my X-ray turned out OK. At least I assume it did. The doc has not telephoned and said something like, "You do have your life insurance up to date, don't you?"

Best of all, I still can't sing Frankie Valli's part in *Sherry*.

Arlo's Grand Plan

I ran into my old pal Arlo Dewberry the other day. He looked terrible.

"What's wrong, 'Lo? You got the flu?"

"No," he replied. "Why do you ask?"

"Your face is swollen, for one thing. Your eyes are puffed up and watery."

"Oh, that. It's an allergic reaction," said Arlo. "I just found out I'm allergic to walnuts."

"So you've gotta take allergy shots?"

"Naaa. Just gotta quit eating walnuts. The doc thinks five pounds a day is excessive."

"*Five pounds of walnuts?*" I screamed. "*A day?* That's not excessive; that's ridiculous! It'd take an imbecile to eat that many walnuts— unless he's part squirrel."

"My doctor's sentiments exactly," Arlo sighed.

"How come you did it?"

Arlo glared at me with one of his patented, boy-are-you-a-dope looks.

"Don't you even read the newspaper?" he snapped. "Walnuts are the latest discovery in the fight against heart disease. According to researchers at Loma Linda University in California, a diet high in walnuts is recommended to reduce levels of cholesterol. So I started eating walnuts. Lots of walnuts. And the next thing I know, I'm allergic to the stupid things."

"Seems to me you've been down this road before, Arlo," I said. "Does the term 'oat bran' ring a bell?"

"Aaak!" he yelled. "Don't ever mention that around me! My colon has never recovered completely. Every time I hear those words, I'm almost overtaken by the quicksteps."

"But I thought oat bran was going to lower your cholesterol for good."

"So did I," said Arlo. "I ate it constantly—plain, in bread and cakes, on top of yogurt."

"Ah, yes," I said. "Yogurt. Wasn't that another of your magic cholesterol cures?"

"Yeah," Arlo agreed. "It came along in the nick of time, too. My guts were so ravaged from oat bran, I could hardly swallow. Thankfully, the yogurt helped calm down my plumbing."

"Did your cholesterol level drop?" I inquired.

"Not immediately. These things take time, you know. But before the yogurt had a chance to work, researchers said red wine would do the trick even better. So I started hitting the jug."

"And?"

"I go to an AA chapter meeting every morning."

"Far be it from me to tell you how to live, Arlo, but did it ever dawn on you that all this low-cholesterol food business has made you weird? The walnuts didn't work. The oat bran didn't work. The yogurt didn't work. The red wine didn't work. Neither did the rice bran, the canola oil, the grapefruit, or the pasta. In fact, just the opposite has happened. You're a label-reading, statistic-spewing, digestive-tract maniac who's scared of his own shadow. Get a grip, man! You want to live longer? Then stop and smell the roses!"

"What's that?" Arlo shouted. "Smelling flowers will lower my cholesterol? Yee-ha! Gotta run, pal. I'm buyin' me a greenhouse!"

Poor Arlo, may he rest in peace. He dashed off so fast he never saw the truck coming.

Presto! No More Pounds!

The weight-loss industry has just unsheathed an inexpensive reduction plan that works faster and easier than all the grapefruit diets, bran diets, rice diets, and fat gram diets ever conceived. You can eat and drink anything you want—pastries, french fries, alcohol, milkshakes, red meat, gravy, eggs aplenty, you name it—and exert no more energy than it takes to walk to the mailbox.

All you need is four dollars, an envelope, and a stamp. Six to eight weeks later, there you are: slim, trim, ready to slither into a skimpy bathing suit and frolic on the beach. Assuming, of course, the beach is on a picture postcard.

This startling news comes courtesy of Ultra Slim-Fast, the liquid-diet company that brought you former Los Angeles Dodger manager Tommy Lasorda delivering eloquent TV commercial lines like, "Hey! That's me!" But instead of asking you to drink its product and take off the weight, the company has an even better deal. They'll shed those ugly pounds for you.

I'm reading the Ultra Slim-Fast ad right now. It says all you gotta do is send these folks a picture of your pudgy little self and tell 'em how much you'd ideally like to weigh. They'll feed the photo into a machine, push a few buttons, and spit out a brand-new, computer-generated you. And you thought the camera never lied.

No doubt the guru who developed this plan figured once people see how attractive they look in a computer-enhanced picture, they'll start dieting big-time. But I'm not so sure. If it's that easy to carve off excess baggage, why mess with counting sit-ups and calories at all? Just hand out pictures to your friends and business associates (additional copies are available, the company points out), and let the image speak for itself.

Don't stop with simple portraits, either. Under the Ultra-Slim Fast plan, it's possible to redesign your entire life.

You know that dusty diploma in the attic, the one you earned through correspondence courses from South Juarez Conservatory of Fingernail Hygiene? What you'd really like to have is a Ph.D. from Harvard, isn't it? No problem. Just mail in the ol' sheepskin and a few bucks, and they'll be calling you "Doc."

Same thing with that oil-burner you've been driving since '71. Rush its picture to the Ultra-Slim Fast folks and let 'em take it for a spin through the computer. Presto! You're behind the wheel of a shiny new Mercedes. Mmmm, I can smell the upholstery now.

The more I think about this concept, the more I realize its potential: Your two-pound trout in last year's vacation snapshot is now a world record; young Billy's buck teeth in the school picture grow arrow-straight; the Timex on your wrist as you accept the softball trophy in the company picnic photo transforms into a Rolex.

This is amazing! It's wonderful! It's fabulous! Smile, America! Put on a happy face!

On second thought, don't smile. We'll let the computer take care of it.

Getting to the Heart of the Matter

I had to take a heart stress test the other day. This procedure is all the rage among us Baby Boomers. It is the line of demarcation between Eternal Youth and Feet of Clay.

When you are young and experience pain in your chest, your natural reaction is to think, "Maybe half a bottle of Tabasco in the fish batter wasn't such a good idea, after all." After you step over the line at fifty and the same pain strikes, you think, "I *did* mail that last insurance payment, didn't I?"

Which is why I found myself attached to a network of IV tubes, extension cords, and jumper cables and galloping along on a high-dollar treadmill as nurses, doctors, and technicians scribbled notes while staring at a bank of computers that beeped to the beat.

But if you want to know the truth, the "stress" part of this procedure was a piece of cake. Walking is what I do for relaxation. So do lots of other folks here in the mountains. If the doctors want to put a patient under real stress—of the palpitating, nail-gnawing variety—they oughta have their fancy equipment available for situations when:

It's thirty minutes before kickoff of the Tennessee-Florida football game, and you're gridlocked two miles from the stadium.

Your secretary sticks her head in the office and says, "IRS on line one."

The sky has become inky black, lightning is dancing across the heavens, you're fifteen miles from the nearest boat dock, and when you turn the ignition key, your outboard motor groans "rrr-rrrrr" and bellies up.

There's a slip of pink paper attached to your paycheck.

The grillwork from an eighteen-wheeler takes up your entire rear-view mirror.

Your daughter whines, "But all of the other kids get to pierce their tongues!"

You are treated to a police blue-light special on the interstate and, patting your back pocket for your billfold, suddenly realize it's still where you left it—on the coffee table at home.

Your proctologist lets out a low whistle and says to himself, "I've never seen anything quite this bad before!"

But in the absence of true experiences in angst and sweat, I suppose the treadmill will suffice. The doc says I passed with flying colors. Like one of John Cameron Swayze's Timex wristwatches, my heart took a licking and kept on ticking.

Maybe I'll use an entire bottle of Tabasco in my fish batter next time.

I Hereby Resolve NOT

I've said this before, and I'll say it again: The best way to avoid breaking New Year's resolutions is to resist the urge to make them. Or, if you simply must, make only those you know you can keep.

Read the previous paragraph again, please. I didn't say to make New Year's resolutions you think you can keep, especially if you try extra-special hard. I said to adopt only those rules for personal living that are iron-clad, 100-percent, lead-pipe-cinch sure bets.

How? By resolving NOT.

I have a proud history in this regard, if I do say so myself. Several years ago, I made a solemn oath NOT to attempt weight loss for the next twelve months. You know what happened? I didn't lose a single ounce. It was wonderful.

I experienced no guilt for backsliding. I experienced no anxiety for not making the grade. I experienced no stress for trying too hard. I did have to buy new pants, of course, but considered it a small price to pay for a job well done.

Take my advice. Work up a list of NOT every New Year, and you'll enjoy fifty-two weeks of pure bliss.

For myownself personally, I hereby resolve to absolutely NOT:

Trust politicians of any stripe on matters of ethics, economics, employment, earnestness, equality, elections, excises, exports, or extra-marital affairs.

Walk into a dimly lit tavern and yell, "I can whip any three men in the house!"

Sing in public.

Give up hunting and fishing.

Believe O.J. is innocent.

Eat brussels sprouts.

Attempt to understand the rules of soccer or hockey.

Use an ATM, wear an IUD, or program a VCR.

Buy a beeper or a dog named "Fifi."

Take up snow skiing.

Get a tattoo or have my ears, nose, tongue, nipples, and other body parts pierced. (Mistakes with hammer and nails don't count.)

Ignore juicy gossip, especially of the office variety.

Sit in front of a computer for one second longer than necessary.

Get serious about home repairs

See? Piece of cake. It's simply a matter of seeing your duty and, by golly, doing it.

Where will All That Fat wind up?

With all the fat-free foods on the market these days, I predict that within ten years the average American adult will weigh somewhere in the neighborhood of ninety-eight pounds. And then—you know this is going to happen—humanitarians in Third World countries will start shipping their pesticide-laden surplus food products across the sea to us. Isn't international cooperation grand?

This nationwide slimdown is going to take some getting used to.

For one thing, men's clothing manufacturers will have to retool to accommodate the industry-standard waistline of twenty-eight inches. Retailers will have to adjust their way of thinking, too. "Big men's" shops will cater only to hideous tubbos in the one hundred forty-five-pound category. For women, the term "mumu" will mean anything above size six.

Sounds exciting. But it begs a very important question: Where will all the fat go?

Let's say the average American adult is waddling around with ten pounds of blubber hanging off his or her belly. "Average," you understand. I haven't checked with medical authorities, but that's probably a conservative figure. Nor does it all hang off the belly. But you get my drift.

Collectively, we are talking about hundreds of millions of tons of grease—saturated, unsaturated, polyunsaturated, partially hydrogenated, and otherwise. Or, roughly enough for one summer's worth of fish fries in Tennessee, Alabama, and Georgia. What's going to happen to it once Americans turn into toothpicks?

Mayhaps it could be burned for fuel to fire power plants. Oil and natural gas supplies are finite, and everyone in the energy business is scrambling to find alternatives. So why not use the lard we won't be wearing anymore?

Fuel for cars and trucks is another possibility. In fact, I daresay it's only a matter of time before the wizards of science perfect a Pork O' Pump, attachable directly to the human body, which transfers unused globules straight into the boiler room of your car. It'll be perfect! Easy, convenient, low cost, and no more waiting impatiently at the gasoline pump, whistling and waving at the clerk inside the store to clear the previous sale.

We could use America's surplus fat to fill potholes, too. Just pour the goo in, smooth it down, and enjoy smooth sailing for months—at least during cold weather when the stuff remains in a congealed state. Summertime would be another story, of course. The fat would start melting, and roads and highway across the country would become pocked with craters. This means repair crews would have to turn out en masse. And set up thousands of huge blinking arrows. And arrange bazillions of orange and white barrels from Miami to Seattle. And force three lanes of traffic into one. And snarl all vehicular movement except between the hours of 3 and 5 A.M.

So? What else is new?

Just Stay at Home

Some common superstitious, along with suppositions and propositions, you might want to ponder before leaving for work on a Friday the 13th:

Step on a crack and you'll break your mother's back.

If your mother is already laid up with a broken back, will stepping on a crack make her condition even worse? Or will it hasten her recovery?

Walking beneath a ladder is unlucky.

What if the only way you can avoid walking under a ladder is by stepping on a crack in the sidewalk?

Carrying a rabbit's foot in your pocket or on a key chain will bring good luck.

What does this say about the luck of rabbits who donated to the cause?

Finding a horseshoe is definitely a sign of good luck.

What if you bend over to pick it up and throw your back out of kilter?

Dropping a salt shaker will bring bad luck.

Does it still count if you were using a salt substitute?

Immediately tossing spilled salt over your shoulder will cancel the curse.

So you're sitting in a restaurant in Minnesota, and you drop the salt shaker, and you decide to toss some salt over your shoulder, and you give the shaker a quick heave, and it flies out of your hand and strikes the diner sitting at the table behind you painfully on the back of his head, and the diner turns out to be Governor Jesse "The Body" Ventura. Would it be considered exceedingly lucky if he only body slams you seven times?

Breaking a mirror will bring bad luck.

What if you happen to be in the mirror-repair business and your livelihood depends on careless people?

It is unlucky for the bride or groom to see each other on their wedding day until the actual wedding ceremony begins.

What if they elope? Are they supposed to drive off staring out opposite windows of the car until they find a justice of the peace?

For good luck, a bride should always walk down the aisle with something blue.

Would spiked, blue hair qualify under this category? What about a blue tattoo on her arm?

Throwing rice on the bride and groom as they leave the wedding ceremony will bring them good luck.

Does it matter if it's wild rice? Brown rice? Uncle Ben's rice? Rice Krispies Treat? Rice pudding? Jerry Rice?

Always knock on wood for good luck.

What if the only wood available is bristling with sharp splinters?

If you find a four-leafed clover, pick it immediately, and carry it with you for good luck the rest of the day.

What if you happen to be standing inside a national park when this magical moment arrives, and a ranger sees you pluck the clover and charges you with stealing public property?

The seventh son of a seventh son is blessed with good luck and wondrous powers to heal.

What does being the seventh son of a seventh son say about luck —good, bad, or otherwise—in matters of family planning?

Bad luck always comes in sets of three.

Does this mean you're immediately going to fold if you're holding two kings and draw three aces?

It is the height of bad luck to light three cigarettes off of the same match.

As if lighting one cigarette is supposed to be lucky?

A caller, noting my occasional tirades about smokers who toss mountains of cigarette butts out the window while sitting at traffic lights and stop signs, left this phone message for an appropriate bumper sticker: "Use Your Ash Tray, Elbow!"

Truthfully, his proposed bumper sticker specified a different region of the human anatomy, an orifice to the south that is not commonly discussed in newspapers. It does, however, rhyme with "elbow." ∼

Artful Alibis

I had to take a physical examination a few days ago. It was required for a life insurance policy I'm buying. After I had answered approximately 14,395 questions about my medical history, my parents' medical history, not to mention the medical histories of Venable ancestors back to colonial America, the nurse handed me two bottles. She told me to go into the bathroom and fill them.

I flirted with the idea of running tap water into the bottles and seeing if the urine analyzing computer—the "Whizometer," as it is known in high-brow scientific circles—would blow a mainspring when it tested my specimens. But I thought better of it when I realized urine analyzing computers, even the budget models, probably cost four hundred kajillion dollars apiece, and I didn't think my insurance agent would see the humor if his client caused that kind of damage. So I recycled my breakfast coffee.

I am not worried about what the Whizometer will reveal. It might show traces of a Twinkie or a jelly biscuit. Perhaps even a stray malt beverage. But because my drug intake is limited to prescription medicine, I have no secrets to hide.

You never know, though. Drugs show up in some of the dangdest places these days. That's why it is imperative to have a plausible excuse.

A few years ago, there was a University of Tennessee football player who tested positive for marijuana. He blamed it on second-hand smoke. According to his agent, the kid was "present in a poorly ventilated room where marijuana was being smoked."

Sounds reasonable to me. If I was a talented college football player with the potential to make millions of dollars as a professional, and I was walking down the street, minding my own business, and someone put a gun to the back of my head and forced me into a tiny room with no windows, and people were smoking marijuana, I would certainly be peeved if an exhaust fan had not been installed.

One excuse won't work on all occasions, of course. And with more employers testing their workers for marijuana, cocaine, and other drugs, it is necessary for excuse-makers to stay on the forefront of technology. Such as:

"The guy who sat next to me on the airplane looked like a drug user, and he breathed in my direction a lot."

"The nose spray I got for my sinus infection must have gone bad."

"My roommate occasionally uses drugs, and she's always borrowing my clothes."

"My mother smoked a lot of grass when she was pregnant with me."

"I walked by the police station when they were burning confiscated dope. It was windy."

"I ran out of chewing tobacco, so I just grabbed a handful of leaves I found growing in the forest."

"I must have picked up somebody else's medicine by mistake."

Then again, there's always the old reliable: "I got it off a toilet seat."

But when all else fails, it's best to come clean. In the words of a great American: "Yes, I smoked, but I didn't inhale."

Yikes! Hospitals Are Full of Sick People!

I recently spent a week in the hospital, and I'm here to tell you it's no picnic. In fact, it was a dreadful experience. My pain and suffering were almost unbearable, and my moaning and groaning—well, they all but woke the dead. Thank heavens my wife was along to get me through the worst of it.

But if you want to know the truth, she wasn't that much assistance. Mostly, she just stayed in bed and made faint croaking noises. Like "Can you grab a towel? I think I'm going to throw up." Or, "Can you help me turn over?"

See what I mean? Is it any wonder I was never able to rest?

As you may have guessed by now, I wasn't the one with a designer bracelet around my wrist. It was Mary Ann. After years of putting up with nagging internal ailments, she decided to avail herself to the delights of a hysterectomy.

This operation is somewhat akin to field-dressing a deer. They make a big long cut and take everything out. Except unlike dressing a deer, they put most of it back in. Then they close the incision with a staple gun, insert approximately thirty seven tubes into various orifices, and wheel the patient back into a room where her husband is desperately trying to catch up on his much-deserved sleep.

When Mary Ann returned from the recovery room, she looked like a science fair project. I've never seen that many wires, tubes, and whatchamacallits attached to a human body. It was as if a committee of electricians from around the world, working with spare parts and communicating via conference call, had hot-wired a '47 Ford.

Mary Ann then wowed everybody with her amazing knot-tying tricks.

The woman has no peer in this regard. In one particularly spectacular session, she managed to twist her tubes and wires into three bowlines, four square knots, a clove hitch, two sheet bends, and a pair of side-by-side half-hitches. Doctors and nurses alike marveled at her skills. I desperately wanted to photograph her performance and sell it to publishers of the Boy Scout manual, but I had forgotten to pack my camera.

Another reason I longed for my camera was to snap a picture of airplanes in the hall.

If you've never stayed overnight with a patient in the hospital, you might not be aware of this phenomenon. But trust the voice of experience: At regular intervals between midnight and 5 A.M., planes take off and land in the hallways. Not itty-bitty stuff, either. I'm talking 747s and the Concorde.

You'll be stretched out of your ergonomically designed Recline-O-Rack, snoring peacefully, when a dull roar emanates from around the bend. In a matter of seconds, this sound builds to ten thousand decibels. Then the walls begin to shake as the plane lumbers past your room. Frantic with fear, you leap to your feet, stagger through the matrix of wires leading to the patient's bed, bolt for the door, fling it open, and—

Too late. The plane is gone.

The only thing in sight is a custodian cleaning the carpet with an industrial-sized vacuum. Or a couple of orderlies pushing an empty gurney. Surely they couldn't have made that kind of racket. So you close the door and curl back up on your Recline-O-Rack, and just about the time your eyelids shut—*rrrrRRRRROAR!*—the airliner that just took off swings back through for more passengers.

I dashed for the door at least a dozen times during our stay, and not once was I actually able to see the airplane. If I'd had my camera, a tripod, and a sensor shutter, I could have captured the event on film and proved to Mary Ann that I wasn't exaggerating.

Of course, the airplanes never bothered her. They always showed up just after she had polished off a McMorphine Happy Meal. The slacker, she slept through every excruciating episode.

But all's well that ends well. Mary Ann and I made it safely back home. Her staples came out. The pathology reports came back negative. The only thing she had to do for six weeks was rest while poor li'l pitiful me cooked, cleaned, shopped, and washed clothes.

She had it so good, I'm thinking about signing up for a hysterectomy myself.

Chapter 3

A Redneck in High Tech

This is a rather embarrassing chapter for me. Even though I take pride in being a jeans-wearing, truck-driving, shotgun-shooting, All-American Baby Boomer of the redneck persuasion, I'm essentially help-less in the tinkering-technology department. This short-coming runs against the grain of many members of my generation.

When I was growing up, the standard birthday or Christmas present for a boy was some type of model plane or car. Your typical 1950s Baby Boomer he-geek could tear into one of these projects shortly after breakfast on a

Saturday, and before the morning's cartoon shows were over, he'd have a Ford Roadster glued together, decaled, and painted. Not me. I hated models, also Lincoln Logs, Erector Sets, and anything else that had to be put together. I was much more at home walking in the woods or sitting beside some neighborhood pond, catching three-inch bluegills one cast after another.

Lord knows I tried. I started any number of model cars as a lad, only to say "phooey!" (this was an innocent age before I discovered the blood pressure-lowering qualities of a good #@$% or *&%!) fifteen minutes later, scrape the whole mess into the trash, and go back outside. It got no better later on. Once, in high school, Dennis Gray and I did spend the better part of an Easter vacation tearing the very real engine out of one very real car and rebuilding it into another—but if the truth be known, Dennis did most of the tearing and rebuilding. I did most of the watching. It's a skill I maintain to this day.

Yet if I thought things were intimidating down there in the bowels of a '55 Chevy in the back of some grimy machine shop, little did I realize the *true* panic awaiting me as an adult when computers came barging into my office and home. These days, I feel about as competent as Daniel Boone in the middle of the Afghan war—a helpless relic from another era, road kill on the superhighway. My technology skills can best be summed up in three words—"not a clue."

This may sound odd to the wizards of society, but I even have trouble staying abreast with advancements in telephones. Once when we changed phone systems at the newspaper, I wound up with a deluxe model bristling with more buttons than a shirt factory. Despite an hour-long tutorial given by the phone folks, I always managed to hit the wrong button for call answering, call holding, call waiting, or call forwarding. Until I finally got the hang of the infernal thing, I said "oops!" into the receiver about as often as "hello." Naturally, once I *did* become competent in its use, the company bought an even newer telephone with more widgets. I'm in favor of a return to smoke signals.

But nothing was as bad as the time I came down with a terrible case of the "hi" virus. Not only did I catch this loathsome disease, I spread it to all manner of people, known and unknown. Happened in December 2001, not long before Christmas. This is a time of year when lots of people get sick. The "hi" virus isn't a toss-your-cookies disease of the human variety, of course. What it does is cause your computer to turn inside out. According to the technology people, this particular virus broke out in Europe. It spread to the United States faster than chicken pox through kindergarten.

Shortly after I arrived at work that morning, a warning was broadcast across our intercom. It said a virulent, international virus was on the loose. Everyone was cautioned to be on the lookout. The danger sign was the word "hi" in the message field. Do not open this message, the directive warned; delete it immediately and alert the technocrats.

Like a good little soldier, I called up my e-mail and scanned up and down the list. There were no "hi" messages. So I went about my daily responsibilities—drinking coffee, gabbing on the telephone, reading the newspaper, engaging in bovine scatology with colleagues, selecting my squares on the weekly football board, and other important columnist tasks. After toiling arduously for a couple of hours, I realized it was time for another important columnist task—lunch. I walked down the street and grabbed a sandwich. Brought it back to my desk. Was munching away when I heard my e-mail bell go "ding." Opened up the program and saw, oh, I dunno, maybe four or five new entries. Started casually scrolling through them.

One of them said "hi" in the message field.

If it had reached out and grabbed my collar and yelled, *"Hey, Buzzard Breath! This is that deadly virus you were warned about this morning! It's a computerized rattlesnake! Stay away!"* I would have deleted it immediately. But since (a) hours had passed since the intercom warning and (b) this surely was a holiday message from a friend, the thought of killing it never crossed my mind. I opened it and saw a bit of text about some kind of "cool screen saver." As unimpressed by high-tech gizmos as I am, I want a "cool screen saver" with the same degree of passion I want a boil on my butt. But out of habit, I clicked the attachment.

And that, dear reader, is when my computer projectile-vomited like it had just crawled off the Tilt-A-Whirl. The cussed cursor started blinking madly. So did the menu (or whatever it's called) that holds my e-mail entries. So did the whatchamacallit on the other side of the screen. A bunch of red-lettered thingamabobs—our techies love it when I use correct nomenclature—flowed downward, like spilled blood.

I said, "Oops, I do believe I've made an itsy-bitsy error," or words to that effect. Then I punched the mayday number on my telephone and screamed, "Haaaaaalp!"

Techno Tim Dinwiddie put on his hazmat suit and sprinted into my office. He yanked wires out of sockets, hosed everything down with digitized Lysol, and dispatched me to another part of the newsroom with orders to repeat, "I will not play with viruses" for the next thirty minutes.

After that, the fun *really* began. Not only did "hi" blow the guts out of my computer, it coughed and sneezed on the rest of our system. Within minutes, monitors all over the building were showing up with "hi" messages from yours truly.

Naturally, Techno Tim got back on the intercom and warned everybody not to open these messages. Naturally, nobody paid any attention. Naturally, other computers started puking. Before the stench cleared, nearly fourteen hundred "hi" messages had bounced back to my computer. It is safe to assume the words "Sam Venable" and "hi" are now considered obscene in many foreign lands and languages.

I strolled back into my office as Techno Tim was wrapping up his delousing duties. I apologized profusely for causing so much trouble. He told me to forget it. All in a day's work, he said. That's what they pay him for.

"Yeah," I replied with a devious smile, "and they pay me to write about it."

Which is what I did. Then I resumed my all-important coffee drinking, newspaper reading, bovine scatologying, and football board square selecting. In the columning business, we call this "multitasking."

Know Thyselves

Richard Seed is a Chicago physicist who wants to clone himself. Recently, he announced that he is ready to start the experiment. His wife will serve as carrier of the embryo.

This is new ground on a variety of fronts. In the scientific community, a lot of folks say it can't be done. In the religious community, a lot of folks say it shouldn't be done. And in the political community, a lot of folks say they're waiting to see which direction the wind is blowing before they are forced into making a decision.

When I first heard about Dr. Seed's plan, I thought making duplicate copies of myself would be nifty. I would have a fitness clone who would be in charge of cholesterol watching and calorie counting. Plus a worker clone who would fret about newspaper deadlines. Plus a money clone who would make me rich. Not to mention a goof clone who would be responsible for all my mistakes.

But then I got to thinking about the movie *Multiplicity,* and I realized what a disaster I'd have on my hands.

Multiplicity starred Michael Keaton as a guy who cloned himself three or four times to help with chores around the house. Naturally, it didn't take long for problems to occur, not the least of which was who's going to share the master bedroom with the missus. I can only imagine the crisis this would create around my place. Mary Ann might even

> **O**utdoor writer Bob Hodge consulted our computer's grammar check function and discovered his use of the word "fisherman" is now a "suspect form of gender bias." Which prompted business writer Jerry Dean to ponder if the politically correct word should be "fish-persons." Jerry also wants to know if biblical style should be altered so believers will become "fishers of folk." I'm almost afraid to ask the techies for an opinion on the matter. ∽

want to set up an audition. In any event, the movie made me realize I'm far better off to leave well enough alone.

For example, I am the most absent-minded person in twelve states. I will be tinkering around the house and idly set a hammer or saw aside to tie my shoes, and then spend an hour trying to find the cussed thing. If one Sam Venable can lose a hand tool in the blink of an eye, imagine what sort of mayhem a crew of me will cause.

I tend to be rather messy, too. Not junkyard messy. Just pair-of-socks-here-and-wet-towel-there-and-underwear-over-yonder messy. If there were three or four of me, I'd have to hire a full-time cleaning service just to keep the sofa and bed from being buried under clothes.

If a bunch of my own clones were running around the house, we'd be constantly bickering over who gets the last chicken leg, who stole my blue jeans, who's going to control the channel clicker, and whose turn it is to mow the lawn.

And, Lord have mercy, I don't even want to *think* about the hassles of traveling together. One of me would be behind the steering wheel, swearing up and down that I know where I'm going. One of me would be digging into the glove compartment for my latest (1973) road map. One of me would be shouting to pull over so we can ask directions. One of me would be cussing at the top of my lungs that we just missed the stupid exit. And another of me would be insisting we turn around and go back home because I think I left the coffee pot on.

For the sake of humanity, someone please stop Dr. Seed before he gets to the lab.

Morse Code, R.I.P.

People who were born technically challenged surely cried for joy when they heard the news that Morse code is dead. This momentous event occurred when an agreement, forged by the United Nations, officially ended the use of those damnable dots and dashes for international communication.

As far as I'm concerned, Morse code should have been eliminated forty years ago, when I was trying to decipher it as a Boy Scout. The Scout people didn't listen to me then, nor to other frustrated campers who followed. In fact, it wasn't until 1991 that Boy Scouting and Morse coding went their separate ways. Apparently it takes the United Nations longer than the Boy Scouts to kick a bad habit.

Morse code is named after Samuel F. B. (which stood for Fried Brain) Morse, who was born on April 27, 1791, (a date that will live in infamy) in Charlestown, Massachusetts. A devious boy, Morse used to aggravate his neighbors by walking around town making strange sounds like *dit-dah-dit-dit-dah-dit* instead of using words.

He patented the telegraph machine in 1840. Alas, nothing much came of his invention until nearly a century later, when Hollywood started cranking out B-grade Western movies. That's when Morse's heirs

Jayne Morgan swears this is true. "My home computer took a jolt during a recent thunderstorm," she told me. "A big bolt of lightning hit nearby, and the computer died instantly. I tried everything to get it going again—new surge protector, new plugs, the works. No luck. It was fried. I loaded it into the car and took it to a repair shop. When I went back to pick it up, the technician said there was nothing wrong with my computer. It was working fine. I was completely baffled and asked him why it wouldn't work at home. The guy looked at me, shrugged, and with a straight face, said, 'Sometimes, they just need to be driven around in a car for awhile.'" ~

reaped millions of dollars in royalties every time someone off camera made the sound of *dit-dah-dit-dit-dah-dit* whenever the marshal had to send an urgent message to the fort in Topeka. (Some fans of B-grade Westerns also credit Morse with the invention of the *chee-oooong!* sound of ricocheting bullets frequently heard during gunfights with the bad guys. This is incorrect. As any B-grade Western scholar will tell you, that sound was first uttered on June 27, 1908, by Milbourne "Spud" Flappe, a studio go-fer, when a metal film canister fell from a shelf and ricocheted violently off his head. But I digress.)

On paper, Morse code is not all that difficult. The letter "a," for instance, translates as dot-dash, or the sound *dit-dah.* The letter "b" is dash-dot-dot-dot, or *dah-dit-dit-dit.* "C" is dash-dot-dash-dot, or the sound *dah-dit-dah-dit.* Given enough time and an ample amount of Milk Duds purchased from the camp store, any fool could sit around in his Boy Scout tent and memorize the system.

But actually use the code for transmitting a message? Impossible. At least it was for me. No matter how carefully I listened, I could never make heads or tails out of those noises.

The Boy Scouts had a signaling merit badge back then. At camp, our instructor would tap out a Morse code message, and all of my buddies would immediately scribble the correct answer—"The black horse just swam across the creek"—on a piece of paper.

I would look studious and chew on my pencil until my mouth was full of wood fibers and graphite. Finally, I'd write something on the order of, "Twisted underwear hurts worse when you bend over."

Then, horror of horrors, we would have to send a message back to the signaling merit badge instructor. All the other happy campers would successfully knock out an interesting ditty like, "Poison ivy has three leaves." The most intelligent word the instructor ever received from me was "farstnagle." Naturally, I never did earn a signaling merit badge.

Not that Boy Scouting was a miserable experience. Quite the contrary. Except for that wretched Morse code business, I learned a lot. I still know how to sharpen knives, pitch tents, cook camp meals, and tie square knots. Speaking of which, I wish somebody had jerked a square knot in Samuel F. B. Morse's farstnagle a long time ago.

Realistic Testing

The people who wreck cars for a living—I'm speaking of highway safety engineers, not NASCAR drivers—have designed a new, five-million-dollar dummy to smash, mash, bash, and crash into itty-bitty pieces.

His name is Thor. He is made by Gesac Incorporated of Boonsboro, Maryland. He is created from a framework of light aluminum and steel and filled with one hundred and twenty sensors to measure the injuries a human being might suffer during an automobile accident. He represents the first major change in crash test body design since the 1970s.

I recently read a detailed report about Thor. It included glowing quotes from Mark Haffner, manager of the crash test dummy program for the National Highway Traffic Safety Administration. The way Haffner put it, Thor and his buddies will provide state-of-the-art information for scientists and engineers to analyze in their pursuit of safer cars and trucks.

No doubt this is true. But if these learned people *really* want to simulate crashes, they'll fling Thor into the scrap heap and start over.

The first thing they should do is give him a realistic name. I have covered the police beat for two major Tennessee newspapers. I have written hundreds of stories about wrecks, everything from fender-benders to absolute holocausts. Not once do I recall writing about anyone—driver, passenger, or bystander—named Thor.

Give this dummy some dignity, for goodness sake. Call him Fred. Or Bill. Or Bobby Joe. Or Bubba. Anything but Thor. Bless his digitized heart, he'd absolutely die to know he bashed out his high-tech brains with a blue-blooded name like Thor.

The highway test experts should give him some realistic body dimensions, too. According to the story I read, Thor is "medium" sized. He stands five feet, nine inches tall and weighs one hundred and sixty-eight pounds.

This is not "medium," at least not in matters of good ol' boy girth. A "medium" person of that height, particularly here in the deep-fat-fry South, is going to have a well-rounded pot belly that will push his bulk well beyond the two-hundred pound mark.

"**A** computer is like an indoor toilet," Carl Thomas was telling me. "It is a great convenience when needed, and I'm certainly glad we have one. Two, actually. But it is not a matter for entertainment or social conversations. I am not interested in getting frequent upgrades to the newer versions. As long as it works reliably, I am quite content."

Now there's a fellow who has it all figured out. ⌒

In addition to different body dimensions, I wish they'd also change his clothing. No more clinical jumpsuits. Instead, put him in blue jeans—low-riders, with ample posterior cleavage—along with a stretched T-shirt, a baseball cap, and a pair of smelly tennis shoes.

Finally, it is of utmost importance that the crash test experts quit positioning their dummies, Thor and otherwise, in an upright manner, with both hands firmly gripping the steering wheel. These tests are supposed to be realistic, aren't they? Then let the dummy be distracted.

Have him jabbering to a buddy about the football game. Have him eating french fries and dribbling ketchup all over his shirt. Have him glancing at the mirror to check the cleanliness of his nose. Have him looking back over his shoulder at the skirt that just crossed the street. Have him yakking on a cell phone and fiddling with the radio dial. Have him arguing with his wife, dope-slapping four whining kids in the back seat, and shouting, "No! We are *not* there yet!" for the fifty-seventh time. Have him flipping a bird to the jerk that nearly ran him off the road. Have him running fifteen minutes late for tee time.

If this guy is destined to wreck, at least it should happen accurately.

you Never Know what's in store 'Til you Try to Pay

Computers and I do not get along. We never have. We never will.

Often they lurk in the shadows, hiding, waiting, plotting, biding their time until I drop my cyberguard. Then they pounce on me like a lion, slashing with fang and claw. They love to watch me wilt as digital blood ebbs from my veins. Other times, I'm a computer-disaster magnet. Call me Venable the Virus. I can walk into any office building at random and fry every hard drive within a three-block radius. It's a gift.

But for reasons unknown, gasoline station computers have largely steered clear of my cosmic powers. Very rarely do they go on the fritz when I'm around. Indeed, the last time a gas station computer threw a hissy fit in my presence was March 1988. I filled up my pickup truck at a convenience store near home and walked inside to pay, only to hear the woman behind the counter explain to the assembled masses that her cash box had just locked itself tighter than a corset on Rosie O'Donnell. She could not compute sales. She could not ring up cash. She could not take credit cards. She was dead in her tracks because the high-tech gizmo that powered her cash register had abruptly gone on strike.

It was a classic showdown, technology versus practicality. The only way the woman could do business was scribble the math on a paper bag and make change with candy bars, smokes, soft drinks, and other spur-of-the-moment forms of currency. A lot of Milky Ways were walking out the door.

The second instance, which occurred recently in Rhea County, was just as bizarre. I was going grouse hunting with a buddy. My truck was running on fumes, so we pulled into one of those gas station–grocery store–deli–video rental–bait shop–tanning bed joints.

Once I wrote a column about an out-dated computer my wife and I had purchased secondhand several years earlier. I mentioned that the monitor had an aggravating habit of fading without warning and that I learned to bring it back to life with a well-timed, well-placed dope slap on the side of the box. Immediately I was deluged with calls from readers who had discovered the same trick. Computers are like mules. You gotta get their attention first. ⁓

I punched the "Pay Inside Credit" button on the machine and pumped twenty-four dollars worth. But when I walked into the store with my credit card, the clerk broke some frightening news in flawless East Tennesseeze: "Oh, Lord, honey! This ain't yore fault! I node you punched 'credit' but I done hit 'cash' on this register, and the dadburn thang has tore up! Hit won't let me go back. Jist pay cash if you don't care to."

I couldn't. I didn't have twenty-four dollars in cash. I had maybe eight or nine bucks, tops. Who needs money in the woods?

"Can't you git it from the IBM?" she asked, pointing to the store's ATM.

"No, ma'am," I replied. "I never use 'em. I don't even have a PIN number."

She looked at me like I had just denounced the church and sworn allegiance to Ralph Nader, PETA, and the ACLU.

"Well, you jist hang on," she finally spoke. "I know somebody who can fix this thang."

She picked up the telephone and dialed a fellow worker. No luck. But from the tone of their conversation, I gathered her fellow worker suggested she call the owner. At home.

"Oh, Lord no!" the clerk screamed. "She'll *keeeel* me if I've ruint this machine again!"

A line of other customers had formed by now. They were becoming impatient. Figuring the boss was the lesser of two evils, the clerk dialed a second number and explained the situation. She and the boss-ma'am tried repeatedly to coax the cash register back to life via telephone. They were not successful. Even worse, the line was growing longer. It stretched beyond the minnow tanks and was fast closing in on the sausage biscuit table.

A good ten minutes had elapsed by this time. My buddy came in to see what was going on. Fortunately, he was flush with cash. We plunked a twenty and four ones on the counter and hoofed, leaving the poor clerk and her ever-growing army of customers to fend for themselves.

I hope she had enough Milky Ways to cover all the other transactions.

A Computerized Saint

Move over St. Francis, St. Christopher, St. Jude, and all the other patron saints of the world. You're about to get a new neighbor. According to press reports out of the Vatican, Pope John Paul II has taken "under active consideration" a proposal to name St. Isidore of Seville the patron saint of the computer and the Internet.

Hallelujah, brothers and sisters! If there's ever a group of people who need protection and intercession from above, it's the multiplied millions of us who tickle a keyboard for work or for pleasure.

(Point of order: The last two words of the previous paragraph constitute blasphemy. As far as I'm concerned, anyone who would log on to a computer for the sheer joy of it needs medical assistance. Yes, I know there are legions who routinely recreate by tinkering with their computers. At the same time, I know there are legions who routinely eat snails, practice nudism, and play the piccolo. I'm not one of them. I accept the computer as a revolutionary labor-saving device, a marvelous tool with

---

In conversation with Lynn Tittsworth the other day, he mentioned he had spilled a cup of Coca-Cola on the keyboard of his home computer. "I had no idea so little Coke could go such a long way," he said. "I wiped and wiped and wiped and thought I had cleaned it up. But then the keys started sticking, and I started getting all kinds of strange messages on the screen. I wound up having to buy a new keyboard."

Lynn said his drink of choice was old-fashioned Coke. He wondered aloud if he'd been drinking Diet Coke, with no sugar, maybe the damage wouldn't have been so severe. On the contrary, I told him, count your blessings. Diet Coke would have shrunk the keyboard, monitor, and software so small, he'd have to buy a complete new machine. ⌒

the potential to accomplish a myriad of tasks in the blink of an eye. But it was and is and ever more shall be just that—a tool. I don't play with my screwdrivers and hammers for fun, and I dang-sure wouldn't sit down in front of a computer screen unless there was work to be done. Just so you understand how I really feel about the matter.)

Support for St. Isidore, who lived in the seventh century, comes from the Spanish Catholic bishops. They say his development of a twenty-volume encyclopedia, *The Etymologies,* was one of the world's first databases. That makes him eminently qualified to watch out for the interests of anyone who walks through the valley of the shadow of digitized death.

Of course a lot has changed since the seventh century. I hope St. Isidore is up to the many challenges that await him.

When he was slaving over *The Etymologies* and his system shut down, all he had to do was stroll into the courtyard, pluck a wing feather from some hapless goose, sharpen the tip, make a slit to carry the ink, and then he was back in business. It's not that simple today.

Still, I like the idea of a patron saint. As anybody who ever stayed on hold for technical services can attest, we need someone to call upon when our computer crashes. Or the system locks up. Or we lose a file. Or we take a wrong turn and, two hundred mouse clicks later, find ourselves hopelessly lost, adrift in cyberspace with the oxygen running low.

I don't scare easily. But when one of those despicable messages that says, "This machine has performed an illegal function and will shut down," appears on my screen, I am frightened nearly to the point of moisture. This is one of the most helpless feelings imaginable for those of us who are computer-challenged. Suddenly we are paralyzed, perhaps through no fault of our own, and life as we know it is about to end.

One of those demons who delights in delivering that evil message lives inside my computer. I am convinced of it.

He waits until I have crafted the most flowing, poetic, and informative gift of literature in the history of modern civilization. And then, before I can hit the "save" button, he throws the switch. My Pulitzer Prize–winning effort goes swirling down the drain, leaving me with nothing but grimy residue. Much like the drivel you are reading right now.

Are you as apprehensive as I about those self-scanning check-out lines at the grocery store? It's bad enough when you're going through a conventional checkout and the bar code refuses to cooperate and the clerk keeps trying it over and over and over and finally gets on the phone and calls back to the meat department to get the correct code to punch in. What's going to happen to those of us who are cyber-impaired when the new process messes up? I say we go back to the barter system. ~

I hope St. Isidore has thick skin, too. Because he's sure going to need it on this job. The air can turn deep blue when someone's computer screen abruptly goes blank. I speak both of personal and observed experience in this regard, and I'm here to tell you it ain't pretty. Maybe it wouldn't hurt to also have a patron saint of cussin'.

An Indication of Trouble

One of the most ingenious developments of our time is the built-in tester on the side of household batteries. Supposedly, this means no more surprises in flashlights, radios, cameras, games, toys, and the jillions of other devices powered by AAAs, AAs, Cs, Ds, and others of their ilk.

Hmmm. Then again, maybe the cure is worse than the ailment. In the old days, we flicked a flashlight on to see if the batteries were charged. It was an alpha-or-omega affair. If the thing worked, we pronounced the batteries healthy and didn't replace them. If it didn't work, we threw out the old batteries and bought replacements. Under this new system, however, we have to wonder if, say, 50 percent is good enough to keep, as opposed to 27 percent or 78 percent. Why does life have to be so complicated?

Nonetheless, it's a step in the right direction. I just hope researchers come up with other items that have built-in gauges to help us shop more wisely. Food is a good place to start.

Right now, most food products come complete with a nutrition label listing fat content, calories, essential vitamins and minerals, and other numbers which allegedly help consumers make healthy choices. Big deal. This information, however factual, has lost its impact. We shoppers have become numb to charts and lists. We need something with flash and color.

Something like a Fat-O-Gauge.

You pick up a box of chocolate chip cookies and squeeze a button on the side. Immediately, it shows the percentage increase in your waistline if you nibble the contents. On more advanced models, two images of your body might appear on the back—one before eating the cookies, one after. Now that's effective consumer information!

The same concept could be incorporated into clothing. Presently, there is no device to prevent the sale of hideous garments to irresponsible adults. We walk into a store and try on a loud, obnoxious sport coat. It looks dashing. We buy it. But when we get home and model it for the rest of the family, disaster strikes. Our spouse faints, and the children run out the door screaming, "Aaaaaiiiiee! The other kids will laugh at me for months!"

Not with the Nerd-O-Gauge.

Just slip the coat on, press the button, and it shows your GQ (Geek Quotient) in big, bold numbers. Press the button again, and it lets you see yourself in the coat through the eyes of everyone else.

This is going to take some fine-tuning, of course, something to tone down the harsh realities. No need to rush into these projects *too* quickly—otherwise, the American food and clothing industries could dry up overnight.

The Corruption of Cotton

On first reading, it looked like the answer to every Southern redneck's prayers: A cotton plant that grows polyester.

In what borders on vegetative alchemy, researchers at a business called Agracetus in Middleton, Wisconsin, isolated bacteria that produce a polyester-like substance. They took the bacteria's DNA and forced it into the stems of cotton seedlings. When the plants matured, they produced a fiber with the potential to be warmer and more wrinkle-resistant than regular cotton.

This procedure is still in the experimental stage, of course. Scientists say it'll take three to five years, minimum, to refine the process to the point that it can be marketed. Nonetheless, they believe this could ultimately revolutionize the agricultural and textiles industries.

Perhaps. But it scares the livin' hell out of me.

I'm all for plant research. Without dedicated plant scientists like George Washington Carver, who spent years studying the lowly peanut, we'd still be eating plain M&M's. But this cotton-polyester business has the potential for out-and-out disaster.

Oh, it'll start innocently enough. Always does. Farmer Brown drops a few seeds into the ground and out comes a cotton-poly plant yielding a miracle fiber that keeps consumers warm, holds color, won't shrink or fade, and doesn't need ironing. Happiness and prosperity will reign from the heartland of America's farm country to the blue-lighted aisles of Kmart.

But then, sure as God and Archer Daniels Midland made little green apples, the evil polyester gene will begin to mutate and take dominion over the cotton gene. The curse will grow like a cancer. Its tentacles will spread further than kudzu, gripping the land in a chokehold like the Mongolian Stomper used to perform every Saturday night on live wrestling.

Thus, when Farmer Brown fires up his combine for the harvest, he'll discover his plants heavy laden not with a high-tech friendly fiber but with (insert blood-curdling shriek here) double-knits.

Overheard on an elevator: "We named our home computer 'Einstein' but our youngest child mispronounced it, 'Frankenstein.' We started to correct him, but then we realized his was a much more accurate description." ～

Yes, itty-bitty leisure suits and bell-bottom pants—lime green, no doubt, with white top-stitching—will dangle from every stem. They will sneer like John Travolta, taunting and mocking whatever fashion progress this country has made in the past twenty years. No plant or acre will be spared. The next thing you know, men will start wearing flare-collared shirts, gold necklaces, and stack-heeled shoes—and they'll be dancing to disco music.

Is this the future you want for your children, America? If not, I urge you to grab a can of week killer and spray with reckless abandon.

Flush with Success

The *Knoxville News-Sentinel* recently undertook a bold and historic move to position itself at the outer limits of technology. It installed automatic flushers in the men's restroom. I haven't spoken to any *News-Sentinel* women about this situation, but since the automatic flushers are limited to urinals, I can only assume this a male-only development. If the women want equal treatment, by golly, let them stand up and be counted. Even if it makes an awful mess.

I realize automatic urinal flushers are not new in regular society, but newspapers loathe change of any kind. Thus, you can understand why several members of our staff are spending more time than normal in the john, getting acquainted. With the new flushers, I mean.

One of our editorial staffers—I am not making this up but won't mention his name because the big cheeses might frown on his research, however noble its intentions—has taken it upon himself to fool the auto-flusher. He told me he stood in front of a urinal, without making a deposit, and then stepped away. No flush.

Then he tried spitting into the porcelain bowl. The flusher immediately activated, leaving: (1) him delighted to have hoodwinked a piece of techno-plumbing and (2) me in awe that a human being can generate such tremendous volume in a single blast of spit.

Alas, when he tried the same test a few days later, the opposite results were noted. Clearly, more experimentation is needed.

After operating the *News-Sentinel*'s old-timey flush urinals for over thirty years, I must admit this abrupt change has taken some getting used to. Old habits are not shed easily. I still find myself reaching for the handle on occasion.

Still, the strangest adjustment involves the gadgets themselves. You see, they have a tiny sensor panel on the front. It's a small, dark piece of plastic that looks exactly like a tiny television screen.

I was, uh, "standing around" in the restroom one day not long ago when another staffer walked up and stood beside me. (Our south wall facilities can accommodate three standers at a time, a condition loudly and painfully referred to as "three of a kind" when a fourth stander enters the room in urgent need of relief.) The guy looked suspiciously at the flusher for a few seconds, then cast his eyes in my direction.

"How you reckon that thing works?" he asked.

"You haven't heard?" I replied. "They sent around a memo on it the other day. All the flushers have a built-in camera. They take pictures of everybody who uses them. Back in the personnel department, they're building a photo file on every man in the house."

Not that I'm making a scientific survey or anything, but I have noticed that ever since, when I happen to be in the restroom and that guy walks in, he always goes into a stall. And shuts the door *very* quickly.

Cars of the Future

A cornpone story made the rounds years ago when automatic transmissions starting showing up on cars. Seems Ol' Zeb bought one of the fancy machines and was real proud of it until the day it blew to pieces during an impromptu drag race.

"Don't rightly know whot went wrong with the ding-blasted thang," he told a police officer in the aftermath of the disaster. "Ah was a'toolin' along when this other feller pulled upside me and gunned his engine. So I gunned mine, and away we went. He was a'pullin' ahead, so I looked down thar on the colyum and seen *L* on the shifter. I figured hit stood for 'leap,' and brother, she shore did leap when I pulled 'er down. Then I seen *R* and figured hit stood for 'race.' That's the last thang I remember."

That story comes to mind every time I hear about research and development of super-smart cars.

These cars are the wave of the future, automotive engineers would have us believe. They will contain all manner of computers to perform functions ranging from routine engine maintenance to map reading. They will be equipped with infrared devices to warn the driver of other vehicles, fore and aft. In short, they will essentially drive themselves.

That's what's so scary. It's just a matter of time before humans are ciphered right out of the equation. If I can't program a VCR in the comfort of my own den, what am I going to do behind the wheel of a hundred-thousand-dollar rolling computer? Wind up in an awful argument, that's what.

"Don't touch that dial!" the car will bark at me when I start to adjust the air conditioner. "It's cool enough in here already. Any change will upset my delicate system."

"Tough for you and your system," I'll tell it. (I assume I will already be used to talking to my car, although the very notion of it makes me tremble in fear.) "I happen to be the boss here, pal, and I'm hotter than a depot stove. So bring it down a few notches."

"You do that, and I won't show you the way to Aunt Ruthie's house."

"How'd you know I was going to Aunt Ruthie's?"

"Because you have on your brown tie, the one she gave you for Christmas two years ago. A statistical analysis of your attire reveals that 97 percent of the time you wear that tie, you are going to visit Aunt Ruthie."

"OK, so I'm going to Aunt Ruthie's," I will concede. "But I don't need you to tell me how to get there. I was driving long before you were a twinkle in some engineer's eye."

"And you were always making wrong turns and getting lost," the smart-aleck car will answer. "My internal map, on the other hand, never errs. Oh, and by the way, forget about turning down Maple Street. It's blocked. The state is doing repair work and faxed me the information last night. . . ."

See what I mean? My car and I will start bickering, and the next thing you know I'll wind up pulling to the curb and beating its digitized brains out with a two-by-four. I just hope Ol' Zeb's around to lend me a hand.

Photos without Fear

I just underwent what used to be one of the most terrifying experiences known to humankind. But, happily, I was surprised to discover things have changed for the better.

This wasn't oral surgery. Or radiation treatment. Or an income tax audit. It was a lot scarier. Yes, even worse than shopping for new clothes. I had to have new photographs made for the church directory and my driver's license.

You remember the drill from the old days, don't you? Of course you do, bless your quaking little heart. You'd sit down in a chair and the camera operator would take dead aim at your innocent face with a device known, technically, as a "lens." Then the operator would make a stupid remark like, "Say cheese!" and you, staring directly into the lens, would flash your pearly whites while the shutter clicked a single time.

Ah-hah! But this was not a *real* camera lens, was it? Noooo! It was an evil instrument of contortion and fabrication. Instead of reproducing an exact image of the beauty and grandeur positioned on the studio chair, the lens played cruel tricks.

It lowered your eyelids to half mast. It took your sexiest Robert Redford smile and turned it into an Alfred E. Neuman grin. It parted your lips and channeled a glistening stream of drool to the side of your mouth. It pulled your ears like taffy. It doubled your chin. It billowed your cheeks like a sail. It reddened your nose. It tussled your slicked-down hair into a Phyllis Diller frizz. It scribbled on your teeth with a yellow crayon. It yanked the designer tie from around your neck and replaced it with a polyester tablecloth. And it drizzled your shirt with ketchup.

Not immediately, of course, at least in the case of church directory photographs. You had to wait several weeks for the proofs to arrive, at which time you leafed through the selection and wondered how the camera company managed to swap your Cleaver family photos with the Munsters.

No more. The wicked witch of the lens is dead, and I have new driver's license and church directory photos to prove it.

I don't understand the technology involved in this miraculous process. It's far beyond my comprehension. All I know is, they use some sort of digitalized camera which produces a finished product in seconds. This doesn't give the evil lens time to cook up devious tricks. If the image doesn't quite meet your standards of beauty and grandeur, they'll shoot another one and deliver it on the spot.

But then again: In a few years, when the time rolls back around for yet another driver's license and church directory photo, I think I'll purposely shut my eyes and drool. I'm such a sucker for nostalgia.

Lost in the Translation

Anybody who ever traveled to a foreign land where mysterious languages are spoken—Michigan or Florida, for instance—is familiar with the problem of inaccurate communication. Just one little misspoken word, inflection, or nuance can leave everyone in the conversation scratching their collective heads and wondering, "What's that guy talking about?"

A few years ago, I happened to be standing near the checkout of a rural grocery store and overheard a man trying to spell a word for the woman behind the counter. She was writing it down, one letter at a time. He came to the letter *q*.

The man, as we are wont to say, wasn't from around here. Thus, he didn't pronounce the letter as "kwew." He said something like "coo."

She stared at him blankly.

"Coo! Coo!" he repeated, like a caged pigeon. "The letter coo!"

The woman behind the counter shook her head in frustration.

"Coo?" she said. "I ain't never heerd of no coo, and I don't know how to make one of 'em."

It also happens at higher levels. Back in the '70s, I remember reading a hilarious news magazine passage about an attempted conversation between two presidents—Jimmy Carter of Georgia and Anwar Sadat of Egypt. Sadat used the word "impotent," but he put the emphasis on the middle syllable.

"Yo' so right," Carter drawled with a broad smile. "I think it's very impo'tant, too!"

Poor Sadat. He probably went to his grave trying to decipher that one.

Too bad the Kwikpoint system wasn't available. Kwikpoint is one of those simple, cheap products that comes along every now and then that makes you slap your noggin and say, "Why didn't I think of this?" It's an eight-panel, laminated card for travelers. It folds up like a road map. It fits easily into a coat pocket. It can be used in a variety of countries and languages because it is based on sketches instead of words.

A Virginia man named Alan Stillman invented this nifty device after traveling fifteen thousand miles on a twenty eight-country bicycle trip. On that journey, he lugged five pounds of dictionaries and translation guides. One day it dawned on him that instead of learning the local pronunciation for common words like, say, "restroom," all he needed was a sketch of a toilet. And Kwikpoint was born.

I am holding a copy of Kwikpoint as we speak. It is indeed ingenious. I wish I'd had something like it when I was Japan a few years ago, and the only thing that looked familiar in any city was McDonald's golden arches. I ate a lot of Big Macs, as I recall.

But even though this handy item might help travelers navigate through Europe, Asia, South America, and other foreign ports, I'm not so certain how it would work in the rural southern United States. I'd love to be standing back in the shadows when someone "not from around here" walks up to a couple of locals and uses the Kwikpoint to inquire about a hotel room (picture of a bed), with smoking (pack of cigarettes) and pets (dog and cat) allowed, plus room service (waiter with tray) while he waits for his vehicle to be repaired (car on jack).

Both good ol' boys study the pictures intently.

"Whut the hale he's sayin', Vern?" one finally asks another.

"I ain't real shore, Corneal, but I think I got it figgured out. I think he's been a'stealin tars off cars, or else runnin' unstamped cig'rettes in from North Car'lina, and needs a place to lay low for awhile."

"Ain't the way I read it," says the first. "He's ferrin, can't you see? He's wantin' to know whar he can get somebody to cook him up one of those ferrin meals. You know—with dogs and cats in it! I say we whup 'im."

A picture may be worth a thousand words, but sometimes the only thing it'll buy is trouble.

The End of Men

The next time scientists gather to consider new entries for the Endangered Species List, they might want to include men.

This is not a political opinion. It has nothing to do with the Angry White Male syndrome. I'm not talking about the alleged endangered status of men in the work force. What I am talking about is the distinct possibility that all of us who belong to the Y-chromosome league —white, black, North American, South American, European, Asian, whatever—may be headed for oblivion.

Why? Because we aren't needed anymore to perform the one basic function that separates men from women, and I don't mean belching.

It's procreating. You know, doing the deed. Based on what I've been reading lately, it won't be long until the rest of the world can get along just fine without our input on the matter.

Consider the sheep-cloning experiments in Europe. I quote directly from a news dispatch describing the procedure: "Scientists took cells from the ewe's udder tissue and cultivated them in a lab, using a treatment that made the cells essentially dormant. They also took unfertilized sheep eggs and removed the nucleus, the cells' central control room that contains the genes. Then they put the udder cells together with the egg cells and used an electric current to make them fuse. The eggs, now equipped with a nucleus, grew into embryos as if they'd been fertilized. The embryos were put into ewes to develop."

Please note the word "male" appears nowhere in this description. This shocking development leads me to the logical conclusion that as cloning procedures become more and more perfected, the word "male" might one day be deleted from the dictionary.

Then again, maybe not—but I daresay most men aren't going to like this idea any better. At Auburn University, someone has found a way to turn she-fish into he-fish. A graduate student named Salam Al-Ablni fed baby crappies a steady diet of male hormones, and before you could say, "Pass me the minnow bucket," they all turned into males. This is big news among fisheries researchers because crappies are very prolific and often reproduce themselves out of house and home. By turning them all into males, however, reproduction is halted, leaving the he-survivors to grow fat on food that formerly was spread around to all the other he-mouths and she-mouths.

Sounds good on the surface, I suppose. Nothing better than hanging out with the guys, stuffing your gut—at least until you decide to swim home to mama and suddenly realize there ain't no more mamas anywhere in the pond!

No, men aren't going to wake up tomorrow morning and discover the world has gone off and left them. But these two developments could spell bad news for men as far as traditional reproduction is concerned. It doesn't take too much imagination to see serious storm clouds forming on the horizon.

(Sigh.) Why can't they like us for our bodies?

Noah Had It Easy

There are many reasons why I don't want to ever ride on one of those space shuttle missions.

For one thing, I have no desire to be an astronaut. Absolutely none. My sense of adventure stops short of the stratosphere. If I want high-flying thrills, I'll take a rope swing off a bluff and drop into the lake below.

I don't think I could stand the confines of that vehicle, either. I'm not claustrophobic, at least not to the point of gasping for breath in elevators and small rooms. But the thought of being cooped up in an airplane with six other folks for two weeks ranks right along with root canals and all-day sermons on the fun-o-meter.

The chow is another concern. To the best of my knowledge, there's not a deep-fat fryer in the cargo hold. Enough said.

Nor would I relish the thought of having every waking and sleeping moment of my life monitored by a bunch of scientists, physicists, physicians, as well as a few million of my closest and dearest friends in TV land. I need a little more privacy for personal matters, if you catch my drift.

But the *main* reason I am delighted to be planted on Mother Earth while the shuttle is Up There is because it is crammed to the hilt with creepy, crawly critters. As a part of NASA's ongoing mission to study weird things in space, they have packed a regular menagerie. According to the space agency, 1,514 crickets, 18 mice, 152 rats, 135 snails, and 233 fish are also on the passenger list.

You *know* what's going to happen, don't you? The shuttle is going to hit a bump—or someone's going to turn around at the wrong time—and crash! Critter soup, up to their helmets. Months from now, those poor astronauts will still be shaking out their clothes.

I speak with experience in this regard. Years ago, back when he was sports editor and I covered the outdoors, Tom Siler and I went bluegill fishing at Lake Tansi near Crossville. I don't recall that we caught an inordinate amount of fish, but I vividly remember we used crickets for bait. Live crickets. Live crickets that came packed in tubes about the size of the cardboard roll inside paper towels. Tubes that had a very flimsy top and an aggravating tendency to tip over every fifteen minutes, slinging their contents across the floor of my boat.

Those crickets took up permanent residence. For weeks, I could walk into the garage and hear a chorus of chirping. I had a regular rolling, floating bait shop until the hateful varmints learned to dart into cracks and crevices anytime I approached with a hook. I swear it was late summer before I caught the last of them.

That was with maybe three or four dozen crickets. Can you imagine the potential mess those folks are going to have with 1,514 crickets? Not to mention rats, mice, snails, and fish?

All I hope is that one of those astronauts had the foresight to sneak a few mouse traps, some bug strips, and a large can of Raid into his luggage.

Check your Local Listings

I am not what you would call a "cable-friendly" person.

Yes, I do subscribe to a cable television service—the limited menu variety, not the one with HBO, UFO, IUD, FBI, CFC, or whatever those movie channels are called. And, yes, I have been known to click up and down the channel selector for a few seconds, just to see what's available. Sorta like window-shopping while walking through the mall. Or glancing at new titles in a bookstore when you stop for an out-of-town newspaper.

But to sit down in front of the tube and make a conscious effort to look at each program long enough to see what's really happening? Heaven forbid. I'd rather be beaten with a stick. That's why I seriously doubt I'll ever subscribe to the five-hundred-channel system. If my present system, with its mere forty or fifty channels, can be so heavy laden with rubbish, I shudder to think what type of programming is possible with five hundred.

Aerobic exercise classes for iguanas and pit bulldogs, perhaps? Cooking with Chef Dahmer? Intestines of the presidents? The cuticle care chronicles? Nature's sizzling secrets: sex life of the carpet flea? Weather forecasts for New Delhi, updated every five minutes?

No! A thousand times no! The more I hear about this five-hundred-channel nonsense, the more I hope Peter D. Hart calls me soon. Hart runs a television research company. Now long ago, he conducted a survey for *TV Guide*. His pollsters asked more than one thousand Americans how much money they'd have to be paid to not watch television. Twenty-five percent of these fools, er, individuals said they would never give up TV, not even for *one million dollars.*

Wait a second. You mean this guy might be willing to pay me one million smackers, and all I gotta do is swear off TV for good? As B'rer Rabbit used to say, "Don't throw me in the briar patch!"

Please call me, Peter Hart. Call collect, if necessary. And let me see the color of your money.

Taking the skill out of a weighty issue

We've been having a lot of snow, sleet, and slush lately, and it has prompted me to start daydreaming great thoughts of spring. *Ahhhhh.* I want to hook up my boat and drive to Douglas Lake and take off my T-shirt and soak up some rays and sip a flagon of barley juice and nibble some Penrose sausage and idle away a warm afternoon casting for bass, crappie, bluegill, or whatever happens to be hungry. At this stage, even a carp will do.

Trouble is, fishing is a lot more complicated than it used to be. A graduate degree from Harvard is required to know how to use many of the gewgaws and do-dads carried by sporting goods stores today. I don't own any new, high-tech gizmos that are absolutely, positively guaranteed to make the big ones bite. Don't need to. My tackle box is overflowing with low-tech gizmos that were absolutely, positively guaranteed to make the big ones bite when I bought them twenty years ago. But even if I did manage to catch a fish, I wouldn't be able to determine its weight with any degree of courtroom accuracy.

During my formative years, anglers used a time-honored method for estimating the size of a whopper bass, trout, or walleye. They lied. It was a wonderful system that worked to perfection.

Let's say Bill was out by himself and caught a bass that, if placed on government-certified scales, would weigh exactly six pounds. Didn't matter. The next day, he told everybody it weighed seven pounds if it weighed an ounce. Or eight. Or nine. Or whatever number he judged necessary to impress that particular audience.

Naturally, everyone who heard the story mentally re-adjusted the weight by a bullshit factor of ten, twenty, thirty, or forty percent, based on their association with Bill. And they all arrived at the exact weight— six pounds—plus a possible two-pound deduction because they never liked Bill in the first place.

This is no longer possible. The tackle market has been flooded with hand-held, digitized scales that calibrate down to the fraction of an ounce. And, should the batteries fail, some cybernerd has perfected a mathematical formula to handle the chore. I read about this process the other day in an outdoor magazine. When I finished the article, I didn't know whether to laugh or cry or immediately sell my boat and take up bowling.

According to the story, hair-splitting weight can be determined by expanding the fish's length (in inches) to the third power, then dividing by a certain number, based on species. The number was 1,600 for bass, 3,500 for elongated fish like pike, 1,200 for panfish, and 2,700 for walleyes. For an eighteen-inch bass—assuming you have a tape measure and pocket calculator on board—the numbers look like this: 18 x 18 x 18 (5,832), divided by 1,600, equaling 3.645 pounds.

Unless there's nobody else in the boat, of course. In which case it weighs seven pounds if it weighs an ounce.

Chapter 4

Less Gravy, More Fiber

Once at the Festival of Appalachian Humor at Berea College, Bill Reed of Lexington, Kentucky, told the story of a farmer who owned a hog that limped around on a wooden leg. A stranger showed up one day and inquired about the animal's unique appendage. The farmer began by recalling how the hog had squealed loudly one night, alerting the family to the fact their house was on fire. Everyone inside was saved from certain death.

"Was the hog injured in the fire?" the stranger wanted to know. "Is that how he got the wooden leg?"

"No," replied the farmer, who then went on to tell about the time his tractor turned over, pinning him to the ground. The hog ran up and grunted and strained and finally pushed the tractor off so the farmer would wiggle free.

"Did the hog get hurt that time?" the stranger asked.

"No."

"Well then, how did it wind up with that wooden leg?"

"Hale far, man!" the farmer exclaimed, "ain't you got no sense? You don't eat a great hog like that all at once!"

OK, so it's a corny joke. But the fact remains we Baby Boomers, rural and urban alike, have been preying on pigs since we were weaned. It ain't right—for the pigs, I mean. The poor things. They've been getting the raw end of the deal coming and going.

We Baby Boomers spent our formative years gorging on bacon, pork chops, country ham, and tenderloin. Then our hearts and arteries started collapsing from all that "other white meat," and it looked like the pigs would finally win a round. Nope. That was just about the time medical science figured out how to make replacement parts for humans out of hog organs. And if that wasn't bad enough from the porcine perspective, researchers at both Penn State and Lehigh universities now believe rendered lard, with a few modifications, can be made into an acceptable fuel substitute. Supposedly it burns hotter than fuel oil, but with no sulfur dioxide and only a third of the nitrogen oxides as petroleum-based products.

See? We play. The pigs pay. It hardly seems fair.

Hogs are but one of the many resources we Baby Boomers have greedily exploited. We have spent a lifetime dashing from one food fad to another—screwball grapefruit diets to flavored coffees to "baby" vegetables to tofu casseroles to fish oil dressings to oatmeal binges to garlic capsules. It's a vain attempt to revitalize our health and stop the aging process, when all along we secretly lust for Mom's pot roast and buttery mashed potatoes.

We have even bastardized the dietary mantra from our parents' generation. Back then, folks used to laugh that if something tasted good, it probably was bad for you. Baby Boomers truly believe if a food item tastes terrible, smells like a sweatshirt, costs a ton of money, and is available only at trendy markets, it *has* to be good for you.

One of the zaniest forms of this feasting I've seen in recent times involves the intentional ingestion of a weed sensible people usually attack with herbicide and a lawnmower. I speak of the stinging nettle, a plant with the most descriptive name in botany. Stinging nettles are covered with tiny hairs that will set your skin on fire. Brush up against one of these babies while hiking, and it will grab your attention faster than a cloud of hornets.

Yet these same loathsome plants are now showing up on the plates of beautiful people in New York and California. I read a story in *Gourmet* magazine that described this delicacy, along with strict precautions to use gloves when handling the plant before cooking.

Which begs two questions: Who was the first person to experiment with this vegetative cobra? And why?

I am neither a picky nor a squeamish eater. With a minimum of arm-twisting, I will explore most new and exotic tastes. Furthermore, I realize society needs an adventuresome diner every now and then to scale new culinary heights. Surely there's not a tomato lover anywhere in the southern United States who doesn't know that until the early 1800s, tomatoes were thought to be poisonous. Then again, the first nibbler might have been attempting to commit suicide.

Nonetheless, I cannot imagine the thought processes at work in these situations. What would possess someone to gaze upon an oak tree, for example, and say to himself, "That bark looks delicious!"? Or swat a housefly and exclaim, "Just what the frying pan called for!"? Or get whacked on the shins by stinging nettles and think, "Yum-yum! Supper!"?

Clearly, these people never heard of pinto beans and cornbread.

I was sitting near the breakfast bar at a restaurant several mornings ago. So near, in fact, that I overheard every conversation the diners had with one another as they made their selections. Almost to the person, they were amazed to see a new item among the meat choices: pork chops. Almost to the person, they said in disbelief, "Who ever heard of pork chops for breakfast?" And almost to the person, each one of them had bacon, ham, or sausage—or a combination thereof—piled high upon their plates. I assume none of these folks holds membership in 4-H. ～

Ol' Red

The first time I saw blue potato chips, I feared the world was headed down a steep path to destruction. This notion was confirmed in my mind when I read that the H. J. Heinz Company is now selling green ketchup.

Heinz reportedly made the move to attract more kids—specifically the four-to-twelve-year-old market—as if children had to be lured to ketchup in the first place. The new green goo comes in a smaller-diameter, easier-to-squirt bottle, perfect for pint-sized hands. Heinz supposedly tested several funky colors for this heresy. Green came out on top.

Lord have mercy. We have lost true north. I feel like my parents' generation must have felt when the Beatles invaded America, birth-control pills were developed, and the anti-war movement was born.

Heinz insists the taste will remain the same, no matter what the hue. The change simply will be a matter of food color. The company also says it will continue to make regular red ketchup—the kind Gawd Hisself squirts on his heavenly fries—for the old fogy market. But I shall have none of it. Any outfit that would stoop to such dietary blasphemy is capable of fomenting evil on all levels. Best to maintain a safe distance from it.

In today's fast-paced, ever-changing world, a world in which entire industries are born at breakfast, make their first billion by lunch, and go bust before supper, some things are supposed to stay the same. Indeed, they *must* stay the same if we are to preserve our collective sanity. Red ketchup is one of them.

Oh, sure ketchup can be fickle. Ketchup can cling like glue to the interior walls and bottom of the bottle, stubbornly refusing to flow until we have banged, tapped, slapped, slammed, and cursed—only to then have it exit forcefully and land, *ker-splat*, halfway across the table.

Ketchup can become watery in the bottle, too. Woe be unto the hungry hamburger connoisseur who exhumes an ancient bottle from hiding in the refrigerator and squirts before shaking. Contrarily, ketchup residue in the neck and lid of the container can form a thick plug that is impervious to acids and abrasives.

Fast-food ketchup can come packed in those insidious, individual-sized packets which invariably (a) squirt across your face when you try to open them with your teeth and (b) run dry when there are still seven fries remaining on your plate.

What's more, ketchup can be controversial. Rare is the talented and well-schooled chef who hasn't watched in horror as his or her culinary masterpiece is covered with a layer of ketchup by some loud-talking, cigar-puffing buffoon at the corner table. Rare, too, is the nutritionist who didn't require smelling salts during the Reagan administration when the federal government officially listed ketchup as a "vegetable" for school lunch programs.

But through all of these dark and stormy seas, ketchup has always been red. Red it should remain, yea, verily until the end of time. Forget what your commie-hating father used to preach back during the '50s. These days, we're better dead than not red.

Clear liquids are the rage these days. Clear cola, clear beer, clear malt liquor. What's next—clear coffee? If so, how are you supposed to order it in a restaurant if you like to drink it black? ～

The Okra Episode

I got into a serious pickle at home the other night, and it wasn't even my fault. This had nothing to do with pickles, by the way. It was okra.

I dearly love okra. Fried okra, that is. No person of respectable breeding would prepare this nectar of the Southern gods without sizzling it in a black iron skillet lubricated liberally with 10W-30 cooking oil of intensely cholesterolic extraction.

Some heathens boil their okra. To them I say, *"pa-tui!"* which not only illustrates my utter disdain for the very notion of boiled okra, but also imitates the sound one makes as he or she spits a slimy pod of the putrid stuff out the nearest window.

Anyhow, I found myself at home the other night, scrounging through the kitchen to rustle up a supper of leftovers. The hunting was spectacular right from the beginning, for on top of the counter sat a red, ripe, bursting-with-flavor, homegrown tomato. Then things got even better. The first piece of Tupperware I checked in the refrigerator was bulging with day-old barbecue. Nestled beside it was another vessel filled with barbecue sauce. From that point on, gastronomical success was a given.

And then—saints be praised!—tucked oh-so-carefully, so as not to damage the precious cargo inside, was a large plastic bag filled to its twist-tie top with cut-up okra, already dusted with cornmeal, salt, and pepper. That's when I remembered Mary Ann had fried up some okra the night before. This was the excess that hadn't made it to the skillet.

Please understand the word "excess." That's exactly what I mean. There was a voluminous amount in the bag, easily enough for two super-sized servings.

Excellent, I thought to myself. By the time Mary Ann gets home from work, I'll have the tomato peeled and sliced, the barbecue heated, and the okra fried. That's precisely what happened, too.

I set a dinner plate for each of us. Fixed the tomato. Dished out the barbecue. Plunked a heaping platter of crisp, fried okra into the midst of everything. And sat down to eat it all by my lonesome. That's how I got into the pickle.

Not because I didn't wait for my wife, you understand. Our work schedules often conflict, so particularly on informal leftover nights, it is perfectly permissible for one to go ahead and eat without the other. It's just that when she *did* finally get home, there was no okra. Not a single, solitary, grease-saturated piece.

I tried to explain to Mary Ann that it was an accident, an honest mistake. I tried to tell her how I had carefully divided the contents of the okra platter right down the middle—my half on one side, her half on the other side. It was a perfect fifty-fifty split. But then, gosh-dang the luck, *I ACCIDENTALLY ATE HER HALF!* Realizing she wouldn't want to compound the problem by eating my half, I reluctantly polished it off, too.

Y'know, once you get used to it, the sofa's not a bad place to sleep.

In Washington, D.C., the Smithsonian unveiled a display honoring the development of the Krispy Kreme doughnut. The next time your nose draws you toward a Krispy Kreme shop, feel free to munch without guilt. You're not pigging out on high-fat junk food; you're studying American history. ～

How to Taste Wine

The first time I went to a wine-tasting party, I didn't have the slightest notion what to expect. I sniffed and sipped and desperately tried to distinguish between Coleman fuel, cleaning fluid, strip mine tailings, bilgewater, and the other fine vintages we sampled. Perhaps that explains why I accurately selected the premier wines.

But then I went for a second round and got cultured. Now I'm an expert.

The taste-off I attended most recently was the Tennessee Wine Festival. It was a civic fund-raiser. In other words, an excuse to drink hooch for benevolent reasons, right there in front of the mayor and everybody. It differed from your standard Tennessee civic fund-raiser because it did not involve the sale of light bulbs, flower seeds, fruit-cakes, chocolate bars, or doughnuts.

Here's how these things work: You buy a twenty-dollar ticket from one of the civic clubs sponsoring the wine tasting. You show up at the right place and time. They give you a glass—it is considered boorish to ask for a Mason jar—and turn you loose on seven hundred wines, plus lots of gooey gourmet treats to eat. And it's all for a good cause. Is this a great country or what?

In the event you get invited to a civic wine-tasting party in the future, allow me to share a few tips I have gleaned over the course of my vast career.

1. Do not enter the room, survey the hundreds of bottles on display, and shout, "So much wine, so little time!" Not only does this peg you as an uncultured goober, it alerts everyone else to your intentions. They'll start slugging it down with both fists, and before you can say "cabernet sauvignon," someone will plug in the Mister Coffee, and you've blown twenty big ones for nothing.

2. When you begin sampling, the first thing to do is check for general appearance. Hold the glass against a contrasting background. Swill the wine gently to see if it "legs" inside the glass.

    Talk about a revelation! Other than watching out for hairballs and floating mice, I'd never looked at my likker before. And the only "leg" I ever worried about was getting jake-leg from lead pipe moonshine. Of course, that was before I became cultured.

3. Judge the aroma and bouquet. In other words, smell it.

    This will be uncomfortable to novices at first. It's seems like sniffing the meatloaf or wiping a spoon on your napkin when you get invited to someone's house for supper. But don't worry. In wine-tasting circles, smelling the goods is considered a compliment. The host won't snap, "Well, I never!" at you.

    When you smell the wine, always speak positively about it—even if it stinks worse than a minnow bucket. Just smile and say something cultured. Like, "What a complex aroma! This little number would be perfect with fish!"

4. Taste the product. This is the good part, the stage where the cheese starts to bind. But unless you know your stuff, you could wind up making a terrible blunder here.

Do not say, "Ashes to ashes, dust to dust, this'll turn yore innards to rust," and toss the glass back. And, by all means, do not holler, "Lordgodalmitey! This'ud peel the varnish off my boat!" afterwards, even if the taste is not up to your standards.

Instead, sip slowly. Pause for a moment and look up—like maybe you're wondering where you left the car keys. Then remark to others, "Lots of character. Bold, but not overpowering. This wine definitely makes a statement." This will really impress everyone within earshot—unless they know you and realize you're already getting a buzz.

5. Spit your wine into another cup at this point. At least that's what the civic fund-raisers expect you to do.

   They are wrong, of course. If they think Tennesseans are going to cough up twenty bucks for likker and then spit it out, the civic fund-raisers have jiggled a bottle once too often themselves.

6. One final category: aftertaste. Good wine is supposed to linger on the tongue, vanishing slowly like the hint of delicate perfume from a passing lady.

   Quite frankly, this was the most startling revelation in all of my wine-tasting experiences. Until I became cultured, I always thought "aftertaste" was something you tried to kill—you know, like when you've just polished off four hot dogs with onions and you've got a hot date in an hour. Why else would they sell chewing gum, mints, and breath spray at the cash register?

   But now that I'm cultured, I know better. Aftertaste is what you get when you wake up from sampling seven hundred wines.

Lean Times in the Land of Plenty

There is a potential crisis hovering over our great nation, and it threatens to undermine everything we Americans hold sacred. They want to put a tax on junk food.

"They" are Michael Jacobson and Kelly Brownell. Jacobson is executive director of the Center for Science in the Public Interest in Washington. Brownell is a psychology professor at Yale University. Not long ago, they wrote a report in the *American Journal of Public Health* that proposed a one-cent tax on soft drinks, candy, chips, and other snack foods, as well as the fats and oils contained therein. They claim Americans' penchant for these goodies costs seventy-one billion dollars annually, and they think sweet-toothed fatties oughta pay.

Are we going to sit still while this lunacy is being discussed? We most certainly are not! We are going to lie down and eat a bag of cheese curls while we collect our thoughts.

How dare these people suggest imposing another sin tax on the American public! Taxing liquor and tobacco is one thing. Taxing the sugar and grease necessary for life, liberty, and the pursuit of XL is unconscionable. Living off the fat of the land is an inalienable right whose roots can be traced back to the founding fathers of this republic. Have you ever seen a picture of a thin Benjamin Franklin? I rest my case.

In addition to its unconstitutional assault on the arteries of America, this nonsense strikes at yet another important element of democracy. It would amount to taxation without representation. If Jacobson and Brownell ultimately are successful in ramming their half-baked plan through Congress, it is only equitable that we junk food junkies have a finger in the frosting bowl as well.

We would insist upon a new cabinet member—Secretary of the Human Interior—who would look after our bulging bellies and bulbous butts with the same care afforded the nation's parks and forests. Among the candidates for the first appointee should be such inspirational icons as Famous Amos, Peter Paul, or, in the name of gender diversity, Dolly Madison.

We would expect statues of the Keebler elves. We would demand that hot dogs, jelly doughnuts, bear claws, Fritos, and Ruffles be served at all state dinners. We would not rest until NASA included Moon Pies on all space shuttle journeys. We would press for the relocation of the White House from Pennsylvania Avenue to 5th Avenue. And on every Pay Day, we would insist upon the super-sized bar with extra nuts.

Thomas Paine was right. These indeed are the times that fry men's souls. Or was it Mr. Goodbar who said that?

Like a lot of other folks, I grimaced when the Centers for Disease Control and Prevention announced that Americans, particularly those of us in the South, are growing heavier by the year. But then my heart, not to mention my belly, fairly leapt for joy when the University of Toronto released results from a study showing potatoes and barley have the power to improve memory. I'm going to write myself a note to be sure to serve an extra helping of mashed 'taters for supper and wash it down with liquefied barley. After a few weeks, my memory will probably be so keen, I can dispense with the note. ⌒

Ancient Cereal

I was in the breakfast foods section of a grocery store the other day when a word on the front of a cereal box caught my eye. "Spelt," it said in bold, black letters.

No, that wasn't the name of the cereal. It was called "Heritage"—which, to someone like me of the Cheerios–Wheaties–Sugar Pops generation, sounded odd for a breakfast food. "Heritage" has a rather historic ring to it, like maybe it's what Betsy Ross ate every morning before she sat down to sew the flag. So I decided to give "Heritage" a shot. I could almost hear a drum and fife corps playing in the background as I put the box into my cart.

But it wasn't necessarily patriotism that compelled me to buy this cereal. It was that strange word, "spelt," plus two others that also jumped off the box: "kamut" and "quinoa." These three words, I discovered on the way home—Mary Ann was driving; I was in the passenger seat, chewing a fresh bagel and reading cereal boxes—are ancient grains. According to the label, they have been known for thousands of years and passed down, generation to generation.

"A mealtime staple in biblical times, spelt is a natural, nonhybrid grain that grows well without artificial fertilizers, pesticides, or insecticides," it read.

I studied further about kamut, which "originated in the Fertile Crescent around 4000 BC. Think of it as an early member of the wheat family with a taste that hasn't been tampered with."

And then there was quinoa, which "the people of the Andes called the 'Mother Grain.' With a naturally fluffy texture, it's an ancient flavor favorite people have savored for centuries."

You sure could have fooled me. I thought breakfast cereals were supposed to contain riboflavin, folic acid, phosphorus, and Vitamin B-12. Plus sugar, of course.

"Spelt" does not sound like something you're supposed to eat. It sounds made-up, like one of those words cartoonists use when Superman lands a punch on the bad guy's jaw.

Oops, wait a second. Now that I think about it, that sound is "splat." "Spelt"—or possibly its derivative, "splort"—is the sound Superman's fist would make when he hits the bad guy on the jaw, only to discover the bad guy is actually a rubber robot, in which case Superman's hand would bounce harmlessly out of the way. In any event, the words would be written out in zigzag type and followed by a couple of exclamation points for added effect.

Then again, "spelt" could be what you do with letters to make a word. Such as, "Cat is not spelt with a *k*."

In the case of "kamut," Superman would be kicking the bad guy into a jail cell: "Here's where you belong—*kamut!!*—so the rest of the world can live in freedom and peace!" (And by the way, where was the "Fertile Crescent" that was described on the cereal box? Was it anywhere near Krypton?)

"Quinoa" doesn't sound very appetizing, either. Wasn't that the name of an Australian airline, the one that featured a koala bear on its TV commercials twenty years ago? Or is it a private region of the body? As in, "Defendant Jones was charged with exposing his quinoa in public"?

As you can imagine, I was less than enthusiastic when I finally poured a bowl full of this cereal. It had brown flakes like Wheaties, but they were thicker. They were exceedingly crunchy, almost to the point of being painfully hard.

Yet I must admit the taste was quite good. There was a hint of sweetness, but I figured no patriotic, wholesome, ancient-grained cereal would stoop to adding sugar to its flakes, would it? No, indeed. According to the list of ingredients, the sweetening comes from "organic, unrefined cane juice." I believe that's what the founding fathers used to call "liquid sugar," but what do I know about historical nomenclature?

All in all, my ancient-grain dining experience was a pleasant one— even though, at my age, *every* dining experience has ancient overtones. Next time I'm at the store, I may even buy another box of "Heritage."

I just wish it came with a magic decoder ring inside, or maybe a mini-comic book, so I could join Superman as he *spelts!!* and *kamuts!!* the bad guys squarely in their quinoas.

Super Bowl Snacks

Before your brain is burdened with meaningless numbers—yards per carry, quarterback sacks, average length of punts, boring stuff like that —let me offer a Super Bowl statistic you can really sink a tooth into: Every time the top two National Football League teams gather to tear each other's head off, Americans tear into 31.7 million pounds of potato chips, pretzels, popcorn, and nuts.

No, 31.7 million pounds isn't an exact number. It's certainly not as precise as when the refs get eye-level with the chain to see if the nose of the football is close enough for a first down. It's an average figure, so maybe it's off a pretzel or three. Nonetheless, it's an educated guess-timation by the folks who bring you these yummies.

"It's based on the increase in sales during Super Bowl week compared to an average, comparable week," says Ann Wilkes, vice president of communications for the Snack Food Association in Alexandria, Virginia. "You assume people who are planning Super Bowl parties will be buying their supplies a few days before the game. In 2000, we estimated 11.8 million pounds of potato chips, nine million pounds of tortilla chips, 3.9 million pounds of pretzels, four million pounds of popcorn, and three million pounds of snack nuts like peanuts and cashews."

I shall leave it to other statisticians, as well as dietitians and demographers, to determine how this translates into calories per household.

But before you start munching, pause for a second and let James Miracle tell you about potato chips that don't come in a fancy, high-priced, shiny plastic bag from the supermarket.

"When you grow up poor, you improvise," he says. "That's the way Mom and Dad taught us."

James is a big, barrel-chested, bushy-bearded craftsman who lives in Bell County, Kentucky, just off U.S. Highway 25E between Middlesboro and Pineville. I got to know him several years ago when photographer Paul Efird and I were doing research for our book, *Mountain Hands.* The chapter about James happens to chronicle his dulcimer-making skills, but this guy is far too talented to be limited to a single discipline. If he put his mind to it, I believe James could prowl through his cluttered workshop for spare parts and then sit down and cobble together a functioning computer. (Who else do you know who whittled a vent valve out of walnut and used it for twenty thousand miles in a '63 Chevy?) I had heard him tell about his mother's homemade potato chips, so when I saw the Super Bowl's snack estimate, I telephoned for an update.

When James was a boy, his mother, Hazel, used home-grown potatoes, a wood-working plane, melted lard, and salt to create "the best chips you ever tasted—I've never eaten chips from the store that were as good as hers," he said.

Mama Miracle would scrub one of her husband's planes squeaky clean and set the blade at an ever-so-fine angle. Then she would rub peeled potatoes across it lengthwise, shaving off chips "so thin, you could see through 'em. She'd drop the chips in hot grease. After that, she'd put 'em out on newspaper to drain—we never could afford paper towels—and then salt 'em. They were crunchy and delicious."

On special occasions like school picnics, Hazel would take an old piece of waxed paper, fold it, and seal the seams with a hot iron to make a bag.

"The other kids at school thought we were something special," he recalled. "They always wanted Mom's 'tater chips instead of theirs that had come from the store."

Maybe Hazel Miracle should have gone into business. Who knows? The snack industry might be headquartered in the steep mountains of southeastern Kentucky instead of the concrete canyons of the

As a proud native son of southern Appalachia, I can tell this joke without worrying about political correctness: An Irishman, a Mexican, and a hillbilly were working on the top floor of a twenty-story building. At lunch break, the Irishman opened his box and screamed, "Corned beef and cabbage again! If I get this one more time, I'm gonna jump off this building!" The Mexican opened his lunch box and screamed, "Burritos again! If I get these one more time, I'm gonna jump off this building!" The hillbilly looked into his bucket and screamed, "Baloney again! If I get this one more time, I'm gonna jump off this building!"

Next day, the Irishman opens his lunch box, finds corned beef and cabbage, and swan dives into space. The Mexican opens his lunch box, finds burritos, and does the same. The hillbilly glances into his bucket, sees baloney, and follows his buddies.

At the funeral, the Irishman's wife is weeping: "Oh, if I'd only known Mick was tired of corned beef and cabbage, I never would have given it to him again!" The Mexican's wife is sobbing: "Oh, if I'd only known Juan was tired of burritos, I never would have given them to him again!" The hillbilly's wife is sitting there, smoking a cigarette: "Hale far! I node I shouldn't a' let Billy Ray fix his own lunch." ∼

Washington Beltway. Or maybe not. You gotta admit "beltway" and "junk food" have a lot in common.

The Tragic Twinkie Recall

There was great weeping and wailing and gnashing of teeth across our great nation in 1998 when Interstate Brands Corporation, manufacturer of HoHo's, Twinkies, and more than a dozen other Hostess goodies, announced a recall of nearly one million snack cakes.

The problem was the possibility these sweet treats were contaminated. The company issued a statement indicating the Twinkies "may have been affected by asbestos fibers in insulation removed from a boiler" at its Schiller Park, Illinois, plant.

Frankly, I wasn't overly concerned. I mean, what's wrong with a few fibers? Shouldn't they help with digestion?

Fortunately, the crisis passed without undue hardships on the bellies of America. But we must be prepared if, God forbid, it ever occurs again. There are other junk foods on the market that provide all the necessary ingredients we humans require for a rich and full, if somewhat short, life. To be certain, I made a spot-check of several Knox-ville truck stops, convenience stores, and supermarkets and discovered a virtual smorgasbord of Twinkie alternatives.

In the category of dairy products, for instance, you can choose between Butterfingers, Milky Ways, and cheese puffs. For meats, I sug-gest several daily servings of Slim Jims, beef jerky, and pork rinds.

Can't forget the veggies, of course. A couple of cans of French's french-fried onions, a large bag of Wavy Lay's potato chips, and a jar of Planter's honey-roasted peanuts should fill the bill nicely.

Fruits? They're everywhere. Krispy Kreme's fried pies are avail-able in apple, peach, and cherry, not to mention raspberry jelly-filled doughnuts. There's also a vast array of Slather's two-for-a-buck bagged fruits, including orange slices, peach rings, lemon drops, strawberry puffs, and Michigan cherries.

Oops. Almost left out the all-important grains. You can't go wrong in this department with Keebler Fudge Shoppe Deluxe Grahams, Oreo Double Stuffs (for twice the nutrition), Little Debbie oatmeal cakes, and at least two six-packs of hops and barley, blended to your individual preference.

Stand firm, America! Our forefathers refused to knuckle under to adversity, and neither should we! May every brave heart keep beating 'til the arteries collapse.

What Are We Supposed to Believe?

There was a silly little story from my childhood about the utter futility of drinking iced tea. Something about how you first have to boil the stuff to make it hot, then add ice to make it cold, then add sugar to make it sweet, then add lemon to make it sour. Far better, the story concluded, not to get thirsty in the first place.

I'm starting to feel the same way about food warnings. We'd save ourselves a heck of a lot of trouble and worry if we'd stop eating immediately, quickly starve to death, and get it over with.

Recently, scientists at the National Cancer Institute in Washington issued a new warning about meat. If you're going to eat meat, they said, for Pete's sake don't cook it through-and-through. Otherwise, you run an increased risk of developing cancer.

I wasn't at all surprised to see this warning. If anything, I thought it was slow to arrive. That's because just over a couple of years ago, the federal government adopted new warning-label guidelines for raw meat. You've probably seen them as you shopped in the meat department of your friendly local supermarket. These labels are plastered on packages of fresh chicken, ground beef, and other animal products. They tell you how dangerous raw meat can be, so for Pete's sake, cook the stuff thoroughly before it touches your lips.

Same song, thousandth verse. I don't know who, or what, to believe about food anymore. Seems like every time I turn around, someone issues a new report about a food product that will either kill me graveyard dead or make me live forever.

In 1996, for instance, we were treated to several breakthrough stories along this line. That was the year that the National Center for Health Statistics in Hyattsville, Maryland, reported findings indicating that certain artificial flavorings can help reduce heart disease. Assuming, of course, that these same artificial flavorings don't send us to the bone yard with cancer.

Same thing with sugar, that old waist-expanding, tooth-rotting menace to society. In 1996, researchers at Duke University said sugar isn't near the dietary villain it's cracked up to be. So spoon up.

Ditto coffee—you know, that ugly brew that tears up your stomach and gives you the jitters by racing your ticker into overdrive. In 1996, the *Journal of the American Medical Association* reported that researchers at the Harvard Medical School could find no relationship between coffee consumption and heart disease.

I'm starting to think this whole business of food warnings is nothing more than a weird game of "Simon Says." It goes like this:

"Simon says don't cook your meat."

"Simon says cook your meat."

"Simon says don't drink coffee."

"Simon says drink coffee."

"Simon says don't eat artificial flavorings."

"Eat artificial flavorings."

Buzzzz! Ha-ha. Simon didn't say to eat artificial flavorings, so you lose the game. Rest in peace.

I Scream, you Scream

In honor of dairy month, I urge everyone out there in readership land to run to the refrigerator and take a long, cold drink of liquid cholester . . . I mean, milk.

Sure hits the spot, doesn't it?

Now for a quick quiz:

1. How many of you people removed the carton from the refrigerator, fetched a glass from the shelf, poured milk into the glass, and then drank the milk?

2. How many drank directly from the carton?

I don't have to ask. I know already. Precisely 51.2 percent opted for Procedure No. 1, while 48.8 percent went the No. 2 route.

I know the answer because, according to the latest information from the *Statistical Abstract of the United States,* 51.2 percent of the American population is female, and 48.8 percent is male. And as anyone who has lived on this planet long enough to get a Social Security number realizes, drinking from the carton is a Guy thing.

This is not opinion on my part. It is fact. Ask any mother-sister-wife or father-brother-husband. This is an act of instinct that comes with the gender territory. It cannot be denied.

Left to their own devices and with no training whatsoever, men who emerge from the womb with their Y-chromosomes hitting on all eight cylinders grow up knowing the proper way to drink milk is straight from the carton (or bottle, in olden days), just as they know how to produce offensive noises from armpits and various orifices, north and south.

A corollary to the drink-from-carton truism involves ice cream. When Jane Doe wants ice cream, she finds a bowl and spoon. Then she goes to the freezer, searches for the ice cream carton, and spoons a serving into her bowl. John Doe will also take the time to locate a spoon—which he uses to eat directly from the carton.

Again, don't take my word for it. Ask any anthropologist. Men and women have exhibited this difference since 5000 B.C., when Ig Westinghouse invented refrigeration.

I mention these tidbits of truth to ridicule the results of a poll I recently read about people's dairy-consumption habits. In this survey, a full 59 percent of respondents admitted to slugging milk directly from the carton. Conversely, only 39 percent reported they had blown milk out of their nose.

Hogwash. These phony-baloney numbers fly in the face of iron-clad statistics from the United States government, and I'll have nothing to do with them.

> **N**early two thousand exhibitors from thirty-six countries converged on Chicago's McCormick Place in 2001 for a housewares show. The new gadgets they displayed included a twenty-six cubic foot refrigerator with these features: "a screen on the front, plus a modem. It can be used for Internet surfing, sending e-mails, and watching television. A digital camera enables two-way video conversations and prints of digital still photos. And it still keeps your food and drinks cold." All for a mere ten thousand dollars.
>
> The only geegaw I'd like to see on a refrigerator is something that automatically takes a new jug of milk to the back and shoves the older, already-opened carton—the one hiding behind the lettuce and mayo—to the front. ⌐

Who conducted this test? The Milk Processor Board from California, that's who. The same state that brings you wine spritzers, roller blades, and earthquakes. You going to believe these fruitcakes or me? I thought so.

Now, let's go check out the freezer. You bring the spoon.

The yummy McPatch

As a lifelong admirer of food—particularly the junk variety—I'm very interested in the Army's plan to fill a combat soldier's belly by slapping a patch on his arm. Researchers at the Defense Department are testing a program to keep troops at the peak of fighting efficiency by having them eat through the skin instead of the more conventional route of mouth, teeth, throat, and stomach.

I am not making this up. Neither, as far as I know, is the Pentagon —although be advised this is the same Pentagon which, in the summer of 1986, repeatedly denied the existence of the F-19 Stealth fighter jet, even though (a) an F-19 had just crashed in the mountains of California and (b) the Testor Corp. was selling 1/48th-scale plastic models of the F-19, one of which was purchased and constructed by my son, who was thirteen years old at the time.

If you want iron-clad proof the Army is testing a food patch, get a load of its official name: "Transdermal Nutrient Delivery System." If that doesn't have "U.S. Bygolly Guvmit" stamped all over it, I'll eat an M-16. Or maybe I'll just eat an M-16 patch.

In any event, this device works like those nicotine patches that are the rage these days among ex-smoker wannabes. It is loaded with high-powered techno-nutrients that ooze into GI Joe's body to keep him alive and kicking when the lead is flying. It is not a permanent substitute for food. Indeed, a publication from the Army's Soldier Systems Center in Natick, Massachusetts, specifies, "The patch would be used to keep the war fighter at optimum performance for a day or two until he or she has access to a real meal and the time to eat it. It is never meant to replace a turkey dinner with all the fixings."

The nutrient patch is years (and Lord knows how many millions of dollars in research grants) away from perfection. The Army thinks it might be ready for combat use by 2025. In the meantime, all I can say is pass the mashed potat—er, I mean, keep up the research.

Like oh-so-many military trinkets, these food patches have a variety of possibilities for civilian use, particularly among campers, hikers, bikers, boaters, bird watchers, nature photographers, anglers, hunters, and other outdoor enthusiasts. I doubt they'll ever replace full-blown campfire feasts, any more than dehydrated meals do now. But for snacks and quick bursts of energy, this will surely beat granola.

I do hope these patches come in several different camouflage patterns. Better yet, they need to be layered with Gore-Tex, wool, goose down, and Thinsulate.

After I cover my body with the Shoney's Breakfast Bar Patch, the Twinkie patch, a dozen Krispy Kreme patches, the Hardee's sausage biscuit patch, the Egg McMuffin patch, two or three raspberry-coconut Zinger patches, the sardine-and-cheese-cracker patch, the Whopper patch, the Thermos of coffee patch, and the ever-popular—*buuuurp!*—six-pack patch, I won't need clothing at all.

Muscle for sale

You may not have noticed, but operating room fads are sweeping America these days. If this trend continues, the conventionally conceived baby will be a thing of the past. Prospective parents will merely drive to the hospital, withdraw all the necessary parts from inventory, sew 'em together like a patchwork quilt and—*ta-dah!*—a perfect, instant human being, just like the blueprints called for.

I got to thinking about this possibility a few nights ago while watching a television news program. An item about plastic surgery for men came on. Not nose jobs and facial reconstructions that transform someone like Michael Jackson from a handsome young man into a grotesque creature from outer space. Instead, this particular type of surgery was directed to the main body. It showed how plastic surgeons are turning ninety-eight-pound Myron Milktoasts into shirt-popping Arnold Schwarzeneggers.

What they do is slice open an arm, chest, or belly and insert artificial biceps, pectorals, and obliques. Bingo, instant hunk. No push-ups or free weights or smelly sweat suits. You merely check into the admitting office looking like a twisted pipe cleaner and re-appear several days later in the form of a rugged metal culvert.

This is the same as putting breast implants in women, except the materials are different. When a flat-chested woman wants a Dolly Parton profile, the surgeon inserts soft, silicone sacs. The stuff that goes into men is hard, like miniature shin guards.

At first glance, this procedure seems like a godsend for pipsqueaks. No more sand in the face for them, by golly. One look at those bulging muscles and every bully within five hundred yards will run for cover.

But did anyone ever stop to think what might happen if these guys actually have to *use* their bionic arms?

It doesn't matter if your biceps look like country hams; they're worthless if you still don't have the strength to open a jar of peanut butter or shift the gears in your car. Even worse, what could be more embarrassing than drawing back to slug the obnoxious oaf who's been picking on you all these years and—*sprooongggg!*—the incision rips and your fake muscles fly across the room like Tonka Toy shrapnel?

What about temperature changes? On real hot days, do plastic muscles melt and leave stains? In winter, is it necessary to move slowly to prevent cracking? If you walk through the room when someone has the TV on, will these new-fangled muscles affect reception? Do they need fifty-thousand-mile servicing? Until somebody can answer these questions satisfactorily, I'll get by with my 100-percent, red-blooded, old-fashioned flesh, thank you just the same.

But that's not the half of it. I picked up the newspaper the other day and read yet another story about operations. Cholesterol control this time. Here's how it works: The doc puts you on an operating table. He slices your guts open. He withdraws the small intestine. He whacks away with his scalpel. He sews you back up.

This process is known as a "partial ileal bypass." It means that one-third of your small intestine is now non-functional. Thus, the amount of cholesterol absorbed into the bloodstream is greatly reduced. A regular miracle of modern medicine.

Except for one teeny-weeny detail. With one-third of your small intestine living on welfare, your digestive system goes haywire. As a result, you suffer chronic diarrhea—*for years!*

"Besides diarrhea," the story said, "those who undergo the surgery are somewhat more prone to have kidney stones, gallstones, and intestinal obstructions."

I happen to have high cholesterol. Through a combination of diet modification, exercise, and prescription drugs, I have been fighting the good battle for a long time. I would welcome any advice the medical profession has to offer. But if I walk into my doctor's office some day and he tells me he's going to "solve" my cholesterol problem with an operation that will give me kidney stones and twenty years of quick-stepping panic, there is every likelihood I will pick up a forty-pound edition of *Gray's Illustrated Anatomy* and tap him lightly across the forehead. Repeatedly.

I will abuse my bodily temple on my own terms, thank you just the same.

The Flavor Parade

I swung by a downtown deli the other day to grab a turkey sandwich for lunch. There was a huge display of potato chips near the counter. One type was dill pickle flavored.

Curious, I purchased the chips and ate them. They were quite tasty. And, yes, they did taste like dill pickles. But as I munched, two questions popped into my head:

1. Why pickle flavored potato chips instead of, say, asparagus flavored or anchovy flavored or banana flavored?
2. Did anybody ever think of developing dill pickles that taste like potato chips?

When I got back to the office with my newfound, but perplexing, discovery, I learned what a sheltered life I've been leading. Pickle flavored potato chips have been around for years, someone told me. What's more, if I wanted something truly exotic, I should try the ketchup flavored potato chip or the "hamburger with all the fixings" potato chip, neither of which am I making up.

"My brother Phil is a potato chip connoisseur," cartoonist Dan Proctor told me. "He found the 'hamburger with all the fixings' chips. They're made with mustard powder, onion powder, and dill powder, and then some grilled flavor has been added. He gave me a few of them to try."

"How'd they taste?" I wanted to know.

Dan made a face. "About like you're eating the grill itself," he replied.

Life used to be *sooooo* simple. How did we get into this mess? We started out with a perfectly good, crunchy, all-American junk food item that dripped with fat, was loaded with preservatives, and filled our bellies with empty calories. But we weren't content with success. We had to start monkeying around with it. I guess barbecue chips came first. Or maybe sour cream. Then salt and vinegar. And now there's no end to the combinations.

Intrigued by my dill pickle discovery, I drove to the supermarket and spent nearly an hour in the junk food section, trying to record the different varieties of corn chips and potato chips on display. It was a daunting experience. Linneaus must have felt the same way when he set out to catalog all those species of plants.

For instance, plain ol' barbecue chips won't do any more. You must choose between mesquite barbecue, hickory barbecue, apple wood smoke and cheddar (not to be confused with jalapeno and cheddar), and barbecue blast (not to be confused with spicy Cajun or extreme fiery ranch.)

Oops. Did I mention chips flavored with ranch dressing? There must be a thousand of 'em. Among other blends, I found zesty ranch, Santa Fe ranch, wild wing and ranch (are we buyin' chickens or chips?), and peppercorn ranch—with a hint of lime and roasted herb and garlic thrown in for good measure.

Then I started looking around the store and found even more examples of this flavor kaleidoscope. Granola, for instance.

I realize plain granola is about as delectable as sawdust. That's why versions like maple and brown sugar were developed. But I also found granola bars flavored like oatmeal cookies, leading me to wonder if anyone ever thought of creating an oatmeal cookie that tastes like a granola bar.

Oh, and check out the popcorn rack. Did you know there's a "Rice Krispies Krunch" type of popcorn?

Huh? If you want the taste of Rice Krispies, why eat popcorn to get it? Does this mean raisin bran popcorn is next? Sugar Pops popcorn? Mini frosted shredded wheat popcorn? Cheerios-with-a-dollop-of-peanut-butter-and-French-onion-dip popcorn?

Staggered by the possibilities, I wandered to the dairy case and stared at regular cream cheese. Plus cheesecake cream cheese, strawberry cream cheese, salmon cream cheese, garden veggie cream cheese, honey nut cream cheese, raspberry cream cheese, and pineapple cream cheese. I was sorely tempted to see if there was cream cheese flavored salmon in the seafood department or cream cheese flavored raspberries in the fruit aisle, but my stomach was churning by then. I had to seek relief.

That's when I made a very comforting discovery. The entire shelf of Pepto-Bismol offered only one flavor. I was back in the pink in no time.

Grocers who sell "seedless" watermelons should be reminded about laws governing truth in advertising. I bought one of these over-priced wonders of agricultural science and discovered "seedless" is a relative word. Instead of countless rows of black seeds, it was filled with countless rows of white seeds, plus a lot of the black ones. I spent just as much time clawing with a fork as I would have with an old-time, cheaper, less-fashionable model. These things should be sold along with the lemons. ⌒

Chapter 5

The "Helpful" Hand of uncle Sam

ace it. Taking potshots at the government is easy. When all else fails, complaining about some alleged misdeed at any level—local, state, or federal —will immediately attract an army of sympathizers.

We Baby Boomers are especially good at carping about the government, and our protests have increased in volume as we've grown older. You thought we raised hell about the draft? Naaa. Just let 'em start messing with pension account regulations, Social Security, and Medicare in a few years, and you'll *really* hear an eruption. We're just like our parents in this regard. We covet our government services, our beloved "entitlements," yet we resent having to fork over the dough to support them.

Talk about naïve. To hear us tell it, presidential prevarication originated in the Nixon administration. We thought those *Saturday Night Live* skits about Gerald Ford's stumbling were the first parody of a standing—or falling, as it were—chief executive. And perhaps because he was one of our generation and we imagined ourselves back in high school, caught in an embarrassing jam, we came close to believing Bill Clinton's "I did not have sex with that woman, Miss Lewinsky" malarkey. At least for the first three minutes.

I have a vested interest in the government. Uncle Sam and his bumbling minions have kept me employed for years. Readers sometimes get the impression that newspaper columnists harbor a seething hatred of bureaucrats and elected officials, but nothing could be further from the truth. Just the opposite, in fact. With no outlet to pillory the distrust, crookedness, and pettiness of people in public office, I'd have to quit my job and go find honest work. God bless these folks! They put food on my table and clothes on my back.

Some writers take the pulpit-pounding approach for redress of grievances. That rarely works for me. Like most Baby Boomers, I was born with a streak of smart-ass eight inches wide. I'd lots rather poke fun at a problem than seriously attempt to find a solution.

During the course of the 2000 Census, for example, there was much debate about how to count. Not surprising. Judging by the way people in Washington blow billions of dollars before the money's even minted, it stands to reason they'd have trouble with anything involving numbers.

As you probably remember from the eighth grade, Uncle Sam counts heads every ten years. The results have a major impact on the future of our country, affecting everything from business interests to the allocation of seats in the House of Representatives. But arriving at the finished product is always difficult because nobody can agree on how to do it.

Last time around, the Republicans insisted on a person-to-person survey, complete with census workers who fan out into every neighborhood with charts and forms. The Democrats said that would be too costly and time consuming. They believed a scientific sampling would provide equal or better results.

Hoo-hum. Same song, umpteenth verse. We go through this debate every decade. Whoever prevails, there are only two things you can truly count on at census time.

1. Nobody's going to be satisfied with the results.
2. It's going to cost out the wazoo.

Thus, I suggested some different methods of countology. Such as:

The Phys Ed Chant—Tell all those government census experts to take a hike, then hire a dozen retired gym teachers. On an appointed census day, have 'em blow a whistle and order everybody to line up single file from New York to Los Angeles, Seattle to Miami, and count off aloud. It would be quick and snappy—although by the time the chant reached the heartbeat of America several hours later, some whiners would complain about having to holler, "Fourteen million, seven-hundred-sixty-two thousand, three-hundred, eighteen!; fourteen million, seven-hundred-sixty-two thousand, three-hundred, nineteen!; fourteen million, seven-hundred-sixty-two thousand, three-hundred, twenty!"

It would have served 'em right for living there in the first place.

The Federal Flush Fusillade—This would have been a breeze now that we've got fancy computers to solve intricate math problems. At a designated time, have the head of every household in America flush the toilet once for each person living under that particular roof. Then simply divide by the average amount of water it takes per flush and—*bingo!*—there's your magic number. This would have cleared the air, not to mention the pipes, about how long it takes to conduct a realistic census.

One possible drawback, though, would be the resulting drought throughout most inland river systems, plus flash flooding along the coast. Big deal. The EPA could have worried about that.

The Give and Take Tally—Easy as pie. So simple, even a bureaucrat could have understood it. Just take the final figure from the previous census, add the number of births (available from every county health office in the land), and subtract the deaths (ditto).

All Grady Griggs wanted was an answer. In July 1991, he received a letter from the southeast regional office of the Social Security Administration. It had been typed on July 12 and signed by the assistant regional administrator. It showed up in his mailbox on July 19. In the letter, Griggs was asked to meet a July 10 deadline.

"I have attended a few county fairs, chicken fights, and goat ropings, and have gone to school a few days," he told me. "But I never could remember any experience that would tell me how to work that sort of problem out. I figured the best thing to do was call for help. Whoever answered the phone wanted to know why I was calling. I told her I wanted to talk to the assistant regional administrator. She asked why. I explained about getting the letter and told her I was having a real problem meeting a deadline that had expired two days before the letter was even written. She said the assistant regional administrator doesn't talk to the public. I told her I understood perfectly. If I made mistakes like that, I wouldn't want to talk to the public, either. And you know what? She hung up on me!"

Who says the government can't take fast action? ⌐

For complete accuracy, it probably wouldn't hurt to throw in a handful of "miscellaneous" on both sides of the equation to account for foreign politicians seeking asylum, illegal immigrants, cemetery inhabitants in Chicago (who are already counted twice in most elections), and religious cultists.

The Junk Mail Marathon—Surely the most accurate method of all. Require sweepstakes companies, politicians, charities, insurance agents, credit card brokers, mail order houses, magazine subscription services, and other users of bulk rate to turn over their address lists. Then run 'em through a computer to remove the duplicates, and every home in America would be present and accounted for.

As usual, nobody in Washington paid any attention whatsoever to my well-thought-out remarks. The ingrates.

A High Water Mark for Candidates

The trouble with political campaigns these days is that nobody uses any imagination.

Oh sure, an occasional candidate will attempt to stray from the fold of conformity—like Lamar Alexander's deliberate choice of a red plaid shirt instead of the obligatory blue suit, white shirt, and red necktie when he ran for governor of Tennessee and president of the United States. But for the most part, all aspirants for public office order off the same campaign menu.

Not so in Puerto Rico. There, Senator Freddie Valentin ushered in a bizarre era of disclosure when he produced a urine sample to defend himself against allegations of drug use.

The word "produced" is key to this discussion. I do not mean Senator Valentin opened a manila envelope and handed out copies of a physical examination by his doctor. Nor do I mean he reached into a paper bag, withdrew a vial of his urine, and presented it to a medical technician for testing. I mean he produced it, *tinkle-tinkle*, right there on the spot. While news cameras rolled above and behind him, the good senator stepped into the stall of a men's restroom and filled a cup. This unique act prompted one radio reporter to announce, "I have just transmitted, for the first time ever, a senator taking a pee before the media."

(For what it's worth, this was one of those "spontaneous" photo-ops that took a few minutes to develop. According to news dispatches out of San Juan, Senator Valentin was self-conscious about the setting and had to drink several cups of water before success was declared. This procedure, in agri-political photographic parlance, is known as priming the pump.)

Perhaps political candidates here on the mainland will also adopt this bold initiative, particularly if they are serious about mainstreaming into the minds of Americans. Indeed, historians fifty years from now will look upon this performance as a watershed event in politics during the final years of the twentieth century.

For one thing, it will give candidates a firm grip on measures to eliminate illegal drugs. As Senator Valentin demonstrated, there is no better way to show voters you are committed to a drug-free society than by proving, conclusively, that your own body is free of any and all controlled substances.

In addition, this new tactic will stimulate the economy as manufacturers of soft drinks, fruit juices, and other liquid refreshments aggressively compete for endorsements. If you don't understand the commercial significance of a seeing a candidate chug-a-lug Diet Pepsi or caffeine-free Coke on nationwide television, you slept through Marketing 111.

At a Christmas lunch in Kingston, Tennessee, I heard the shortest speech ever delivered by a politician. Ken Yeager, the Roane County executive, was introduced and, as is customary, was asked if he'd like to offer "a few words." For most politicians, this is interpreted as, "I'll only take twenty minutes." Not Yeager. He stepped to the microphone, said "Merry Christmas," and sat down. Now I know why he got re-elected. ⌒

But perhaps most important, this unique twist in electioneering will pump renewed life into worn-out clichés. If a candidate steps to the podium and declares, "I have nothing to hide!" he can prove it beyond a shadow of a doubt.

Pest Taxes

Way back in the summer of 1988, when George Bush (His Elderness) and Michael Dukakis were campaigning for the White House, both men made tax promises to the people.

Bush told us to read his lips: No new taxes. No way, no shape, no how. Zip. Nada. Absolutely *not,* never-ever. Period.

Dukakis took a different approach. Yes, he said, taxes would most definitely rise under his administration—and that they also would if George Bush was elected. The difference, said Dukakis, was that he wasn't going to lie about it in order to win votes.

You know what happened, of course. Dukakis's little exercise in truth failed miserably, and he was forced into exile in Boston. But his prediction about taxes came true. President Bush flip-flopped worse than a fish fillet in hot grease, much to the chagrin of Republicans everywhere.

Dukakis kept his word, too. As governor of Massachusetts, he began milking the tax machine with practiced hands. An array of new taxes, which produced over one billion dollars the first year, was approved by the Massachusetts legislature. The measure generated money from nearly six hundred new areas, mainly in the service industry.

What kind of services? You name it. Taxes were levied on such bizarre occupations as telephone booth cleaner, trampoline operator, fortune teller, yoga teacher, vendor of piped-in music, mattress renovator, baking pan re-glazer, textile sponger, and tent repairer, to name just a few. It wouldn't have surprised me if the movement had kicked off a second Boston Tea Party—although the thought of baking pan re-glazers flinging cases of Pam into Boston Harbor isn't the kind of civil disobedience that makes tyrants quake.

Nonetheless, the idea of innovative taxation is intriguing. I'm not talking about service taxes, however. I'm talking about pest taxes. I say we stick it to jerks, fools, idiots, and other forms of fungal life who

Every time I read one of those fancy business stories out of Washington about the "government's index of leading economic indicators," I am forced to wade through rivers of drool about stock prices, housing starts, adjustments for inflation, blah-blah-blah. Why not stand at a grocery checkout counter and see how many people are buying generic peanut butter? ～

make things miserable for the rest of us. Lord knows there are hundreds of sources.

For starters, I say we levy a high tax on: grocery shoppers who sneak through the express line with more than fifteen items, browsers who tie up the lone salesclerk to try on seven pairs of pants while you're holding cash for socks, football fans who start "The Wave" two minutes after kickoff and insist on keeping it going throughout the game, telemarketers in general, athletes and actors who forget the little people who pay hard-earned money to watch them perform, cell phone users who don't have the decency to walk around the corner and speak quietly, joke tellers who feel compelled to explain the punch line, diners who describe their hemorrhoidectomy while you're attempting to eat at the next table, e-mailers who send chain messages with dozens of attachments, dolts who block intersections, interstate tailgaters, fast-food customers who order a twelve-course meal in the drive-through, pathetic public speakers who write hour-long speeches, sales people who scream on radio and TV commercials, waiters who don't realize "iced" tea should contain ice cubes, and grocers who sell cardboard tomatoes and peaches labeled as "fresh produce."

When the treasury overflows with money, you'll thank me for this.

A Few Other "Declarations"

The more selfish, scandalous and scurrilous behavior I see from politicians, the more I start to question those lessons I learned in American history about the pious patriots who founded our republic. Makes me wonder what *really* happened back then. Have times changed that much?

Maybe. Maybe not.

If you had been a fly on the wall of Independence Hall in Philadelphia on July 4, 1776, you might—might, I reiterate—have heard comments like these:

"What's with Hancock? Just because he gets to sign first, does he have to take up half the damn page? Where are the rest of us supposed to write—over in the margin? Hey, John! It's only your signature, for cryin' out loud! You don't have to make a production out of it!"

"Did anybody trot this thing by the guys in Legal and let them have a look at it?"

"I'm not touching that document till I see how the polls are leaning. We've got an election coming up, you know."

"Pssst! Make certain you sign with a goose quill, not a turkey quill. The goose producers' PAC out-contributes the turkey PAC, three to one."

"Is my wig on straight? My staff tells me this is an important portrait-op, and I need to look good for the folks back home."

"Get a load of Franklin! How much more weight you reckon he's going to gain? Another pork pie and—*ka-boom!*—he's gonna blow from sea to shining sea!"

"It's stifling in this room! What's so all-fired important that we have to convene now? Can't this wait until October or November, when we're not swimming in sweat?"

"Who was the idiot who proposed we say 'all people are created equal' instead of 'all men'? Let those liberals get a foot in the door, and the next thing you know they'll be talking outright treason—like giving women a say-so. Hoo-boy, what lunatics!"

"This better turn the economy around, or else I'm toast in my district."

"I'm still not comfortable with that 'God' and 'Creator' and 'Divine Providence' language. Isn't there any way we can mute those passages? I know we must appease the religious right, but a lot of atheists vote, too."

"Life and liberty are OK, but that 'pursuit of happiness' nonsense is just going to breed trouble down the line. Mark my word. This new generation of youngsters will take that phrase and turn it around to suit their own hedonistic desires."

"Whadaya mean we gotta step outside into the alley if we want a pinch of snuff? Geeze! Next thing you know, they'll be saying we can't smoke our pipes!"

"Did you get an eyeful of that new intern when she leaned over the desk? Wow! Talk about a pair of self-evident truths!"

"Is it 'unalienable', 'inalienable' or 'non-alienable'? Where's Webster when we need him?"

"Call me superstitious if you want to, but I'm tellin' you we need to wait until another colony signs on before we go forward with this independence business. Thirteen is unlucky any way you look at it. It's not good for commerce, and it's not good for agriculture. Let's just wait till we have fourteen."

"Has anybody ever told Samuel Adams his name sounds great for a brand of beer?"

"Now that we've got this 'taxation without representation' issue settled, nobody will ever complain about paying the cost of running the government."

"Just my luck—the inkwell goes dry the moment I start to sign. This new high-tech equipment is going to be the ruination of us all."

Politics is the only line of work where you can stay on the payroll in one job while actively seeking another. In the spring of 2000, for instance, Vice President Al Gore, Texas Governor George W. Bush, and Arizona Senator John McCain were still on the clock in their respective jobs while campaigning for president of the United States. Does this form of occupational double-dipping rile your taxpaying piles? Or does it give you great comfort knowing that the offices of the vice president, Texas governor, and Arizona senator can function quite smoothly with nobody behind the desk? ∼

"I'd like that smarty-pants Jefferson to explain to me what, 'Prudence, indeed, will dictate governments long established should not be changed for light and transient causes; and accordingly all experience hath shewn, that mankind are more disposed to suffer, while evils are sufferable, than to right themselves by abolishing the forms to which they accustomed' actually *means!*"

The Bottle Battle

Tennessee's beer industry has finally caught up with Tennessee's likker industry.

Note I said "likker." I did not say "liquor." Aside from the fact that both involve firewater, there are several distinct differences between these two products.

Liquor is high-class hooch. Likker is a pedestrian potion.

Liquor is advertised in newspapers and magazines. Likker is advertised by word of mouth.

Liquor is sold at licensed stores where the sin tax is so high it will drive you to drink, even if you're buying the stuff for medicinal purposes only. Likker is sold cheaply, on the sly.

Liquor comes in a fancy bottle that has been stamped by the state. Likker comes in a variety of containers, none of which bears a stamp of any description.

One of these very containers is at the center of a political fight between Tennessee's liquor industry and Tennessee's beer industry. Officials of the beer industry—technically known as the "malt beverage" people—are joyous because of a new law. It eliminates a lot of old restrictions governing the size, shape, and color of containers for malt beverages. Tennessee's liquor people don't like the new law. They claim the beer people will use it to sell beverages that deceive customers.

Specifically, the liquor people believe the beer people will start peddling dark green bottles filled with an elixir that looks, smells, and tastes like a wine cooler. But since it is malt-based, it won't really be wine. Nor will it be taxed like wine. Thus, it can be sold inexpensively in grocery stores.

Confused? Of course you are. Everybody is confused—except for the beer lobbyists, the liquor lobbyists, and the politicians who keep them in business. The other 99.9999 percent of us are confused to the point of chucking the entire mess into a garbage can and starting happy hour right away, and I say we join 'em.

As we enjoy the cooling beverage(s) of our choice, we should bear in mind that the likker industry has been ahead of this curve for many years. The likker people have never concerned themselves about the size, shape, and color of their containers. Although the Mason jar achieved legendary status in this regard, the likker people have employed a wide variety of vessels to convey their handiwork, including once-used mayonnaise jars, milk jugs, coffee cans, and soft drink bottles, to name a very few. Not that I have vast experience in this area, you understand, but a twenty-ounce tea jar or Coke bottle with a twist-off, twist-on lid is hard to beat.

As the man who occasionally transfers these containers to me will tell you, "Fergit the bottle, son. Hit's what's on the inside that counts. And this stuff here? Hit'll knock you on your ass."

How to Get Rich Filthily

For approximately the four-hundredth time, the news on air quality in the Great Smoky Mountains National Park is not good. In fact, it's downright awful.

According to the Environmental Protection Agency, ozone levels in the Smokies are "particularly high." In fact, our ozone levels are "the highest in a decade and thirty to forty percent higher than the national ozone standard." In matters of overall dirty air, the Great Smokies continues to get bad grades. The EPA says, "Eastern visibility on the haziest days has worsened."

Sadly, none of this is new to residents of the Tennessee Valley. In study after study for more than two decades, the story's the same. It all boils down to too many people. Too many cars. Too many air conditioners. Too many power plants belching too many tons of pollutants into the atmosphere. And too many clouds dumping too much acid rain upon the highlands.

What in the world to do? In dire situations, when fate has stomped nearly every ounce of strength out of your body, when it looks like things can't possibly get worse, when all hope for a brighter tomorrow has vanished, I like to hark back to those wise words of encouragement fathers everywhere impart to their children: "A bird in the hand is worth. . . ."

Oops, wrong page in the fatherly advice book. The wise saying I *meant* to impart for rough times like these is, "When life gives you lemons, make lemonade." Instead of trying in vain to preserve the pristine wilderness environment of our mountains, we should immediately begin to:

Promote this area as the world's greatest test site for skin cancer research. What's the good of having all that ozone if we don't use it? Blast a hole in it, by gum, and then invite pharmaceutical companies from around the globe to come in. Let 'em dole out a few billion shekels to gauge the effectiveness of their sun screen products.

Court high-dollar defense contractors who specialize in gas masks and night-vision eyewear. Charge 'em big bucks to field test their

During Halloween 2000, there was a weird light bulb incident at Horace Maynard High School. Seems that whenever people attended a night basketball game, some of them developed a sunburn-like condition. The school's gymnasium was given a thorough cleaning and ventilation, yet the irritating symptoms continued. Not until principal Jimmy Carter put two and two together and realized the burns only occurred at night and only in a certain area did the light fixtures come into question. He instructed workers to inspect and replace bulbs. That's when someone read the instructions on one of the boxes and realized that broken bulbs can emit short-wave, ultraviolet radiation. Problem solved. But the devil in me couldn't help but ask that age-old question: How many people does it take to change a light bulb in Union County? ∽

prototypes in the broad "daylight" of a typical Smokies summer afternoon, when visibility usually is limited to the end of one's nose.

Contact the folks from Guinness to see if we can establish a new record for the world's longest continual parking lot: Highway 411 from Gatlinburg, Tennessee, to Cherokee, North Carolina.

See what I mean? With just a bit of innovative thinking, we can bleed this environmental tragedy for all it is worth and rid our mountains of the nattering nabobs of negativism at the same time. I'll think of a few more tips as soon as I take another hit off my oxygen tank.

Making "Adjustments"

I am going to do things differently this year when Tax Guy and I sit down to determine how large a siphon Uncle Sam intends to stick into my billfold. I'm not going to bring any records. No W-2s, no W-9s, no expense accounts, no receipts, no nothin'. I have no need for records this year, thank you very much.

That's because I have discovered a new method of accounting, and I urge my fellow Amurikans, red-blooded and otherwise, to follow suit. It is called "making adjustments."

I learned about this exciting new system from the United States government. Specifically, the Pentagon. Not long ago, Pentagon officials probed through their records for some receipts. They came up short. Something like $2.3 trillion short.

I can sympathize, of course. Any homeowner can. Receipts, vouchers, and other official documents have a way of slipping through our fingers, too. You find a good deal on a couple of used stealth fighters or cruise missiles, and you've bought and paid for the crazy things before you know it, and now, gosh-dangit, where are those fool receipts?

No problem for the Pentagon. It simply "made adjustments" in its financial ledgers—on the order of seven trillion bucks. Give or take a few billion.

None other than the Pentagon's inspector general announced these "adjustments" in his report. In part, the announcement said the Defense Department's "internal controls were not adequate to ensure that resources were properly managed and accounted for, that DOD complied with applicable laws and regulations, and that the financial statements were free of material misstatements." Which amounts to thirty-three words of governmental gobbledygook meaning, "Your guess is as good as ours."

Initially, I was smitten with an overwhelming wish that the Pentagon would roll its official report into the shape of a large lance and deposit it, making no "adjustments" whatsoever for comfort and ease of insertion, where the sun doesn't shine. But then I got to thinking, "Hey! If this 'adjustment-making' business is good enough for the feds, it's good enough for me."

Thus, when Tax Guy tells me my business expenses are too low, I'll instruct him to "make adjustments" in my books. That way, I hope to turn $14.78 worth of pens and paper into at least $5.87 million in travel, office supplies, publications, and postage.

Furthermore, I want Tax Guy to "adjust" my income tax return to show that I worked my buns off twenty-four hours a day, seven days a week, gave everything to charity, and posted a net profit of thirty-seven cents for the entire year. That should put me in good shape for a healthy refund. Which, of course, I expect to receive in cash.

This will enable me to make significant "adjustments" in my style of living.

> **W**ouldn't it restore your faith in humanity if someone took a poll showing that ninety nine percent of Americans wished poll taking was a crime? ～

Third Place Has a Nice, Cozy Feel of Home

When Census 2000 figures for Tennessee were announced, the Nashville metropolitan area had eclipsed Memphis metro in population. Oh, how the mighty have fallen!

Memphis had been at the top of the heap for quite some time. So long, in fact, that reference staff at Lawson McGhee Library couldn't pinpoint an exact date. The best they could find was a notation in an early history book stating Memphis had the highest Tennessee population "in the 1860s." After the new figures were released, however, Nashville added "most populated" to its list of credits, along with "seat of state government" and "home of country music."

From a political standpoint, this shift resulted in some redistricting for seats in state and federal offices. From a regional pride standpoint, it resulted in a realignment of egos. Sorta like the shock Texans felt when Alaska joined the union.

Here in Knoxville, we're still Number Three, and I hope we stay that way. Politicians, business leaders, and other big wheels may celebrate a ballooning population, but I'm content with a lower level of growth. I'm already up to my armpits in highway construction and urban sprawl. Besides, being Number Three ain't all that bad.

I thumbed through several statistical lists while I was at the library, and I realized that the Number Three entries are buffeted from the worst of the bad, yet are still close enough to the pinnacle of the good to enjoy a taste of gravy. For instance, the worst oil tanker spill of all time occurred in Trinidad on July 19, 1979, when the *Atlantic Empress* and the *Aegean Captain* collided, spilling three hundred, thirty-thousand tons of crude. In second place was the *Castillo de Bellver,* off Cape Town, South Africa, on August 6, 1983, with two hundred, eighty-one thousand tons. But way down yonder in third, at a piddling two hundred, seventy-five thousand tons of spillage, was the crash of the *Olympic Bravery* off Ushant, France, on January 24, 1976.

See? Don't you feel better already? Now, look on the happy side of the coin.

According to the stats I found, the highest paid American athlete was Michael Jordan, at sixty-nine million dollars. In second was hockey player Sergei Federov of the Detroit Red Wings, at thirty million. But just an itty-bitty drop lower, at a whopping twenty-seven million, was golfer Tiger Woods. Wouldn't you settle for that?

The more I got to reading about good ol' Number Three, the more joyful I became. I discovered Miller Lite is the third-most popular beer in the United States. Diet Coke ranks third in soft drinks. Third Street is the third-most commonly named street in America. Caribou,

Maine, is the third-coldest. Hampton, Virginia, is the third-oldest. Oak Grove is the third-most common city name. "Buddy" is the third-most popular name for a dog; "Max" has the honor for cats. Episode eight of *Roots* captured the third-largest television audience of all time. "Love Me Tender" was the third-best selling single by Elvis.

On the dark side of the ledger: Acute lower respiratory infections are the third-most common illnesses in the United States. Illinois is the third-worst state for murder. The bubonic plague in India, 1896–1948, was the third-worst epidemic of all time. The fear of flying is the third-most common phobia. Knees are the third-most common sports injuries. Mozambique is the third-poorest country. Russell's viper is the third-deadliest snake in the world.

And in a category that makes me think statistical researchers really need to find honest work, the third-longest word in the English language came from medieval times and describes a superstition. It has 310 letters and is much too long to be reprinted here. Suffice to say it looks like a pack of chipmunks was turned loose on the keyboard. If

In 1941, the city of Knoxville's secondary school needs were met by four large facilities: Stair Tech, Rule High, Austin High, and Knoxville High. But like many other southern towns, Knoxville experienced a huge expansion after World War II. Not only were Baby Boomers birthed by the thousands, the city's growth began to radiate away from its original core. Thus, small, neighborhood schools sprang up all over the map.

Half a century later, Knoxville found itself a full-fledged southern metropolitan area with tens of thousands of second-generation Baby Boomers bulging at the seams. So how did the city meet the educational needs of these far-flung masses? By closing the neighborhood schools and consolidating everyone back into a handful of mega-schools. Just like the old days.

No wonder we're so hesitant to teach evolution. It shows what monkeys we still are. ⌣

you think that's bad, the second-place finisher has 1,185 letters. The first has 1,909.

Thankfully, none will be included in this year's spelling bee championships.

Candidates Abound for This "Official" Honor

Members of the Tennessee House and Senate missed a golden opportunity when they interrupted their traditional trivialities long enough to pass a piece of serious legislation. By unanimous vote, they designated the Tennessee Walking Horse as the "official state horse" of this sovereign territory.

Not "official state animal," mind you. Tennessee has more official state animals than Noah could have crammed onto the ark. Such as an official state bird (mockingbird), not to be confused with official state game bird (bobwhite quail). Plus an official state sport fish (largemouth bass), not to be confused with an official state commercial fish (channel catfish). As well as official state insects (firefly and ladybug), not to be confused with the official state agricultural insect (honey bee) or the official state butterfly (zebra swallowtail). With the occasional official state wild animal (raccoon), official state amphibian (Tennessee cave salamander), and official state reptile (eastern box turtle) thrown in for good measure.

An official state horse is harmless fun. But lawmakers failed to go the extra mile. They should also have named the official state horse's ass. The sheer number of potential recipients could keep committees and subcommittees tied up in discussions for months. That way, the damage from other legislative actions would be lessened.

Where to start looking? Just about anywhere.

Right off the bat, I'm thinking of everyday crooks, particularly the flim-flam artists who prey on old people. Computer hackers also deserve a shot. So do litterbugs. And anybody connected with those *Who Wants To Be a Millionaire?*, *Weakest Link*, and *Survivor* television programs.

Excellent candidates all. Yet there is an even finer cadre of honorees, a group of men and women whose very actions make them the hands-down peoples' choice for this award. I speak, of course, of the

> **D**id you know that when the Tennessee Wildlife Resources Agency, headquartered in Nashville, mails out boat registration renewal notices to Tennessee skippers, they come from Ohio? A reader alerted me to this geographic puzzle and asked why. I contacted the TWRA and was told it simply was a matter of economics. The Ohio company out-bid everyone else in Tennessee. I suppose that with all the rivers, lakes, ponds, and streams Tennessee is blessed with, folks would rather be on the water than at work. Can't say that I blame 'em, either. ⌇

members of the Tennessee General Assembly. These folks, who rarely meet a lobbyist they don't like, have a habit of enacting rules that apply to everyone but themselves. Perhaps they take their cue from members of the United States Congress. In any event, their latest venture into the land of do-as-I-say-not-as-I-do occurred when they were being visited by a bunch of high school students from Obion County.

As anyone who ever flicked a Bic knows, state buildings have been smoke-free for years. But when the kids ventured into the Capitol and Legislative Plaza—*hack! wheeze!*—they ran into the fumes of legislators, lobbyists, and anyone else who wanted to puff. Seems these areas are specifically exempt from no-smoking regulations.

That little bit of sleight-of-hand alone should qualify lawmakers for the coveted "official state horse's ass" designation. But if you think I'm being overly harsh, let's try another honor for the fearless elected leaders of Tennessee government: official state jellyfish.

Weeding Out a Thorny Issue

There are several reasons why I didn't buy a new lawnmower this spring.

I didn't have a mountain of spare cash sitting around, for one thing. For another, my old mower, though slow and clunky, still cuts grass reasonably well. Especially if my son is running it instead of me.

I didn't want to mess with the hassle of shopping, either. Spending two days comparing the qualities of a Goatmeister, with its patented skozjamflagit maniflobulator for easier handling, to a Super Snipper, with its revolutionary new whipdoodle hookdingie for precision cutting, interests me almost as much as a butt full of boils. So I put off the task for another year.

Now, I'm starting to think this was a serious tactical error. I should have made a purchase while soon-to-be-antiques were still on the market.

The Environmental Protection Agency recently announced sweeping emissions standards for lawnmowers, chain saws, weed trimmers, and similar products. You better believe the folks in small engine research and development are slaving over their drawing boards as we speak, creating new whingdingles and wangnuggets guaranteed to make the air spewing from their exhaust pipes cleaner than April in the Alps.

Fine. I understand all that. I realize carbon monoxide and other pollutants from these pint-sized engines, when magnified by the multiple millions in use across the country, contribute significantly to dirty air. At the same time, though, I have difficulty swallowing all of EPA's figures on the matter. Having grown up in the shadow of TVA, I instinctively reach for my gun any time I hear statistics quoted by the federal government.

According to EPA, one hour of lawn mowing creates as much pollution as driving a new car for eleven and a half hours. The same amount of time with a weed trimmer is equal to twenty-one hours behind the wheel. With a leaf blower, it's thirty-four. And with a chain saw, the EPA's figure leaps to sixty-three. C'mon. If that were true, we'd need gas masks to walk to the mail box.

Still, I realize the need to control all sources of pollution, and I'm willing to do my part. I just shudder to think how many bugs must be worked out before clean air grass cutters sweep across the land. If you will remember with automobiles, it took several years of experimentation before Detroit produced vehicles that would run smoothly, powerfully, and maintain any semblance of gasoline efficiency—all at the same time, I mean.

The best thing for me to do is kick back and let the regulatory-manufacturing processes thrash themselves into shape. Give the designers several years to perfect a clean, efficient lawnmower that, hopefully, will be (1) smaller than a cement mixer and (2) operable by cretins who have not graduated with honors from MIT.

For lawn control in the meantime, I'm seriously considering the purchase of a cow. Assuming the EPA doesn't complain about Bossy's methane emissions.

You can't escape big brother on land or water. During the 2000 Census, I heard from a man and woman who were camped in a public park on Melton Hill Lake. They said two men bearing Census Bureau identification badges worked their way through the campground making sure campers had filled out the necessary forms to be counted. ∿

A Different Approach

If I were in charge of the Internal Revenue Service, I'd take a hint from Publishers Clearing House and change the way taxpayers are contacted. I'd promise 'em anything they want to hear.

Currently, the IRS sends out an incredibly complicated tax form, accompanied by a lifeless letter accentuated with veiled threats, and expects everyone from Seattle to Sarasota to gleefully open their billfolds. That's not the way we human beings operate. We need to be stroked. We need to be comforted. We need to be baited.

Imagine how delighted taxpayers would be if they went to their mailboxes in January and discovered the same type of letter Publishers Clearing House sends to households all over America.

"Dear MILTON R. FIGWHISTLE:

"Congratulations! You may be on the brink of receiving a million-dollar refund this year!

"You are extremely lucky, MILTON R. FIGWHISTLE! Thousands of other taxpayers have been eliminated through a special selection process. But you are still in contention! And if your name is chosen, the President of the United States will personally drive to your home at 482

BEANSPROUT BOULEVARD in FLEABITE, MISSISSIPPI, and award you the refund himself!

"But you have to act quickly, MILTON R. FIGWHISTLE! We must hear from you by April 15, or that refund will go to someone else!

"Please take time to browse through the enclosed catalog and see the important federal services that make FLEABITE, MISSISSIPPI, such a great place to live! Then fill out the attached 1040 form and return it to us, along with our low shipping and handling fee based on your income.

"Who knows? MILTON R. FIGWHISTLE could be the envy of all his neighbors on BEANSPROUT BOULEVARD when the president pulls into his driveway with that check! (See official rules for details. Neither void nor prohibited. Non-participants subject to jail time.)"

Sure, this approach is hokey. Sure, it stinks worse than a chemical spill. Sure, it makes an alleged promise that doesn't have one chance in one-hundred million of coming true.

So? What's the problem?

Truly the government works in mysterious ways. Knoxvillian Ted Buel went to his mailbox one day and found a letter addressed to a company in Palm Bay, Florida. Buel knew nothing about the company. He had never conducted business with it. He had never communicated with it. Indeed, the only thing he had in common with the company was the same street number: 1648. Not same street name, mind you. Just the number. Everything else—name, address, city, state, ZIP code—was different.

Buel wrote "Mis-delivered, forward" on the outside of the envelope and dropped it into a Postal Service bin. The next day, it was right back in his mailbox. It took a second mailing before the letter disappeared. He's not certain it reached the company in Florida, of course. Just think how many streets across America have a location with the number "1648." This thing could bounce around for decades. ⌒

Chapter 6

No Longer a Slave to Fashion

There is one clothing problem I don't have. I never have to sit around and worry about when *Gentlemen's Quarterly* will call and ask for an interview. When you make sartorial statements with blue jeans, T-shirts, and camo shirts, the only people who notice tend to frequent sporting goods stores.

Aside from a brief moment of insanity in college, I've never been a fashion plate. Never intend to be. Bully for the men and women who are, though. More power to them if they feel compelled to stay abreast of the latest fabrics and styles. They help keep the economy strong. I'll stay happily hidden among the unwashed masses.

One reason I resist high fashion is because I'm cheap. If I'm going to plunk down several thousand dollars on a store counter, I expect something more than a business suit in return. A bass boat, perhaps.

Even if money was no object, I cannot imagine cloaking my body in expensive finery. In August 1990, I was sent to California by the *News-Sentinel* to write columns and color stories surrounding the Kickoff Classic football game between the universities of Tennessee and Colorado. For one dispatch, I cruised the trendy clothing stores along Rodeo Drive in Beverly Hills. I came away from that experience convinced this country would be better off, from a clothing standpoint, if California sank immediately into the Pacific.

At one store I was greeted by a sales clerk named "Imtiaz." At least that's what it said on his shiny gold tag. He walked up while I was looking at a pair of eight hundred fifty-dollar shoes. I stammered out words to the effect that I really wasn't interested in shoes.

No doubt Imtiaz pegged me for a rube from the get-go, but you couldn't tell it by his lavish attention and service. He was exceedingly polite and helpful as he led me to another section of the store. I might as well have been Bill Gates—although I doubt Bill Gates needs smelling salts when he is handed a cardigan sweater priced at over one thousand dollars.

Assuming that one was a bit too steep, Imtiaz then showed me a pullover version of the same sweater. It was a mere five hundred twenty-nine bucks. Then he reached for some wool trousers. "Feel the fabric," he said. I felt the fabric. I also felt the price tag and without benefit of Braille immediately detected a figure of two hundred eighty-nine dollars.

Something to keep the trousers in place? Imtiaz handed me an ostrich skin belt. Only two hundred ninety-nine dollars. Silently, I reasoned that no man should wear britches that cost less than the belt. Besides, I wasn't sure how those fancy pants would hold up in the washing machine back home. I said no thanks.

Imtiaz was not one to give up quickly. He sprayed my wrist with cologne. "On sale today for only forty-nine dollars," he said with a smile.

I smiled, too. Then I said, "Feet, get me outta here." My feet responded, despite the fact they weren't equipped with eight hundred and fifty-dollar shoes.

Another problem I have with "the look" is dealing with discomfort. Why would otherwise sane people subject themselves to pain in order to be chic? Women in high-heeled shoes, for example. There's no way walking around on those inclined stilts can be anything but excruciating. And the kids who wrap themselves up in horribly baggy pants? Spare me. No wonder preachers keep warning about the end of time.

Once at a grocery store, I saw a teenaged boy whose pants were so baggy, he had to grip his waist with one hand at all times to keep 'em from falling off. This kid was built along the lines of Barney Fife, yet his pants would have easily held Otis Campbell and Sheriff Taylor with enough room for Opie to squeeze in on the side. There was sufficient material piled up around his ankles for Aunt Bee to make an apron. Despite such torture, I'm sure this pimply faced stud thought he was the most dashing figure ever to grace the aisle of a Kroger.

Of course, neither I nor any other Baby Boomer has a right to criticize the clothing style of youths. Not after we assaulted the eyes of our sovereign nation with tie-dyed shirts and, later, polyester leisure suits. In fact, I always get a kick out of listening to fossils like myself harp about whatever it is the youngsters happen to be wearing. When will it ever dawn on us that the main reason they choose such hideous stuff is to watch us recoil in horror?

All across America right now, there's a big push for dress codes in public schools. It is a wasted effort. Parents and school administrators might as well save their breath about forcing students to wear uniforms. Ain't gonna happen that way.

But there is a trick to make the hellions clean up. Simply pass a regulation stating they absolutely, positively must wear the grungiest, nastiest, baggiest, ragged, worn-out articles of clothing they can find. No exceptions. Violators will be tossed out of class without prior warning.

You know what'll happen? The students will run out and buy blue blazers, khaki pants, white shirts, and neckties and wear 'em as a form of protest. It's in the genes.

Riches in Britches

A pair of old blue jeans recently sold on eBay for $46,532. When the story and photographs about this historic auction were published, Baby Boomers all over the United States had three immediate reactions:

1. "So *that's* where the jeans that got stolen from my dorm room wound up."
2. "Maybe my retirement won't be so bleak, after all. If those beat-up britches went for forty-six grand, I must have half a million bucks' worth of antiques hanging in my closet."
3. "Ain't it great to be over fifty and still wearing blue jeans?"

True, these $46,532 classics weren't your everyday blue-light specials. They had been found in the ruins of a Nevada mining town. Estimated age: one hundred and twenty years. Levi Strauss & Company, the original manufacturer, purchased these jeans for a corporate collection. An eBay spokeswoman described them as being faded, ripped in the inseam, but still intact and even wearable. Meaning any kid could have put 'em on and worn 'em around town, and no one would have been the wiser. Compare that with, say, a celluloid collar or bustled dress or other dapper item of turn-of-the-last-century clothing.

Fashions come and fashions go, but, thankfully, we've always got jeans. They're a security blanket for the millions of sartorially impaired—and we know who we are—who couldn't make the Top Ten Best-Dressed List in a nine-person town.

Sure, there have been subtle changes in jean styles through the years. The width of the legs is subject to periods of ebb and flow, just like the tides. Sometimes the butt is baggy; sometimes it's tighter than a drumhead. The design of the fly switches back and forth between button-up and zipper. But despite those changes, good ol' faded blue jeans—with the emphasis on old and faded—are about as close to clothing nirvana as humans will ever come. If Adam and Eve had chosen blue jeans instead of fig leaves, they might have gotten a reprieve.

The only aspect of the jeans experience I dislike is the acquisition itself. I always have two strikes against me in this department because I'm not a shopper at heart. If I had my druthers, I would just wave a magic wand periodically, and the next set of comfortable, familiar, broken-in jeans would suddenly appear in my closet.

The newer relaxed and faded denims they have these days are better than those indigo stovepipes from the '50s. But even if they've been acid-washed or stone-washed or beaten with sticks during the manufacturing process, new jeans are still that: new. They take some getting used to. That's why I refuse to give them up until they're in tatters. Only then will I bite the bullet and start working on another pair.

Contrary to what many Yankees believe, we southern Appalachians know how to tie our shoes. Indeed, this is a skill most of us have mastered by the time we finish high school. Assuming, of course, we finish high school.

Nonetheless, I have a question for shoe makers, particularly the makers of athletic shoes: Why are the dadblamed strings so long? This phenomenon remains the same across the board, despite the brand of shoe. When I lace up a pair of running shoes, there's enough string left over to fly a kite. What are you supposed to do with the excess? Wrap it around your legs two or three times like Roman soldiers?

A suggestion to manufacturers: Why not cut back on the length of each string and pass some of the savings along to us customers? ～

I'd like to think those eBay Levi's were originally owned by some old coot who hit it big in the mines and spent the rest of his days paying someone else to buy and break-in jeans for him. Even with inflation, though, I doubt it set him back $46,532.

The worst kind of water pollution

Attention, men. In case you're sitting around the pool wondering, "Is there any way I can embarrass myself further?" the answer is an unequivocal yes. Grandpa's swimming suits are coming back in style.

Actually, they're already back, at least in the cutting-edge market. Highly competitive swimmers, the kind of fools who think nothing of a brisk ten or fifteen miles in the pool every morning before sitting down to a delicious breakfast of tofu and beet juice, have been wearing them for quite some time. That, plus the worldwide television exposure they got in the Olympics, should have couch potatoes everywhere saying to themselves, "Hey, with a suit like that, *(buuurp!)* I can look cool, too!"

Of course, these people should be dragged out of their homes and summarily executed. But that's not the way punishment works in America. Instead, the guilty go free while the rest of society is tortured, in a most cruel and inhumane fashion, by the sight of hippos waddling around in garments designed to fit hummingbirds. Does the term "short shorts" come to mind?

The most radical item in this new breed of swimwear comes from the Speedo Company. It is called "Fastskin" and is stitched with surface indentations that supposedly work like sharkskin. This is known in the trade as a "bio-medic" design because it directs the flow of water over the body.

What's more, this type of suit supports muscles up and down the body. It's the same principle as a weightlifter's belt. With conventional swim trunks or those hideous peanut-shell-and-rubber-band triangles, muscles tend to flop aimlessly in the water, wasting precious energy with each stroke and grossing out everyone within a thirty-mile radius of the pool.

These new suits aren't cheap. We're talking three hundred dollars for an ankles-to-neck cover up. But, as jelly bellies everywhere are wont to say about these matters, "What's a few extra bucks if it hides more skin?"

So consider yourself warned. Before long, swimming holes all across America will probably be XXL-rated.

No matter that it will take a crane and erection service to hoist these men into place—plus an all-terrain vehicle with the transmission geared to low range to stretch one of the new outfits across ten acres of flab. No matter that poolside mothers will be forced to cover the eyes of their children, lest they suffer permanent visual and psychological damage from gazing at the ugly sight. No matter that rock-ribbed teenagers will laugh until they vomit.

We fashion-conscious mature figures have an image to uphold. If our fathers had the guts to parade around poolside in high rider black socks and wing-tipped dress shoes, the least we can do is squirm into one of these skin-tight babies. This is our heritage. This is our solemn duty.

Surely you've seen the "No Fear" logo on the back window of cars and trucks. For those of you who are hopelessly out of touch with the times—I had to ask one of the young pups on our staff—"No Fear" is a line of clothing that has taken on a life of its own. The wording has become somewhat of a motto for the twenty-something crowd.

A buddy of mine recently saw the east Tennessee version of "No Fear" on the back of a pickup truck. Hand-lettered, it read, "Ain't Skeered." ⌇

The Right Stuff

As anyone of the male persuasion will tell you, it is not uncommon to see men attending to certain cosmetic and personal hygiene duties in public restrooms. Besides the *really* personal hygiene duties that take place inside the stall, I mean.

The activities I'm talking about are usually carried out at the sink, in front of the mirror. Hair combing, for instance. How many times have you—I'm speaking to men in the audience right now—walked into a public john and noticed some guy standing before the mirror, comb or brush in hand, sculpting his locks? Hundreds, at least.

I, myownself, have witnessed this activity along all points of the hair-combing spectrum, and I'm certain other men have, too. Some guys will pluck a comb from a hip or shirt pocket, run it under the tap water, swipe a couple of times across their scalp, re-pocket the comb, and be on their way. Others are more deliberate. They stare at the mirror intently, cocking their head from side to side, slowly coifing each individual fiber until it has been perfectly positioned. Like Kookie Burns on *77 Sunset Strip* or the Fonz on *Happy Days*.

Tooth brushing is another activity often seen in public facilities, particularly along the interstate highway system and other major thoroughfares frequented by travelers. Makes sense. If a guy's on the road for the day and has just downed a couple of Quarter Pounders for lunch, chances are he'll want to stop at the next rest area and scrub his choppers.

You've probably seen men shaving or sponge-bathing at public sinks, as well. I know I have. Whenever I'm on the road, it is not uncommon for me to fill my stomach and my gas tank at a truck stop. Invariably, one or two long-haul jockeys will be in the john, scraping away three days' worth of whiskers or throwing a few hasty splashes of water on their face and armpits before climbing back into the cab.

Now that I put my mind to it, I can rattle off three or four other duties—shoe shining, clothes repairing, clothes changing, for example —that commonly occur in public facilities. But I recently saw a cosmetic activity in a men's restroom that was an all-time first for me.

Eyelash curling. I am as serious as a train wreck.

This occurred a few mornings ago at a Knoxville hotel. I had just concluded a breakfast business meeting and, en route to my vehicle, swung by the privy for coffee recycling. I opened the door, stepped inside the room, and nearly bumped into a man who was curling his lashes with one of those little scissors-like tools. He went at it just as casually as anyone else might comb his hair or brush his teeth. He finished, tucked the curling tool into his travel kit, and walked out the door. I nearly peed on myself.

Please understand. I make no judgment whatsoever about this matter. If that fellow had a need to curl his lashes, more power to him. Who knows? Maybe eyelash curling has become the in thing for beautiful people to do these days.

Then again, I am typing these words while keeping one eye glued to the television as John Glenn is being blasted back into space. I figure if any man on this planet has been given a thorough bodily going-over, it's the senator and former astronaut from Ohio. I daresay every square inch of his torso and his spacesuit was checked and re-checked for functional, hygienic, and cosmetic purposes. And I'm willing to bet fifty bucks that eyelash-curling tools were nowhere on the checklist.

Non-Doohickey Shoes

I would like to pose a question that has bothered me for most of a half-century. It is not an earth-shattering matter by any stretch of the imagination. It ranks well below more important quests for knowledge such as, "What is the meaning of life?" or "Is supper ready yet?" or "Do you think the fights are rigged on the *Jerry Springer Show*?"

Nonetheless, I simply must ask: How in the name of common sense can people stand to wear flip-flops, sandals, and other shoes with that little doohickey sticking between their toes?

Not all types of casual footwear come equipped with those infernal doohickeys. It's important that you understand the difference.

The regular kind, the non-doohickey kind which Gawd Hisself intended for us mortals to wear, have straps that go across the feet. I own bunches of them, both of the el-cheapo, flip-flop variety, as well as the fancy "river sandal" genre featuring self-stick straps to keep them on my feet when I'm launching a boat.

The doohickey kind, which were inspired by Satan, have this hateful two-by-four that runs between your big toe and the next toe. I do not own any of these awful devices. For the life of me, I don't see how other people can bear to put them on their feet.

When I was a child, then later as a teenager, I desperately tried to wear the doohickey demons. But the dadburned things alternately pinched and tickled with each step I took. These same problems persisted into adulthood. That's why I cannot understand how other people manage to wear them.

Maybe the space between my toes is super-sensitive. Or maybe I was born with a rare toe impairment and should urge my congressman to fund a hundred-million-dollar research project to study it. Then again, maybe this is one of those culture things you're supposed to acquire with maturity—like developing a taste for scotch whiskey. If that's the case, I will happily spend the rest of my non-doohickey flip-flop and sandal days drinking beer.

I've never made a scientific study of this situation, but casual observation tells me I'm in a distinct minority here. Particularly in matters of flip-flops. Far more people seem to wear the doohickey kind than the non-doohickey kind. Meaning, of course, that the non-doohickey kind is exceedingly difficult to locate.

No problem. We non-doohickey wearers know how to cope with adversity. Whenever I'm in a tourist town, I check out all the cheap shops till I find one that carries non-doohickey flip-flops. Then I buy about twenty dollars' worth.

Keep your exquisite wine cellars and pricey stamp collections. I own a better investment, thank you. The shoe shelf in my garage contains three pairs of pristine, never-worn, mint-condition, non-doohickey flip-flops, still in their original plastic sleeve. I face the summer with confidence.

I'm FREE to Put My Best Foot Forward

I recently received great news in the mail, and I couldn't be more excited if I'd won the lottery.

If I had won the lottery, all I'd get is some money that the government would take back in taxes. But with this wonderful offer, I can save money and time, get convenience and a daily massage, and I'll always look my best. All for no cost or obligation. Such a deal!

This incredible offer came to me from L'eggs Brands, Incorporated. It is for pantyhose.

I am not lying. Everything is right here in a computer-generated letter. It is not addressed to my wife. Or my daughter. It is addressed to me.

"Dear Sam Venable," it starts, "want to look your best, save time and money, and get something FREE? Many women in Tennessee have already received a FREE sample of L'eggs pantyhose because they want to take advantage of our FREE introductory offer on America's No. 1 style, Sheer Energy, and to try the best, most convenient, first quality hosiery program around."

The letter goes on to describe how my FREE (federal advertising law requires this word to be spelled in capital letters) pantyhose will give me "unique morning-to-midnight massaging benefits" that will keep my legs "invigorated and refreshed."

Excellent. If there's anything I like better than saving time and money and getting something FREE, it's having invigorated legs. That's why I can't wait to fill out the form and send it back.

Naturally, there's a catch. A couple of them, actually. Since I've never ordered pantyhose, I'm not familiar with some of these complexities. Should I select control tops with the reinforced toe? Or support legs with the sandal foot?

Size is another problem. L'eggs sent a chart, but my dimensions aren't listed on it. I'm five-foot, nine inches tall, and the heaviest weight in that category is one hundred, seventy-five pounds. The last time I weighed one-seventy-five, Jimmy Carter was president.

But the biggest choice is color. Sheer Energy comes in seven shades, so I asked a few *News-Sentinel* colleagues to help me decide.

Cartoonist Dan Proctor suggested navy "so your leg hairs won't show." Outdoor editor Bob Hodge went for off-white "because it'll give you that perfect slutty look." Projects editor Babs Asbury opted for coffee "because that's what you're drinking all the time." Copy editor Donna Cruze said black was a must since "you can wear it to work or after hours, and it gives a long, lean appearance." Special Publications editor Vivian Vega also voted for black "because it goes so well with your sandals, yellow coach's shorts, and blue Hawaiian shirt." Copy editor Fatima Hyder insisted on suntan; she also recommended I shave my legs "with a razor, not Nair."

Marvelous advice, and I appreciate these people taking time from their schedules to guide me through this quandary. But with a decision as important as pantyhose, I really ought to seek a higher authority. An expert. A pro whose leg wear knowledge is legendary in the industry.

Anybody got Joe Namath's phone number?

The Hunt for the Perfect Fit

Archaeologists in Switzerland have just announced what may be the strangest discovery of the new millennium. They have dug up a shoe insole believed to be 5,200 years old.

According to the Associated Press, the insole—about ten inches long and made out of moss—was discovered under a road along the shores of a lake near Zug, a town in central Switzerland. This area was the site of a Neolithic settlement. Stefan Hochuli, a Swiss scientist, says about ten shoes from the period have been unearthed so far, but this is the first insole.

(I wonder if Stefan Hochuli and his fellow archaeologists, shortly after making their remarkable discovery, set an international record for the longest and loudest exclamation of the term, *"aaaiiiiaarrrgh-sheeeew-eee!"* An old tennis shoe or sock that remains entombed in a gym locker over summer vacation is bad enough. Can you imagine the impact of an insole that managed to stay hidden for fifty-two centuries? This would likely win the Nobel Prize in medicine as a permanent cure for blocked sinuses. But I digress.)

Whoever the ancient insole maker happened to be—do you suppose he was known by other villagers as "Scholl, the physician"?— he surely is the patron saint of everyone who suffers from ill-fitting shoes and boots.

I speak with vast experience on this matter. I have never figured out how footwear manages to change sizes on me as soon as I make my purchase and walk out the door. This trickery never occurs with other types of clothing—with the possible exception of pants, which can hang in my closet up to a full three weeks before beginning to show signs of shrinkage.

With shoes and boots, however, the change is exceedingly faster. Inside the store, they fit wondrously. Not too tight up front. Not too loose in the back. Just the right amount of wiggle room all around.

Good ankle support. I even take a test walk around the joint just to make sure.

For all the good it does. As soon as I get home and lace them up again, it's as if somebody switched packages with me at the cash register. Either that, or the crazy things took a horrific growth spurt while they were in transit. This seems especially true with boots.

I'm in the woods quite a bit. I own nearly a dozen pairs of boots. I can't tell you the number of times they have changed sizes on me less than half a mile down the trail. Invariably they start feeling loose around the heels. Even though they appeared to fit marvelously at the store—tried on while I was wearing thick boot socks, you understand—the heel suddenly becomes too loose, too tight, too narrow, or too wide, depending on the whim of that particular pair.

Which is why, in addition to owning a king's ransom in footwear, I have a small fortune invested in insoles. We're talking store-bought insoles. Custom-made insoles. Heel inserts. Arch supports. Leather insoles. Closed-cell foam insoles. Gel insoles. Felt-padded insoles. I store all of these products in a big box in the garage and pick and choose from the inventory as needed in my eternal quest for the ever-elusive "perfect" fit.

I haven't tried moss insoles. Yet. But I'm here to tell you the next velvety green patch I stumble across is in danger. Like Sir Galahad searching for the Holy Grail, I shall keep wandering. Or limping, as the case may be.

A Bulge in the Buns

Most men have a royal pain in the butt.

Please note I did not use the verb "are"—although a vast number of men qualify for the honor—because we aren't talking about character flaws. We're talking about that thick, bulging, agonizing hump of leather riding on most men's hips. The billfold.

What started as a simple container for currency has ballooned over the generations into a pocket-sized version of the suitcase. As a result, males of our species are metamorphosing into a pitiful lot of off-balance, twisted-spine cripples who will never know the joy of standing, walking, or sitting in comfort.

I got to thinking about this phenomenon the other day after getting a telephone call from Bob Luttrell. He had just returned from the doctor's office, where he had been forced to produce a stack of plasticized verifications and identifications.

"First, they wanted my driver's license," he said. "Then my Medicare card. Then any supplemental insurance cards I might have. Then a charge card. Finally, I said, 'If you'll wait long enough, I've probably got a card somewhere in this billfold that tells how many days a week I have sex.'"

"How did we get into this mess?" Bob asked me. "When did we go from name, rank, and serial number to a wad of cards the size of a football?"

He's right. Why, indeed? Isn't there a better way? In this high-tech, digitized, bar-coded world, can't somebody invent a single card that does it all—fishing license to voter registration to AARP membership to fast-food coupon?

To quantify this bulky trend, I grabbed a ruler and note pad and took some informal, uh, "male measurements" around the *News-Sentinel's* editorial office. I asked a dozen male colleagues to give me their billfolds. With rare exceptions, they produced without asking why. This is not because I exude an air of universal trust. It is because newsmen are too poor to carry much money. Plus, their credit cards are permanently stressed to the point red lights would flash if someone attempted to add any charge greater than two bucks.

The thickness of these twelve billfolds ranged from one-half inch to over two inches.

Mike Silence, Mike Flannagan, and Mike Strange had the slimmest—leading me to the immediate conclusion that the key to hip pain relief is to be named Mike. Actually, Eric Vreeland's billfold also was a slender one-half inch, but I nullified the entry since (a) his billfold was the larger, inside coat pocket style not designed for hip wear and (b) his name is not Mike.

Among the big boys were Johnathan Tipton (one and a half inches), Don Jacobs and Bob Hodge (one and a quarter inches), and Dan Proctor (one and an eighth inches). The champion was J. Miles Cary, who unsheathed a horse-choker slightly over two inches thick. Then again, Miles has great experience in carrying heavy loads. He's one of those news photographers who feels naked unless he's packing fifty pounds of lenses, tripods, filters, and attachments.

What's buried inside these tombs?

Virtually the same in each case, in greater or lesser volumes: Photos of the wife and kids, credit cards, those insidious grocery store "discount" (insert laughter here) cards, ID cards, insurance cards, drivers license, ATM card, business cards, membership cards—plus the occasional nameless telephone number, circa 1975, and Visa receipts generated during the first Bush administration.

Stan DeLozier (three-quarters of an inch) would have won the record for moldy oldie, but he confessed to recently cleaning out some dated material, including his old Selective Service registration card. Sounds reasonable enough. At age sixty-one, the only draft notice DeLozier should expect is from Civil War re-enactors.

Still, the questions remain: Why do we shackle ourselves to this butt-busting menace? Why don't we strike a blow for freedom? Why don't we follow the brave lead of bra-burning women and strike a match to our billfolds?

Ah, yes. Bra-burning women. Maybe that's where those nameless telephone numbers came from.

How Many Lawyers Does It Take to Tell Time?

If you think a dollar doesn't go far any more, you obviously haven't bought a wristwatch. I shelled out $17.96, plus tax, the other day, and in addition to a serviceable timepiece, I also received a partial law degree and instructions in how to speak eight foreign languages. Show me a better bargain anywhere.

As you can tell from the outlandish price, my choice of wristwatches tends to run on the lower side of the economic curve. Translation: cheap. I have never understood why someone would pay hundreds, thousands, even tens of thousands, of dollars to know the time of day. Nor, apparently, do I have an appreciation for status symbols. A friend who moves in more affluent circles than I once explained to me that high-dollar lawyers have a reputation to uphold. They need to wear a fifteen-thousand-dollar wristwatch, he said, because their clients expect their attorneys to have the best of everything. Including the highest fees. Go figure.

I bought an el-cheapo Timex to replace the el-cheapo Timex I had been wearing for the last two or three years. These are bottom-of-the-barrel discount store watches. They come in one color—olive drab—and have a plain face with a minute, hour, and second hand.

These el-cheapo Timexes used to operate the way wristwatches were supposed to. They had to be wound daily. Now, they are battery operated, a change for the worse as far as I'm concerned.

I could get six or seven years out of the wind-up el-cheapo Timexes before they broke. The battery el-cheapoes don't last that long. Maybe Timex should update its motto to: "It takes a licking and eventually quits ticking." Once, I managed to wear out both the battery and the watchband at the same time and realized replacing these bum parts would constitute nearly three-fourths of the price a brand new watch. And to think we still laugh as the Russians experiment with capitalism.

In any event, when I got home with my newest OD el-cheapo, I noticed a small, thick wedge of paper attached to it. Curious, I started unfolding it.

I kept unfolding it. And kept unfolding it. And kept unfolding it.

At long last, I finally wound up with a thirteen-by-seven-inch sheet, printed on both sides in itty-bitty type. It contained the operating instructions and warranty for my watch. After perusing this document, I am convinced Timex is owned by the United States government, for no entity in the private sector could come up with something so convoluted.

Each step was spelled out in English, French, Spanish, German, Japanese, Chinese, and three other languages I couldn't identify. But instead of having sections for the different languages, each step had its own interpreter, resulting in the most dizzying array of engineering instructions and legalisms, foreign and domestic, my eyes had ever seen. I nearly grew carsick scanning the text for a familiar-looking word.

"Please read instructions to understand how to operate your Timex watch," one line said.

Not possible. If I took enough time to wade through this mumbo-jumbo, the battery would be dead, and I'd have to go through the entire watch-purchase process once again.

But I did cover enough ground to finally locate the warranty. There, I discovered my $17.96 watch is covered against defects and damage for one year—but only if I kick in seven dollars for shipping and handling if and when I return the thing. Oh, and for an extra five bucks, I can extend the warranty for four more years.

Thanks, but no thanks. I like to live dangerously. The very idea of stepping out boldly into the world without backup protection for my $17.96 wristwatch is heady wine.

Besides, just like those lawyers with their fifteen-thousand-dollar wristwatches, I've got a reputation to uphold.

It's So Easy for a Guy to Shop

You'd think after more than thirty years of marriage I'd know better. Indeed, I do know better. I just wasn't paying attention to business.

Oh, how I wish someone had sat me down and said, "Think, man, think! Use your noodle! You're a Guy who's about to enter the Non-Guy world! For Pete's sake, don't blow it!" But someone didn't say that to me, and it led to a crisis.

What happened was, I went fabric shopping with my wife.

Please understand. That, in and of itself, was not the issue. There's nothing in the Guy Book of Rules that says you can't shop for fabric, with or without your wife. In fact, I was the instigator of the fabric shopping trip in the first place. For over a year, I've wanted curtains in my office at home. Mary Ann has had dozens of other chores on her to-do list, and, frankly, this was not a high priority item for either of us. A few days ago, we finally got around to acquiring the raw materials.

That's when I committed the cardinal sin of Non-Guy shopping. I walked into the store, which was stocked with approximately 856,732 bolts of cloth in 417,964 different patterns and textures. I looked around for, oh, ninety seconds. Two minutes, tops. Then I announced, "Here's what I want for my curtains. Let's take it to the counter and ring it up."

Mary Ann looked at me in horror, like I'd just been visited, publicly, by the Three-Bean Chili Emission Monster.

"What did you just say?" she asked.

"I said I found what I want. Let's go."

"*Go?*" she demanded. "We just got here!"

"So? I found what I like. Let's buy it and leave."

"You couldn't have found what you liked!" she insisted. "You've hardly looked at all!"

"How hard can this be?" I replied. "All I needed was something brownish with Guy Stuff on it. This material is tan, and it's covered with a fishing lure pattern. It's perfect."

"But what if you find something you like better?"

"I won't."

"How do you know if you don't shop?"

"I don't need to shop! I came here for brownish Guy Stuff curtain material, and I found some!"

Our debate had attracted some of the sales clerks by then. They took Mary Ann's side. In fact, they appeared to feel quite sorry for her. Of course they would. They were all Non-Guys.

To placate the entire lot of them, I paced up and down seven or eight aisles, nodding this way and that. After fifteen excruciating minutes, I finally was able to herd the Non-Guy caravan toward the cash register, where my originally selected material was measured, cut, and put into a bag.

"Honestly!" Mary Ann said as we exited. "I can't take you anywhere!"

And, wow, you should have heard what she said a few seconds later, when the Three-Bean Chili Emission Monster *did* rear his ugly head. The Guys would have loved it.

Hey, Bubba! yore Nails Are Mighty Purty!

I was standing in the stall of a men's rest room, doing what men normally do in this position, when I happened to glance down at the floor of the stall next to me and saw something—ten somethings, actually—that very nearly caused me to make a mess of the situation.

Purple toenails.

We are not talking about purple that resulted from an accident—say, a two-by-four that tumbled off the workbench. We are talking about purple that resulted from the deft application of nail polish.

I didn't do a lot of research after that. This may come as a surprise to members of the audience who don't stand in rest rooms, but men generally avoid eye contact in this environment. Suffice to say I studied just long enough to note that the purple toenails were attached to feet that were wearing sandals, and the feet were connected to a set of hairy legs.

This occurred a few nights ago at the Knoxville Convention Center. I'd gone there to make a speech. A rock concert was in progress next door at World's Fair Park. Judging from the conversation the Prince of Purple was having with two guys in adjacent stalls—I didn't see their feet—that's where they all were headed.

Hoo-boy. I am *so* far behind the times. No parts of my body have been pierced (stray fishing hooks don't count) or tattooed. And now I must add toenail polish to the not-done-yet list.

But based on spot checks at a half-dozen Knoxville nail salons, I have concluded that the vast majority of other men haven't added nail coloring to their list, either. Most of the locations reported no male clients at all. But there were exceptions.

Lisa Huffman, a nail technician at Belleza Salon and Spa on Kingston Pike, said she's had one male customer who requested painted toenails. He chose red. At Fancy Nails on Chapman Highway, Tracy Vu told me she puts colored polish on men's fingernails and toenails "a couple of times a year." Purple is the color of choice. And at 18 Karat Spa on Deane Hill Drive, Michelle Pritchard said she has a twenty-two-year-old customer who gets his fingernails colored for "special occasions." Some of his choices have been black and white, gold stripes, and neon green with white stripes.

Of course, you wouldn't expect Knoxvillians to be at the cutting edge of any trend, much less one this radical. Our time-honored method is to wait until the big city folks have beaten a fad to pieces and discarded it for something even newer; then we convert. According to a recent story in *Time* magazine, nail art is catching on in Los Angeles,

New York, Dallas, and other locations—meaning the craze will probably filter down to K'town by turn of the century. That's the twenty-*second* century, you understand.

Then again, what do I know? I still think men with earrings look weird. But trust me on this: When the good ol' boys quit field-dressing their deer, grabbling for catfish, and tinkering with engines because it messes up their nails, society will surely be sucking its last gasp of air.

Zippers Just Don't Measure up Anymore

When Ivar Carlson goes shopping for trousers these days, he carries something much more important than cash, credit cards, and his checkbook. He takes a ruler. And he pays a lot closer attention to something besides the fabric, the color, and the price. He checks the zipper.

"Other men ought to start checking, too," he says. "Otherwise, they're going to be in for a big surprise."

Make that a *little* surprise.

Carlson is a retired General Motors executive who lives in Tellico Village, near Knoxville. He remembers the day when he put on a spanking new pair of pants and made the sobering discovery that all was not well down below.

"The zipper was way too short," he said. "I didn't think much about it at first. I thought maybe these pants had a defect or something. Then I started checking around and realized the same thing was happening to lots of pants."

Let us make one thing perfectly clear. Carlson's complaint is not rooted in the relative differences between certain portions of individual male anatomies. This has nothing whatsoever to do with "distinguishing characteristics," as they say in certain Arkansas and Washington, D.C., legal circles. What he's talking about is an aperture in the garment that is sufficient enough to do the job without bodily contortions and undue stress on the cargo.

"I started measuring some older pants," he told me. "They had zippers eight and nine inches long. The ones made today run five-and-a-half inches up to eight. That's quite a change. Unless you've tried these pants on yourself, you can't get a real feel for the problem."

I reckon not.

Carlson even took his complaint to the men's clothing section of a local department store. The clerk agreed with him. "He said, yes, the zippers are getting shorter. He said it's because women are designing and manufacturing these pants, and they don't understand the need for a longer zipper."

Perhaps. Or perhaps this is a long-awaited payback by women for having to suffer through years of behind-the-back bra snap torture.

"Then again, maybe it doesn't have anything to do with women," Carlson continued. "Maybe it's a cost-saving thing. Maybe the manufacturers can save a few pennies on each pair of pants by cutting an inch or two off the zipper. Either way, it's an injustice to men."

Here is Ivar Carlson's guideline for worry-free wearing: "Be sure to carry a ruler into the store, and use it. Individual pants are going to vary by style and cut and whether they're trim-fit or pleated or whatever. But under no circumstances would I buy anything with a zipper shorter than seven inches."

What if the clerk thinks you're nuts and tries to argue? Tell him he's all wet—which is the very situation you're trying to avoid in the first place.

Al Kinser of Kingston wishes the textile industry would make an important change in production. "Have the people assigned to sewing labels in shirts start sewing on the buttons," he says. "The way it is now, those neck-scratching labels are sewed on so tightly you can't hardly cut 'em off with a razor blade. Yet the buttons fall off the first time they go through a washer and dryer." ～

The Lawrence Principle

A manufacturer of women's clothing in New York City has answered the question that's burning in everyone's mind up there: How can fur garments be safely worn in public?

On the outside chance you don't keep up with fur fashion news, I should point out that strolling down Main Street in an ermine coat can be risky business in New York and other large cities. That's because anti-fur activists take a dim view of bashing an animal in the head, peeling its hide like a banana, and turning it into clothing. These people have developed a nasty habit of walking up to women wearing fur coats and cursing them loudly.

At least that's what the "passive" activists do. The more active ones are a bit more aggressive. They throw paint. In my All-Time List of Things That Will Get Your Attention in a Hurry, a streak of red Lucite across the front of a thirty-thousand-dollar coat ranks second only to gently settling onto the bear trap you've mistaken for a toilet seat.

(Oddly enough, I've never heard of anyone getting cursed or painted for wearing leather that came from a head-bashed, banana-skinned cow. Or for poisoning rats, for that matter. When it comes to killing animals, anti-fur activists, passive and active, enjoy a unique double standard. But I digress.)

If a fur coat paint assault took place in Knoxville, the response would be predictable. The assaultee would grab the assaulter in a strangle hold and tap lightly about the head, face, and neck for approximately thirty minutes—or until thirty-thousand dollars worth of satisfaction was achieved, whichever took longer. In civilized New York City, however, people allegedly behave in a more mature manner. At least that's what clothier Norman J. Lawrence is banking on.

Lawrence specializes in rainwear. High-dollar rainwear. This is not your $7.95 plastic model off the bargain counter. His cheapest, unlined version checks in at seven hundred dollars. But for about fifteen hundred dollars more, Lawrence will make you a rain suit lined with your own fur.

"Avoid the fur controversy," proclaimed one of his ads in the *New York Times*. "Conceal your old fur in a new silk raincoat!"

In other words, hide your shame. If you're afraid to show the fur in public, wrap it in cotton velveteen or silk broadcloth, and no one will be the wiser. This approach not only keeps your fur undercover, it also affords extra protection should the paint patrol get a glimpse of your secret lining. Quite ingenious.

But why limit this high-tech camouflage to furs? Why not apply the Lawrence Principle to other facets of life?

Let's say you've been lusting for a gas-guzzling sport utility vehicle. No more mousy sewing machine engines for you, mister. You want a road hog that responds—*varrroom!*—when you punch it.

But wait. What are you, some kind of fossil fuel Benedict Arnold? You gonna be unpatriotic and burn more than your fair share of fuel right there in front of Green Peace and everybody? Certainly not. You're going to purchase a new Lawrencemobile, the car that's milk toast on the outside but macho under the hood.

Or say you've got a craving for a cheeseburger. An all-American, grease-dripping, 100 percent, clog-those-arteries-till-they-wilt cheeseburger, with a super-sized order of forty-weight onion rings on the side. Unfortunately, all of your fellow diners are nibbling spinach salad and sipping bottled water. Do you want to look like an unhealthy, beer-bellied oaf? Of course not. Just tell the waiter, wink-wink, you'll be having a Lawrence Lunch.

When your order arrives, it'll look exactly like a spinach salad. But you know better. Nestled deep inside the bowl, protected by plastic film from those disgusting green leaves and all that tasteless dressing, is your cheeseburger and onion rings. You savor every sinful bite without so much as a snobbish glance from others at the table.

This is known as having your cake and hiding it, too.

Pierced by the Need to Look Cool

Ever since bell-bottom pants and polyester shirts with tablecloth collars drifted—thank you, dear Lord—into the dusty pages of sartorial history books, I have done my absolute best to avoid fads.

Such wisdom comes with middle age, I suspect. You wake up one morning and start to climb into yet another a piece of insidious beautiful people clothing, and all of a sudden your head lunges backward, as if you've been fiercely smitten across the brow by the broad side of a shelving board. Stunned momentarily, you break into a broad grin. "Wow!" you remark to yourself, "I don't have to do this!" And from that moment on, you are cured of the curse.

Fad avoidance has spared me the embarrassment of pinkie rings, ear studs, gold necklaces, ponytails, tattoos, pleated trousers, baggy-legged blue jeans, double-breasted suits, pointy-toed shoes, and bruise-colored neckties, to name only a few. Furthermore, I have never been attracted to bottled water—these people don't know about beer?—or brie, tofu, kiwi fruit, sushi, and any cuisine, nouvelle or otherwise, that has not been rolled in cornmeal and deep-fried in grease as the founders of our republic intended.

Thus, it is correct to assume I will not be swept into the body-piercing fad that is gaining momentum as we speak. Body piercing takes up where ear studs left off, the apparent logic being that if a gold ring looks handsome in a man's ear, a sixteen-penny nail through the cheek turns him into a god of love.

Not long ago, our newspaper carried a picture of a man, nailed through the tongue, who was about to marry a woman who looked like a walking pin cushion. The story did not go into detail about their romance—did they meet in the fastener aisle at Home Depot?—nor did it specify where they had chosen to spend their honeymoon. I daresay the sparks flew, literally, on their wedding night.

Nonetheless, I am indebted to Allan Hjerpe of Sevierville, who recently sent me some guidelines about body piercing. It listed several buzzwords used in skewer society. Such as:

Cart—piercing that punctures cartilage.

Hafada—side or center scrotal piercing, *yeeiii!!,* that originated in Arab countries. (And you wondered why Saddam is so testy?)

Labret—traditional Eskimo piercing in the center of the lower lip.

Madison—piercing at the base of the front of the neck.

No thanks. If a nail ever punctures my body, it will be a testament to my carpentry clumsiness, not a statement of fashion. Still, I must admit to being intrigued by body piercing on other people. Once, when

I know this certifies me as a card-carrying geezer, totally out of touch with the body-art fashions of this era, but I can remember when the only time you could see humans covered in acres of tattoos was by paying a quarter at the freak show every fall when the fair came to town. ⌒

Jim Walls and I were doing a TV fund-raiser, there was a woman in the crowd who had a nail in her nose.

"I wonder how much that cost," I remarked to Jim. "I wonder how much it hurt."

Jim, a very practical man, stared intently at the woman, rubbing his chin in deep thought. "What I wonder," he finally said, "is how she picks her nose."

My Frowns Are Fine

On my personal list of the Top One Hundred Things Not To Do Anytime Soon, you will find "get a Botox shot" in the high nineties. It's somewhere between "spend twenty million bucks to ride on the space shuttle" and "climb into a boxing ring with Mike Tyson and wiggle my ears."

Botox is the hottest news since Viagra. It eliminates wrinkles. Which, now that I think about it, also can be said for Viagra, but forget I mentioned it. Unlike Viagra, however, Botox doesn't come in pill form. It has to be injected, just under the skin, usually on the forehead or around the eyes. A few hours later—*shazam!*—no more wrinkles. No more frown lines. No more crow's feet.

That's the good news.

The bad news is that these treatments (a) only last about six months, (b) will set you back anywhere from three hundred to one thousand dollar per pop, and (c) have the potential to backfire worse than a Jerry Jones facelift. The fact that Botox is made from a diluted form of the deadly toxin that causes botulism will make you sit up and pay attention, too.

I happen to enjoy my wrinkles and frown lines. I've spent a lifetime developing them and, by gum, I'm not going to fritter them away on the latest dermatological geegaw.

Frowns are one of the benefits of growing older. You're *supposed* to look grouchy at my age, for Pete's sake. It's part of the deal, and no perky teenager is going to run up, punch you on the shoulder, and say, "Smile, darn ya, smile!" Even if you're in top humor, everyone expects you to grump, so why disappoint them?

Besides, there's nothing more pathetic than a GIT (Geezer In Training) like me trying to wipe twenty-five years off the slate. It's like "fixing" a worn-out automobile by installing a brand new engine. Unless you also install new brakes, new clutch, new suspension, new transmission, new air conditioner, and new everything else, you haven't accomplished much.

I think about this every time I see a man my age sporting a goatee.

(Point of order: Technically, the facial hair young males are growing these days—a moustache that flows southward around the mouth and into chin whiskers—is known as a "Vandyke." A goatee is merely a plain tuft of hair on the chin. But if you say "Vandyke," nobody knows what you're talking, so I'll just use "goatee." This is another GITism. You get to correct everyone's speech, and you need a well-furrowed frown to do it properly. If you're trying to bark out an admonishment and can't wrinkle up your face because it's been riddled with Botox, you wind up looking like some kind of goofy Mr. Rogers instead of an irritable Mr. Wilson. Just ain't natural.)

Goatees are a facial statement for the under-thirty crowd, the same as moustaches and sideburns were a facial statement way back when. These things do not transcend generations. Salt and pepper is OK, ahem, in a moustache. Not in a goatee. It looks bogus. The same goes for white-maned men in ponytails and beer-bellied swimmers in Speedos. Sticks out worse than Granny with a boob job.

But the scariest thing I've been reading about Botox is how it can literally freeze a person's face in place, especially after repeated injections. And if the doctor happens to be off the mark by a teeny-tiny fraction of an inch, the results can turn you into a sure-enough freak.

Consider this gentle warning I saw in *Newsweek:* "Too much Botox in the forehead can cause an eerie mask-like expression. Too much around the mouth can cause slackness and drooling."

Or how about this quote in the *Knoxville News-Sentinel* from Dr. Richard Glogau, a clinical professor of dermatology at the University of California, San Francisco: "The face has forty-four muscles. Hitting the wrong ones can cause droopy eyelids, asymmetric smiles, or even drooling."

No thanks. When you get to be a full-fledged geezer, weird expressions and drooling come with the territory. No way I'm going to spend thousands of dollars for these privileges ahead of schedule.

If boxing promoter Don King married singer Sinead O'Connor, and they had a child, do you think they'd always argue about how to style the kid's hair? ⌣

Chapter 7

A Flat Tire on the Road to Riches

Just my luck. The Fabulous Nineties came roaring along and made millionaires out of every Gen-X geek who owned a computer, knew how to design a web page, and was slick enough to talk some gullible venture capitalist out of his life savings. But it didn't help me one lousy bit. I limped out of the Nineties the same way I crawled in—nearly broke, paying bills, burdened with a mortgage.

This is the universal fate of writers. For every Stephen King and Tom Clancy, there are thousands of Sam Venables. Probably tens of thousands is more like it. The closest I ever came, literally, to literary riches was the night I dined with Alex Haley at his farmhouse in Norris, Tennessee. Yet even Haley, for all of his *Roots* success, was feeling a serious financial pinch by the time of his death in 1992. I drove back to Alex's farm for the auction of his estate and could all but taste the bitter irony. Here was a man who had made an internationally famous name for himself by writing how his ancestors were sold like merchandise, yet his final possessions went up on the block just like them—ten dollars here, twenty dollars there. At least Haley had good literary company. None other than Mark Twain, surely the most widely read and wealthy writer of his era, went bust around the end of the nineteenth century.

Some of my *News-Sentinel* colleagues and I attempted to break this cycle in the spring of 2000. When the multi-state Big Game Lottery reached an astronomical level, seventeen of us kicked in five bucks apiece and purchased eighty-five dollars worth of tickets from a store in Virginia. Lowell Branham, the copy editor who masterminded our investment scheme and drove to the state line for procurement, then photocopied all seventeen Big Game tickets so we could keep track of our winnings.

No, we didn't hit the top prize for millions. Nor some of the smaller prizes worth a few hundred-thousand dollars, either. We did, however, have two correct Big Game numbers.

They were worth a dollar apiece.

To redeem them, we had to send the two winning tickets back to Virginia and wait several weeks for the arrival of our two-dollar check—which then had to be divided seventeen ways. After deducting the price of postage to mail the tickets to Virginia, our eighty-five-dollar investment had boiled down to just under a dime per person. Thus ended our big-time economic ventures.

None of this would have been necessary if my stupid Uncle Willis had played his cards right back in the 1880s. I could be loaded by now. But riches eluded me once again.

I speak of Willis Venable, a pharmacist at Jacob's Drug Store in Atlanta. He was one of the creators of Coca-Cola. I am not making this up. Check any soft drink industry history book. A chemist named John Styth Pemberton came up with the first formula for Coke. He envisioned a health drink and called his product "French Wine of Coca." Pemberton kept tinkering with the recipe, adding sugared water, removing the wine, then blending with a kola nut extract for caffeine. His bookkeeper, Frank Robinson, coined the catchy alliteration "Coca-Cola" to accompany a flowing script logo now known 'round the world.

Enter Uncle Willis. He dreamed up the idea of adding carbonated water to Pemberton's cola syrup to give it fizz. This dark joy juice enjoyed modest sales at the drug store; but, hey, it wasn't sarsaparilla. Finally, in 1887, Pemberton and Robinson sold their secret formula to Uncle Willis and his partner, a man named George Lowndes.

And what did Uncle Willis do?

HE SOLD THE $%#@! THING FIVE MONTHS LATER— THAT'S WHAT!

Arrrgh! Blew it all for us deserving Venable descendants down through the ages! Robbed us of our billions! Cheated us out of our stock options! Deprived us of our yachts, our mansions, our villas by the sea! Double-arrrgh! Triple-arrrgh!

Oh, well. What's done is done. I suppose there's no use cryin' over spilled Coke. To be truthful, I don't know if I'm even remotely related to Willis Venable. Even if I am, there's no reason to think so much as one drop of the Coca-Cola empire would ever have trickled down to this distant root of the family tree.

But on lazy summer evenings when the sun is sinking low and the stars are peeking out and the crickets are chirping and a gentle, peaceful feeling starts settling like the dew across Dixie, it's one of those things that crosses my mind. And I think to myself, "Uncle Willis, wherever you are, I hope they're serving Pepsi."

In 1993, every man, woman, and child in Alaska received a check for $949.46. It was their cut of the state's oil profits. This dividend program began twelve years earlier to ensure Alaskan citizens were compensated for their state's vast petroleum riches.

Tennessee once had a windfall like this. There used to be a unique, revenue-producing program, funded by the sale of high-octane fuel, that brought wealth into impoverished mountain regions. Then the dang revenuers got wind of it and ruined everything. ⌒

Money Does Grow on Trees, After All

The first time I saw bottled water for sale, I laughed out loud. I was convinced this had to be a joke. Or else the water was flavored with an exotic ingredient or laced with hooch. I was certain nobody would pay ninety-nine cents for a bottle of plain ol' drinking water, unless maybe they were stranded in the desert.

Shows how little I know about consumers. Shows how little I know about making money, too. If I had spent less time laughing at water bottlers back then and more time investing my meager savings in their crazy scheme, I would be writing this book right now from my villa in France. Actually, I wouldn't even be doing that. I would be telling one of my servants to write the stupid book.

As I grow older, everyone else's bottled water success stories seem to haunt me with greater frequency. I never would have thought people would shop online, for example. I never would have thought students—kindergarten to college—would carry their books in backpacks. I never would have thought suburbanites whose idea of "off-road adventure" is navigating a gravel driveway would buy outrageously expensive sport utility vehicles capable of climbing Mount Rainer. And now I'll be danged if I ain't "never-would-have-thought" myself out of another fortune.

Question: What dazzles us with vivid colors every autumn, then tumbles to the ground in great abundance?

Answer: Leaves. Multiplied millions of them. We'll love 'em briefly, then we cuss 'em mightily.

Between Halloween and Thanksgiving, there's no telling how many homeowners will use a leaf rake to turn their arms and backs into quivering masses of sore muscles. Some of the leaves from these efforts will be composted to help build the soil in gardens and flower beds. More of them will wind up in black plastic bags and hauled off in garbage trucks to take up precious space in landfills. I daresay a few will even be burned, despite air pollution laws to the contrary. And it'll all be like throwing away fistfuls of dollars.

I realized this shocking truth a couple of days ago when a friend showed me the latest catalog from the Orvis Company in Manchester, Vermont. There, in the midst of boots and sweaters and blankets and other winter items, was the latest play-pretty for the beautiful people to hang on their walls.

Pressed leaves.

I am not teasing. You can have delivered to your door a mounted selection of leaves—maple or Bradford pear—attractively displayed in an eleven-by-fourteen-inch wooden frame. For ninety-five dollars. Each. Plus shipping.

I'd sit down and cry, except I'm sure that somewhere, some marketing genius is bottling tears for ten thousand dollars a pop.

Don't wind up All wet

Forget stocks, bonds, mutual funds, gold, dot.coms, aluminum siding, velvet Elvises, chinchillas, solar-powered can openers, Last Supper blankets, and other traditional investment opportunities. Unless I miss my hunch, the surest bet for fortune in the immediate future will be water retention devices. If you've got a couple of hundred-thousand bucks gathering dust under your sofa and want to turn them into a couple of million, my advice is to rush out and buy all the Pampers, Huggies, and Depends you can find.

But don't stop there.

Buy water bottles, too. And canteens. And super-blaster water pistols. And sponges. And paper towels. And sand bags. In short, if it'll hold water, buy it.

Do it now. Time is wasting. If you don't seize the moment, a bunch of Johnny-come-latelies—or is it Johnnies-come-lately? I always forget. Must have skipped English class that day—will corner the market and spoil the opportunity of a lifetime.

If you follow scientific news, you know why I am issuing this advisory. Polar ice is melting faster than Brown Cows at a Labor Day picnic. Before long, even the people living on mountaintops will be up to their ankles in water. According to aerial surveys by the National Aeronautics and Space Administration, eleven cubic miles of ice, containing fifty billion tons of water, disappear every year from the Greenland ice sheet alone.

(Then again, since NASA is doing the calculations, one is tempted to ask if the figures have been accurately converted from metric to English, and vice versa. Even then, I reckon any way you slice it, we're talking about a huge volume of moisture. Enough, NASA claims, to raise sea levels by five-thousandths of an inch annually, flood low-lying areas, and displace literally millions of people who live in coastal regions around the world. So forget I mentioned the potential for math errors. Nothing to worry about, I'm sure.)

When this disaster does occur, water retention devices will command premium prices. And that's when we smart investors will reap humongous profits—but not before we apologize for making a windfall at the expense of the less-fortunate. Like the big oil companies do.

I figure it will take five-hundred bazillion Pampers—or, roughly, the amount found inside any outdoor trash receptacle at a McDonald's near the interstate—to line the Atlantic, Pacific, and Gulf coasts of the United States. That should stem the floods temporarily.

After that, the bucket brigade will have to take over. With the deft deployment of bottles, pails, water pistols, hoses, sponges, and other receptacles, the excess dampness can be funneled inland and buried like toxic waste.

I, myownself, am so convinced this get-rich-quick project will work, I am going to sink my entire personal fortune into it. Just as soon as I sell off my last four dozen Pet Rocks and free up some working capital.

I s there anyone in America whose mailbox doesn't overflow with credit card applications? I get at least one or two a week. Sometimes, that many arrive on the same day. I am seriously considering filling out each and every one of them, going on a whale of a shopping spree, then use one card to pay off the others' debts, right down the line, until all are maxed out.

Sure, that's liable to get me into a legal-financial stew, but what the heck. If Congress can live on bogus credit all these years, why can't I? ⌒

Funny Money

Even though the "new" money has been in circulation for awhile, I still do a double-take every time I see it. This stuff looks fake, like something kids would get in a toy set. The first time I held some of it in my hands, I swore it was counterfeit.

One reason the new fives, tens, twenties, fifties, and hundreds don't seem official is because the background on each of them is plain. Over the years, we Americans have grown accustomed to busy backdrops on our filthy lucre. This new stuff looks like it was cut off a fresh ream of white paper.

But the biggest difference is the makeover on the respective faces of Abraham Lincoln, Alexander Hamilton, Andrew Jackson, Ulysses Grant, and Benjamin Franklin. Those images did not come out of a history book. They came off a Chippendale's calendar. At least they did in Alexander Hamilton's case.

On the old tens, Hamilton looks like a frilly laced mama's boy who spent his afternoons at tea parties and piano recitals. In the new incarnation, he's a stud muffin who could fit into the cast of *Baywatch*.

Lincoln's makeover is quite flattering, too. In fact, the Ol' Railsplitter, who—at least from every sketch and grainy photograph I've ever seen—was plainer than a bowling shoe, actually looks handsome this time around. The sharp edges on his face have been smoothed. And his receding hairline has re-sprouted so vigorously, the guy now qualifies for membership in Hair Club for Men.

The artist(s) also gave Jackson a long bath in the Fountain of Youth. The prez on the twenty looks a good twenty years younger. His billowing hair has a fuller, more Hollywood flair to it. But for some reason, the gaze in his right eye doesn't seem to follow his left eye. Given Jackson's reputed love for horse racing, maybe he's trying to catch the attention of a bookie.

Grant seems to be the least changed of any. About all I could detect was a slight narrowing of the eyes. Then again, maybe that was just my imagination because I had to temporarily borrow a fifty and a hundred from the tellers at my bank and was afraid they'd think I was going to dash out the door. We ink-stained wretches don't get our paws on fifties and hundreds very often.

Ah, yes. The hundred. Even the makeover magicians at the United States Mint couldn't do much to improve the looks of Ben Franklin. The guy never was a walk on the beach in the first place. They have tried, however. Franklin's hair is darker than before. His new face seems fuller, less pasty. And in what surely must be a nod to political correctness, the fur collar around Ben's coat is missing in the new version.

Oddly enough, Franklin's right eye also has that wandering look about it, just like Jackson's. Mayhaps, in true Washington style, those fellows are watching our money while it's still in our billfolds.

Tax Time Tribulations

I sat down to figure my federal income tax a few nights ago and started by doing the same thing I've done for years. I emptied The Envelope very carefully.

(Clarification: I don't mean to imply that I, dumber-than-a-fence-post-in-matters-mathematical, actually fill out forms and compute what I owe the feds. Heaven forbid. It would be easier for me to hot-wire a 747. What I mean is that I start the process. Then I take everything to Tax Guy's office, throw it inside the door, scream, and run. But back to The Envelope.)

The reason I have to open it carefully is because it is crammed far beyond capacity with receipts, cancelled checks, photocopies, notes, writs, forms, and everything else related to the taxpaying procedure.

Each January, I start collecting these papers in a plain, crisp, nine-by-twelve-inch envelope. Well, technically, I think it's 8¾-by-11¾, but the IRS requires you to round off. As the weeks and months go by, The Envelope swells fatter and fatter. Its once-sharp edges develop love handles, the flap displays the backbone of a busted balloon, and the metal clasp ascends to that great wastebasket in the sky.

Sometime in early autumn, The Envelope begins to fall apart at the seams. By Thanksgiving, it is a manila time bomb. If you dare to open the file cabinet between Christmas and New Year's, you do so at your own risk.

By the following April, however, The Envelope can be ignored no longer. I must ease it from the cabinet and, stepping oh-so-deliberately so as not to trip on the carpet and lose my balance, carry it to the dining room table. There, I give it one teeny, tiny shake.

Wooooosh!

For the next few nights, the top of the dining room table is barely visible as I sort and stack, index and file, and arrange and collate the flood of paper that emerges. Shortly before the tax deadline, I will have those contents in the closest semblance of order they'll ever achieve and hie myself off to Tax Guy's office.

Of course, The Envelope is destroyed in the opening process, and all those stacks of paper must be assigned to *three* other envelopes the same size. It's a phenomenon of packaging, just like how a rain parka large enough to cover two football spectators can be packed—the first time—into a plastic sleeve the size of a postage stamp. Forever after, the parka will barely fit into a cigar box, not matter how carefully you try to fold it.

But why am I telling you all of this? You probably have a primitive filing system all your own. According to a national survey by an accounting firm, the vast majority of Americans are exceedingly low-tech in matters of financial record keeping. Forty-eight percent of respondents in this survey said they crammed their papers into a file drawer. Seventeen percent used a shoe box, desk drawer, or cardboard box. Way on down the list, each in single-digit percentages, were bank safety deposit box, strong box, various hidey holes at work, and an accountant's office.

You know what the smallest category was? A personal computer. Cross my heart. According to the poll, only one percent of taxpayers were geeky enough to sink to such a low level of cyberfoolishness.

God bless America, land that I love.

Holding Our Country Together

I'm going to give you a bit of stock market advice. Put your money in coat hangers and watch your net worth mushroom. With the possible exception of duct tape and WD-40, there's not another commodity Americans use more often or for as many purposes.

There can never be too many coat hangers, either. As a nation, we must go through millions of them every day. Not for hanging clothes, of course. If you will check your hall and bedroom closets, you will probably find coat hangers that have been serving continuous clothing duties since the Truman administration. I'm talking about all those other important missions for coat hangers. This is what keeps them in constant demand and makes them the linchpin of the national economy.

I got to thinking about this notion few days ago when I was on my knees beside the open door of my pickup truck, carefully inserting a length of straightened coat hanger through a hole in the bottom of my dashboard. Way down in there somewhere was the latch doohickey on my parking brake. The hateful cable on this brake had just broken— for the second time in as many years, I might point out to Detroit— and I was attempting to snag the doohickey with the end of a coat hanger I had bent into a small hook.

Now that I'm doling out stock advice, let me mention over-the-counter reading glasses. This is a particularly good investment for geezers in training like me who have recently discovered that thousands of items, including parking brake latch doohickeys, are a lot smaller than they used to be. With Baby Boomers buying over-the-counter reading glasses at the rate of approximately ten million pairs a day, this is also a potentially lucrative market.

Yes, I was successful at making repairs to the parking brake. So successful, in fact, I haven't bothered taking my truck to a mechanic for an official going-over. The coat hanger works marvelously. I ought to take the twenty-five bucks or so a mechanic would charge me and add it to my coat hanger portfolio.

Of course, coat hangers have far more uses than automotive repairs. That's why they are such an important segment of our lives. What would a school science project be without a lattice of coat hangers to hold it together? How could we roast hot dogs and marshmallows? Is there any other way to unclog a drain? How else would we replace broken radio antennas? Where else is there a ready source of utility wire for countless jobs around the garage, from attaching a can of paint to the rung of a ladder to making a plant holder to fixing a busted lawn mower handle?

Keep America strong. Invest in coat hangers.

Every year when the National Insurance Crime Bureau's report of the most-stolen cars and trucks comes out, motorists frantically check to see if their fancy sports cars and SUVs are listed. I never have that worry. When you drive a dented, faded, eleven-year-old pickup truck with over one hundred and seventy-five thousand miles on the odometer and a non-matching camper cover bolted to the bed, you can park it at the mall—with the engine running and a sign in the window saying, "Steal me!"—and not fret about theft. This is one of the benefits of being broke. ⌒

Up to Our Knees in Riches

The people of East Tennessee are wealthy and don't know it. I came to this startling conclusion after viewing a display at the Knoxville Museum of Art. It was called "Trashformations," and it was the most bizarre assortment of jewelry, furniture, clothing, and household decorations I'd ever seen.

That's because it was made entirely from junk.

Yes, the same type of rubbish, garbage, litter, and trash found along every ditch, lakeshore, and woodland of this area. I'm talkin' bottles, cans, newspapers, milk cartons, waste paper, broken glass, busted crates, car parts, tires, cardboard, kitchen utensils, wire, coffee filters, and Lord-only-knows-what-else.

There was a necklace made from a sink drain, paper clips, and bead chain. A crystal cabinet pieced entirely from scrap wood. A kitchen counter created from kazillions of tin cans. A chair supported by gearshift levers and a motorcycle kickstand. A "stuffed" rhinoceros head that somehow had come together from a fire hose, kettle, mailbox, golf balls, and tricycle parts. A Christmas tree garland crafted from chewing gum wrappers. An evening gown woven from plastic grocery bags. Oh, yes, and a "Marilyn Monrobot" anatomically assembled from scrap aluminum, a coffee pot, light bulbs, and drawer handles. Dolly Parton would be jealous if she saw this baby.

Walking and gawking through the museum, I couldn't help but think how much valuable junk is going to waste out there in the woods and fields. Actually, I did more than think. I did a bit of ciphering.

There were roughly eighty exhibits in this collection, which was on loan from a museum in Bellingham, Washington. I couldn't find out what they are collectively worth—it's not the sort of thing artsy folks discuss openly with commoners—but a member of the Knoxville museum's staff told me the whole she-bang is insured "well into the six-figure range." Meaning that no matter how you slice it, these pieces might sell for at least a few G's per pop.

Are the little wheels and gears in your noggin starting to turn? Are they telling you something? I reckon they are! And you need to fling those wheels and gears into the briar patch because we're sitting on the most extensive art supply warehouse in the United States!

Our mission is two-fold. First, we need to spread the word to artisans far and wide to shop for their raw materials in East Tennessee. Tell them to bring plenty of money because we have the greatest inventory ack Lail, who runs the on-line division for our newspaper, researched the Amazon.com book list to see how my literary pearls of wisdom were faring in the universal marketplace. "Congratulations!" he e-mailed me. "You are the 404,018th best-selling author in America!"

As my pappy used to say, be proud of any accomplishment. ～

in the industry. Second, we must encourage East Tennesseans to litter on every occasion. I know many people already practice this civic duty on a regular basis, but what we need is a huge, concerted push by the entire tribe.

Sling those old bedsprings to the side of the road! Dump that refrigerator into the creek! Let fly with your beer bottles!

Remember: You're not doing it for yourself. You're doing it for the good of our region.

Darkness Is Coming!

Today's consumer tip is buy white. White shirts. White pants. White suits. White belts. White hats. White shoes and socks. Whatever the garment happens to be, if it's white, bring it to the cash register.

This has nothing to do with fashion. Instead, it's going to be a matter of convenience sometime in the future. The world is going to get dark one of these days, so unless you want to get bumped into and run over by goofs who are blundering around in the void, I say put your mitts on all the white clothing you can afford. True, it's going to be a while before darkness falls. But you can never be too prepared for any emergency. So buy now, while the selection is still good.

I learned about this impending situation recently while perusing news from the American Astronomical Society's winter meeting in Toronto. Two astrophysicists from the University of Michigan, Fred Adams and Greg Laughlin, reported that the universe is going to shut down, turning everything into one gigantic black hole.

Frankly, I can't wait.

It'll give me a good chance to catch up on my sleep, for one thing. For reasons unknown—maybe I've been eating too late or drinking too much coffee—I've been having a difficult time nodding off at bedtime. I figure once everything is dark, day or night, I'll be more inclined to snooze.

Another reason I'm excited about total darkness is that I enjoy fishing at night, and this will give me additional opportunities to be on the water. Ask any bass angler. Often, the best action occurs during the dead of night, particularly during the summer months. That makes it tough on working folks who must punch a clock at 6:30 the next morning. But with permanent darkness, no problem. We'll be able to fish just as effectively at 4:00 P.M. as we would at 4:00 A.M.

What's more, without sunlight, the grass won't grow, giving us even more free time for sleeping, fishing, or, ahem, other nighttime recreation.

Want yet another reason to rejoice at the thought of twenty-four-hour darkness? How about no more sunburn? Nor will the paint on our houses and cars fade from the sun's relentless rays. I'm telling you —it just doesn't get any better than this.

How long before complete darkness settles on the universe? Oh, a wee bit. Astrophysicists Adams and Laughlin estimate it'll happen in the year ten to the two-hundredth power. That's the numeral one, followed by a couple of hundred zeroes—give or take an hour or two.

In 1999, a California promoter convinced some super-models to donate several human eggs, which he auctioned on the Internet for prices ranging as high as forty-two thousand dollars each. I suppose the idea, however disgusting, has a statistical chance of working. But as anyone who has ever bred dogs, horses, cattle, and other animals will attest, championship bloodlines don't guarantee championship offspring. How'd you like to spend forty-two grand engineering a kid like this, and he turns out looking like Alfred E. Neuman? ⌣

No, this isn't a date you can count on as assuredly as, say, Christmas or the Super Bowl. But it's going to roll around sometime, and I intend to be ready by stocking up on white clothes. I might even buy a new flashlight and some reflector tape, just in case.

Thanks, but we'll just pass

After thoroughly examining our options, my wife and I have decided not to become millionaires. We looked at both sides of the coin, so to speak, and came to the conclusion that being millionaires was going to be too much trouble. We'd just as soon not fool with it.

Actually "millionaires" doesn't touch it. As Leona Helmsley might say, only the little people are mere millionaires. What Mary Ann and I turned down was the opportunity to be millionaires thirty-one times over. That's how much money the folks from Publishers Clearing House were going to give us on Super Bowl Sunday. They sent us a letter about it. It had our name on it and everything.

What's that? Well, yes, now that you mention it, there may have been some details down in the fine print. But I'm sure they didn't mean anything because the rest of the letter gushed over and over about how Mary Ann and I were soon to be mega-rich. According to the letter, all we had to do was walk to the front door, hold out our hands, and they'd fork over the dough.

Initially, the thought of being kajillionaires was tempting. That sure would take a chunk out of our Christmas bills. But the more we thought about all the strings attached to this windfall, the more we were convinced it wasn't worth it. We tossed the letter into the fire and went on with our business.

Why turn down thirty-one million? Two reasons.

First, we'd have to give ten percent of it to the Lord. We have no objection to tithing, but this would mean a cool $3.1 million to the church, cash, right out of the blue.

Can you imagine what kind of cat fight this would start? One group would want to add on to the sanctuary. Another would want to hire three more preachers. Yet another would want new choir robes. Or

Two jock jokes: A football player's father dies. The dutiful son calls the fanciest funeral home in town and tells 'em to spare no expense. Some weeks later, he gets a bill for twenty-seven thousand dollars and pays it from the estate. One month later, he gets another bill for seventy-five bucks. He pays it, too. The next month, another one for seven-five dollars arrives. Then another. Finally, he calls the funeral home to see what's going on.

"You said you wanted the best for your daddy," the under-taker explains, "so I rented him a tux."

"Oh, OK," the jock replies. "But to save us both a lot of trouble, couldn't you just put it on my automatic checking withdrawal?"

And did you hear about the jock who won three million dollars in the state lottery? To avoid taxes, he decided to take his money in payments over a long period of time—three bucks a year for a million years. ⌣

new chairs for the fellowship hall—the new and improved fellowship hall, that is. Before the dust cleared, half the congregation would have left in a huff, and the other half wouldn't be speaking to each other. Thanks to our wise decision to nix the money, Mary Ann and I stopped this holy war before the first shot was fired.

The other reason we don't want all that money can be summed up in a single word. Telemarketers.

Mary Ann and I are broker than convicts, and yet we are besieged with supper-hour calls from people selling life insurance, siding, heat and air systems, mortgage refinance, and all manner of other goods and services. If the word got out we were sitting atop a mountain of moolah, the calls would be nonstop.

Thanks for the offer, Publishers Clearing House, but no thanks. We're happy the way things are right now. Go knock on somebody else's door and give them thirty-one million bucks' worth of trouble.

Seven Hundred Good Reasons to Stick Around

I desperately want to live until the year 2005.

Hmmm, now that I mention it, I'd like to make it a lot longer. Just because 2005 rolls around, that doesn't mean Saint Peter is required to scribble my name on his list. If he wants to wait thirty years—or more—beyond 2005 before swinging the gate open, fine by me. It is imperative, however, that I stick around these parts at least until then.

Why? Because I'm so dang cheap. I have just written the state of Tennessee a check for seven hundred dollars. It's for a lifetime hunting and fishing license, and I want to make sure I get my money's worth.

You gotta pay for your outdoor play in any state, and the cost keeps going up. When I first started buying hunting and fishing licenses—this would have been in the late 1950s—the annual fee was three dollars. It has risen to one hundred now because I always buy a Tennessee "sportsman's license," an all-inclusive document that covers everything from snail darters to Cape buffalo.

The Tennessee General Assembly passed the lifetime license law in 1998, but I waited until the following year to get mine. I'd already bought my 1998 sportsman's license by the time the lifetime bill worked its way through the legislature. But there was a far more important reasons for waiting until 1999. It saved me an extra five hundred smackers.

You see, there's a system of staggered fees for this thing, depending on age. For wee ones up to age three, it's two hundred dollars. From there to age twelve, it's six hundred. Between thirteen and fifty, it's a staggering twelve-hundred. But at fifty-one, it drops back to seven hundred. And after age sixty-five, there's no charge at all. I turned fifty-one only six weeks after the new law went into effect, but that was too far into the cycle of 1998 hunting and fishing seasons to go without a license. Thus, 1999 was the first time I qualified at the "cheap" rate.

Agreed, seven hundred bucks is a lot to plunk down for fun afield. But I'm hedging my bets against both the Grim Reaper and the political system. Figuring a C-note per year for a sportsman's license, I will have paid off my seven-hundred-dollar lifetime license by the year 2005. That's assuming the sportsman's license fee doesn't increase before then, which it is likely to do, making my decision an even wiser one.

After that, I can hunt and fish forever throughout Tennessee for free. Unless, of course, you include a few details.

Such as boats, motors, trailers, boat registration fees, boat launching fees, gasoline, oil, bearing grease, shotguns, rifles, shotgun shells, rifle ammunition, rifle scopes, gun cleaning equipment, targets, black powder, smokeless powder, shot, wads, bullets, slings, hip boots, woods boots, chest waders, duck decoys, goose decoys, decoy bags, decoy string, decoy anchors, duck calls, goose calls, turkey calls, portable deer stands, permanent deer stands, lease fees, out-of-state license fees, federal duck stamps, dog food, vet bills, brush pants, chamois shirts, goose down coats, camouflage coats, camouflage pants, rain suits, gloves, socks, longhandles, hats, coffee jugs, tackle boxes, filet knives, pocket knives, skinning knives, ropes, tents, tarps, sleeping bags, nightcrawlers, crickets, crankbaits, jerkbaits, top-water baits, spinnerbaits, hooks, pork rind, hair jigs, plastic jigs, plastic worms, dry flies, wet flies, nymphs, popping bugs, spinning rods, spinning reels, casting rods, casting reels, fly rods, fly reels, jig poles, frog gigs, approximately five hundred miles of line in various weights and tests, landing nets, magazine subscriptions, books, membership fees for Ducks Unlimited, Trout Unlimited, Quail Unlimited, the Ruffed Grouse Society, and the National Wild Turkey Federation, not to mention Penrose sausages, coconut-raspberry Zingers, Little Debbie raisin cakes, barley juice, and a few other incidental items that make hunting and fishing such a simple, innocent, inexpensive pleasure.

No problem. As I've been telling my wife for years, the cost of that stuff doesn't count.

> **T**rue story: A reader from Jefferson County, who didn't want to be identified in print, made a one-cent error when she deposited her paycheck. The bank caught her mistake and corrected it with an official "miscellaneous debt" voucher made out for one penny. It took seventy-eight cents worth of postage to conclude the transaction. ⌣

The Kudzu Cure

The latest news from Harvard Medical School is spreading through the South like kudzu in July. Researchers have isolated a substance in kudzu roots that helps curb the appetite for alcohol. Although kudzu treatment for alcoholism has been used in the Orient for centuries, this apparently is the first time it has been tested in the United States.

What an ironic breakthrough! Trying to control the spread of this vegetative octopus has driven many a southerner to drink. Now kudzu may return the favor.

Assuming, of course, that boozy humans react like boozy hamsters when they drink a tea made of root squeezins. In results published in the *Proceedings of the National Academy of Sciences,* researchers said that after treatment with kudzu extract, test animals reduced their alcohol consumption fifty percent. Not bad at all. But it won't prove of much significance if human subjects suddenly start filling their cheeks with food, rolling around in cedar chips, and running ceaselessly on a wire wheel at all hours of the night.

My advice is for southern entrepreneurs to get their act together. If I had several thousand dollars burning a hole in my pocket, I'd start visiting some of Dixie's most prolific kudzu zones and get friendly with the landowners. Maybe plunk down a buck or two of earnest money. By all means, do it before some carpet bagging no-good from up north sneaks in and tries to corner the kudzu market.

But be careful. People unfamiliar with this fast-growing vine have no idea of the inherent dangers involved. When you come to an area of particularly lush growth, do not stop your car and try to walk near the stuff, especially if there are small children, senior citizens, and slow-moving dogs in your party. You turn your head for one second and—*schllooooop!*—Uncle Asa and Arf will be history.

I hope this discovery pans out. I really do. Not only will it help legions of people lessen their craving for alcohol, it will also turn a southern botanical embarrassment into a very lucrative cash crop. Who needs cotton when you've got King Kudzu?

Naturally, the kudzu cure won't be on the American market anytime soon. It'll take years of further testing, public hearings, blah-blah-drone-snore-blah-wheeze, before the treatment gets a green light from the Food and Drug Administration and everyone else in Washington.

Even then, you never know what might happen. Be just like the feds to suddenly decide kudzu is an endangered species.

Chapter 8

Misplaced in Modern Society

I don't fit in any more. Nobody my age does. (Except maybe Dick Clark. But now that I think about it, he's not our age. Just how old *is* Dick Clark—eighteen or eighty?)

This is a common complaint among Baby Boomers. We thought we had been paying societal dues all these years so we could enjoy a comfortable, carefree adulthood. Then just about the time we settled into the good life, the account turned up woefully short of funds. Sorta like Enron's 401(k).

All things change, of course. We understand that. Indeed, Baby Boomers were the leading proponents of change back when we were the young pups and wrinkled, stuck-in-the-past dolts were running the show. Now that we wise Baby Boomers have climbed to the top of the heap, we've discovered change isn't all it's cracked up to be. We want things to work like they did back in the good ol' days.

For example, most Baby Boomers embraced the concept of handicapped parking spaces when they came into vogue more than twenty years ago. This was the solution to a problem the older, insensitive generation had blithely ignored. Unlike those Neanderthals, we understood what a burden the people in wheelchairs and crutches had to endure to gain access to buildings. It did not aggravate us to park our cars in the lower forty at a shopping center. Furthermore, we would roll our eyes in irritation when some perfectly healthy coot, who had to walk an extra fifty yards, proclaimed aloud, "My feet still hurt from marching through France in World War II! How come they don't have a special place for me? Huh? Answer that!"

Now, it's our turn to take up the cry. You know what I recently saw in a shopping mall parking lot? A sign that marked off half a dozen perfectly good spots for expectant mothers, that's what.

Agreed, pregnancy isn't a picnic. But think about the ramifications. How "expectant" does a woman have to be to qualify for this courtesy? As soon as the home pregnancy test shows positive? At the onset of morning sickness? Just beginning to show? Eight months along? Fully dilated and screaming at her husband/boyfriend to stay away from her for the next twenty years? And how do you know a woman who whips her car into one of these slots is indeed with child? Will the pregnancy police descend upon her with test kits? What about beer-bellied men in T-shirts and coaches' shorts—or cellulite queens in Spandex, for that matter—who look for all the world like they're going to deliver quintuplets within the hour?

See what I mean? That's just a minor example, but it proves when you start messing with the established order, you wind up with chaos. The scary thing is, this fruit-basket-turn-over phenomenon is everywhere. Even the little changes are beginning to irritate me.

For instance, when did they start making it OK to write the numeral seven with a line through it? Anytime I see at a handwritten message these days—whether it contains a telephone number, an address, a price, whatever—there will be that silly looking seven.

This is not a 7. At least not a God-fearing 7 like they used to teach in schools. The purveyors of this travesty take a perfectly good 7 and then ruin it by drawing a line, horizontally, about halfway up the shaft. What results is an oddball pen stroke that looks somewhat like a capital *F* in cursive.

Not only does this look strange to the eye, it is confusing to the brain. If I'm reading a telephone number that starts with "577," my brain says, "5FF." It's sorta like the old-timey way the letter *s* occasionally appears in handwritten versions of the Declaration of Independence. You know—"self-evident" shows up as "felf-evident" and "separation" looks like "feparation."

I tried to run down the source (or "fource," if you prefer) of the line-through seven but was not fucceffful. (Forgive me; I couldn't ftop myfelf.) I checked with the mathematics department at the University of Tennessee, the reference desk at Lawson McGhee Library, and my son, Clay, who holds a math degree from UT. They all said this is the European way of writing a 7.

So? What does that prove? Just because the Europeans make their sevens that way, we're supposed to as well? I assume we should also start eating kidney pie and driving on the left side of the road?

Clay theorized this designation helps distinguish the numeral seven from the numeral one, in the same way a line-through zero helps distinguish it from the capital letter *O*. I don't buy it. Yes, a zero, particularly in this day of computereze, might be mistaken for an *O* and vice-versa. But a *7* is a *7* and a *1* is a *1*. No line-throughs needed, thank you.

Perhaps there is hope. As you know, the singer named Prince dropped his name several years ago and adopted a sign instead. It looked somewhat like a cross between an ampersand (&) and the biological sign for female. Since this sign was not pronounceable, writers had to refer to him as "the artist formerly known as Prince." Then "the artist formerly known as Prince" quit using the sign and officially declared himself "Prince" once again. So maybe this line-through craziness will eventually run its course, and we can go back to plain ol' sevens and zeroes.

Not to confuse the issue further, but technically, Prince should now be referred to as "Formerly the artist formerly known as Prince." Just in case you're keeping fcore.

Nothing Opens Easily

There is a special place in hell for the people who design and manufacture "easy-open" (their term, not mine) packages, bottles, boxes, cartons, and other containers. If not assigned to hell, at least these miscreants

Back in the late 1990s, when Y2K hysteria gripped the land, Floyd Anderson sent me this warning: "Please make sure your toilet paper is Y2K-compliant. If not, on New Year's Day it will turn into a 1900 Sears-Roebuck catalog." ~

should be subpoenaed before a congressional subcommittee and forced to demonstrate—publicly and without benefit of claw hammer and acetylene torch—how to unlock the seals they have created.

This thought comes to mind every time I attempt to fight my way past one of these damnable entries. The exact language varies by container and manufacturer, but it usually goes along the lines of, "Insert finger under flap (indicated by an arrow) and gently slide along length of seam. After opening, insert tab (another arrow) into slot (third arrow) to keep contents fresh."

Horsepuckey. Those words constitute the most shameless fabrication since, "Why, of course I'll respect you in the morning."

With the possible exception of Edward Scissorhands, nobody can "gently slide" a finger beneath the flap. That's because the flap was cemented in place at the factory with a compound whose secret ingredients are guarded more closely than those of Kentucky Fried Chicken. The human finger is no match for this adhesive substance. It isn't even a contest. You might as well try rapping your knuckles against the bole of an eighty-year-old white oak and expect it to come crashing to the ground.

Case in point: I reached into a kitchen cabinet the other night and retrieved a recently purchased box of cellophane food wrap. Foolishly (I never learn; no one does), I attempted to "gently slide" my finger beneath the flap. It would not budge. It could just as well have been welded shut. Not until I savagely attacked with a butter knife did it start to yield. The flap, I mean. The seal and the adhesive compound remained an impenetrable blob. The hateful flap was no longer a thing of beauty by that time. It looked like it had been assaulted with a chain saw.

At least I was then able to use the cellophane wrap. Had this been a box of potato chips, crackers, or cereal, my work would only have begun. That's because food products are further entombed inside a bag that is surely made of the same material as nuclear warheads.

Remember back in the good ol' days, when you could open one of these bags with a quick rip? Or, in extreme cases, your teeth? Those days are gone. Not even Jimmy Carter's impressive ivories could prevail against this stuff. It must be sliced open with a knife sharp enough to perform surgery.

All of which results in a classic Catch-22: You will surely lacerate your hand in the process, but you can't treat the wound until you hack your way into a bandage box and a bandage wrapper, both of which have been sealed—hermetically, genetically, and phonetically—against all invaders, foreign and domestic.

Truly amazing. If mad scientists can spawn something this impervious for a stupid box of saltines, why can't they cook up a batch of asphalt that doesn't crack and buckle fifteen minutes after being poured?

> **I** ordered coffee at a fast food drive-through in Sevierville one day. It came in a foam cup festooned with admonitions about the potential for burns. It had not one, not two, but three advisories —two printed on the side of the cup (one in English, the other in Spanish), plus a florescent red sticker on the lid. Sufficiently warned, I pulled back into traffic, resumed driving, and pried off the lid for a sip. The coffee was stone cold. Not even remotely lukewarm. Maybe I should sue for getting chilled. ⌁

The Short and Long of It

I was driving through a stretch of western North Carolina a few days ago when a sign outside a rural hardware store caught my eye. Apparently there was an inventory reduction sale going on. Among the clearance items listed on the sign were—I'm quoting verbatim here—"bolts and nuts."

"Did you see that?" I asked myself.

"Yes," myself replied. "Maybe we oughta go back. There might be some great bargains."

"Bargains butt!" I barked to myself. "I'm talkin' about the sign itself. Why didn't it say 'nuts and bolts'? Isn't that the way the term is usually pronounced?"

Myself thought about it for a moment. "I suppose so," myself finally responded.

"Then how come they turned it around?"

"Maybe the hardware store folks are aware of that. Maybe it's just an advertising ploy to catch people's attention. Then again, maybe they're trying to make a statement within a statement. Something to shake up the language patterns around here."

"Not likely," myself spoke back. "I bet ten dollars the owner simply handed the letters to some kid, told him to go outside and put 'em on the sign, and that's how they turned out."

"You ain't got ten dollars to bet on anything," myself said with contempt. "You spent our last dime on breakfast this morning."

Myself and I continued to debate the situation, but we never reached a logical conclusion. We rarely do. That's what happens when you attempt to argue with an idiot.

Nonetheless, I'm still intrigued by that sign. The more I think about it, the more I realize all manner of everyday terms would sound strange if the words were simply reversed, even though the text remained factually correct.

Have you ever heard of anybody fixing a jelly and peanut butter sandwich for lunch? Or ordering an LTB on wheat toast? Or making dumplings and chicken? Do they ever ask you to pass the pepper and salt so they can season their beans and pork?

Of course not. For that matter, how come you never hear people say stuff like:

Getting down to the gritty nitty?

Falling for something line, sinker, and hook?

Haircut and a shave, twenty-five cents?

A dent-and-scratch sale?

Knack-knicks?

White and black photography?

Forth and back?

Flop-flipping?

A system of balances and checks?

Gentlemen and ladies?

Every Dick, Harry, and Tom?

A socket and ball joint?

Comparing oranges and apples?

Wait and hurry up?

South, east, north, and west?

An ink and pen sketch?

Batten and board siding?

Telling Junior about the bees and birds?

I could keep rattling off this silliness until the cows come home, but I just noticed my glass is empty. Think I'll go fix another tonic and gin. Which is one of the few things myself and I always agree on, barrel, lock, and stock.

> I thought civilized society could not sink lower into the mire of degradation. But I was wrong. While perusing the overalls (as in blue denim bibs) section of a Loudon County hardware store, I saw a manufacturer's label touting an exciting new feature: a special pocket to hold a cell phone. One of these days, I reckon they'll offer sterling silver tobacco-spitting cups. Monogrammed, of course. ⌣

The Metric Martyr

All of us antiques who are eternally stymied by the metric system should raise a pint of foamy beverage in honor of Steve Thorborn.

Please understand that I said pint. As in sixteen liquid ounces. If you feel passionately about Steve Thorborn and his noble cause and want to raise two pints—that's thirty-two liquid ounces—or even more, be my guest. Just don't attempt to drive afterward. However you choose to celebrate this guy's name, please refrain from hoisting your beverage, foamy or otherwise, in units of liters. It would defeat the purpose.

Steve Thorborn is a British fruit vendor who locked horns with the legal system in his country for failure to adhere to the metric system of measure. His shop was raided by the authorities, his scales were

seized, and he got hauled into court. All because of a British law man-
dating a nationwide conversion to metric. Thorborn resisted the new
regulation, saying it kept him from conducting business "in the way my
customers want me to work." Dubbed the "metric martyr" by the British
press, he became something of a celebrity.

I hope Steve Thorborn winds up planting one foot—I speak here
of the terminal portion of the human leg, not a twelve-inch length of
measure—swiftly and forcefully against the blue-blooded tush of his
prosecutors. As long as the net weight remains constant, if he and his
customers want their bananas in pounds and ounces instead of kilo-
grams and grams, so be it.

Agreed, having several different systems of weights and measures
floating around the world can cause problems. But normally, we humans
can work around these differences without much hassle.

To illustrate: In the rivers and lakes of this country swims a very
popular game fish. Its technical name, immediately recognized by scientists from Europe to South America, is *Pomoxis annularis.* This fish
is an important piece of economic work. There's no telling how many
multiplied millions of dollars are spent annually in the pursuit of it.

We know it around Tennessee as the white crappie. We pronounce the word "CROP-ee." Deeper into the Southeast, the pronunciation changes to "CRAP-ee." And in other parts of the country, it goes by
a wide variety of handles. Everything from "calico bass" to "white perch"
to "papermouth" to "strawberry bass" to "chinquapin" to "sacalait" (a
Cajun French term meaning "sack of milk" in deference to its white,
delectable flesh.)

Confusing, perhaps. But nothing earth shattering. There's never
been a concerted effort to centralize the name. Nor should there be. I
feel the same way about Steve Thorborn's fruit-weighing scales.

Of course, learned members of the international monetary, commerce, and scientific communities will disagree. As always, they will howl
and harrumph and continually remind us that metric makes more sense,
is more logical, and is easier to comprehend than any other form of
measurement. And, and always, we crappie-catching, unwashed, non-
metricified masses will remind the learned members of the international

> **C**arl Porter offers a sure-fire method for getting your grass cut frequently and without charge. Just buy one of those old-time, non-motorized, reel-type lawn mowers that are so popular among the beautiful people these days. None of the kids in your neighborhood will have ever seen such a contraption, he says. They'll be amazed by it and veritably beg you to let them take a few rounds. Sure worked for him. ⌁

monetary, commerce, and scientific communities that they may kiss the collective surface of our American rear ends—a fleshy region of, oh, roughly two-hundred and fifty-thousand square acres.

Repeat: *acres,* not hectares.

Changing the Games

Anytime I turn on the television to watch the Olympics—summer or winter—I never cease to be amazed by the camera work. For decades, going back to the "agony of defeat," the talented men and women who broadcast Olympic images into our homes have done an outstanding job of showcasing the winners and losers with close-ups, slow-motions, stop-actions, and other tricks of their trade.

Matter of fact, those frontal slow-mo's of sprinters running toward the finish line illustrate the most amazing contortion of muscles this side of a circus. Until now, I never realized the human mouth and nose twisted, curved, arched, and bent in so many weird positions during the course of a foot race. If somebody set these gyrations to music, I'm sure it would spark a new dance craze.

But as interesting as these events are, and as impressed as I am by the physical skills of the contestants, I'm starting to get bored. Why not incorporate some new events into the games? Not trampoline and ballroom dancing, either. I'm talking about an entirely fresh slate of competition that is more relevant to modern society.

Archery was essential before the invention of gunpowder. So was discus before God gave us Frisbees. Pole-vaulting came in handy when it was necessary to cross the moat during a friendly round of castle pillaging. The triple jump, no doubt, was riotously funny back when the first ancient Greek happened to stumble while running. And synchronized swimming was good for—well, *surely* it had a reason for being invented way back in the dusty pages of athletic history. But that's the point. Traditional Olympic events are old hat. We need sports that are more related to contemporary living. Such as:

Computer Toss. Contestants square off to see (a) how quickly their screens will flash with the maddening message, "Illegal Operation— About To Shut Down" and (b) how far they can heave the infernal machine. For heightened viewer appreciation, this contest should take place atop a platform forty feet above an asphalt surface.

Mouse Throw. Contestants swing a computer mouse round and round, like the old time hammer throw, and let 'er rip. Again, in consideration of the TV audience, this event could be coupled with skeet shooting. Trust me on this. You show a computer mouse being blasted out of the sky with a shotgun, and one-hundred million voices throughout the world will scream "YES!" in unison.

Baby Juggling. Primarily an event for women, but surely a limited men's division can be created, even though men are generations behind the training curve. Contestants race through a supermarket to see who can most quickly and efficiently purchase one hundred dollars worth of groceries while simultaneously balancing an infant on one hip, attending to a toddler in the shopping cart, yelling "*I said no!*" to a four-year-old who is hanging off the front of the cart, and spanking a seven-year-old who keeps jerking candy and toys off the shelves. In this event, doping is allowed. Indeed, contestants will be plied with Prozac before the starting gun.

Cell Phone Marathon. This can be a 5K, 10K, or conventional marathon distance. Whatever the length, competitors are required to keep at last three conversations going through deft use of the "hold" and "call waiting" buttons.

Don't wait. Start your training regimen today.

Esther Rainwater of Dandridge answered her telephone one night. It was a telemarketer, calling for her husband, Charles, who had died two years earlier. "He's deceased," she told the caller. "No problem," the drone on the other end replied, "I'll call him back later." ∽

A Perfect Cup Holder

Hello. My name is Sam, and I have a drinking problem. I drink when I drive. I drink when I drive to work. I drink when I drive to the store. I drink when I drive on vacation. I even drink when I drive to church.

Coffee, that is. (What? You were expecting something else?)

My wife insists the keys to any vehicle I'm driving will flat-out refuse to turn in the ignition switch unless I am holding a steaming cup of joe in the other hand. It's hard to argue with her. She is an observant woman.

I don't know when I fell into this habit. I've been drinking coffee and driving so long, one seems impossible without the other. It's a Pavlovian response. Whenever I hear an engine fire up, my left arm automatically arcs toward my mouth, the hand crooked in position to hold a foam cup. This causes strange looks from passersby if I happen to be standing on a street curb at the time.

At least I'm not alone. Recently, the automotive research firm of J. D. Power and Associates asked forty-seven thousand new-car owners to rank problems they had discovered with their vehicles. This was not a random quest, either—as in, "Anything wrong with your car?" No, indeed. The J. D. Power people came up with a list of—I am not exaggerating—one *hundred and thirty five* possible complaints.

(Holy hubcap! I can't think of a hundred and thirty five complaints I've had in my all my years of vehicle ownership! If the thing starts, stops, runs smoothly, doesn't burn an extraordinary amount of gasoline, and the AC blows cold air, I'm usually content. Maybe my expectation level is far below the curve. But I digress.)

You know what ranked in the top twenty among problems? Cup holders. There weren't enough of them. Or they didn't work properly. Or they were in the wrong place. In fact, 63 percent of respondents said the cup holders on their vehicles were inconveniently located, making them difficult to use.

Said Dave Spykerman, engineering manager for Johnson Controls, a Milwaukee-based auto industry supplier, "The pursuit of the cup holder, the perfect cup holder, is often referred to as the search for the Holy Grail in our business. Everybody's looked for it, but nobody's found it yet. It's a never-ending battle."

How well I know. I've never been overly fond of built-in cup holders on any vehicle. I'm a dashboard-windshield man myself. With few exceptions, there's always a place—a sweet spot, as it were—along the top of the dashboard where a foam cup can be wedged against the windshield.

This varies by cup and dashboard, of course. Those jumbo mega-gulp containers you get at some fast-food outlets are eternally too tall to fit anywhere. And those itty-bitty, communion-sized shot cups that qualify as a "small coffee" in some cheap joints are eternally too short. But with enough experimentation, you'll eventually come up with a cup and a sweet spot that work. Your coffee cup or tobacco spit cup— I speak with vast experience in this regard, too, before I took the pledge —will stick tightly in place, despite bumps and curves.

The only cup holder I ever liked better was a homemade one. I built it three or four trucks ago after getting the idea while shopping at a marine supply store. I bought one of those drink holders for boats

I was driving along the interstate one day when I got passed, in succession, by three of those shiny, over-priced, gas-guzzling, mile-high, knobby-tired SUVs. You reckon twenty years from now we'll look back on those things like those block-long, tail-finned, chrome-domed, rolling fortresses from the 1950s and laugh ourselves silly? ⌣

and bolted it on the control panel, right next to the ashtray. The thing worked like a gyroscope. No matter how abruptly my truck turned, it always stayed level. That little gem must have handled ten thousand gallons of coffee (and Lord only knows how much tobacco juice) without spilling a drop.

Are you listening, auto makers? The people have spoken. Or slurped, as the case may be.

Lashing Out against Cell Phone Misuse

Cellular phone manners—or, specifically, the lack of same—are such a worn-out topic of discussion these days, I'm hesitant to even broach the subject.

Well, almost hesitant. The louts who misuse cell phones are cut from the same bolt of ragged cloth as litterbugs, loudmouths, linebreakers, and other loathsome lowlifes who care not one whit about their fellow human beings.

My latest encounter with one of these miscreants occurred in the Atlanta airport. I was waiting at the gate for my flight, along with approximately two hundred strangers, when this she-wolf reached for her malfunctioning cell phone, placed a call to some distant friend, and then proceeded to chronicle her holiday vacation, hour by hour.

Actually, I'm only guessing (a) her phone wasn't working properly and (b) she was calling North Dakota or some other foreign outpost. That's because this hussy spent the next twenty minutes *YELLING AT THE TOP OF HER LUNGS ABOUT ALL THE FOOD SHE HAD BEEN EATING AND ALL THE RELATIVES SHE HAD BEEN VISITING.*

I'm serious. This woman was so loud and so obnoxious, she brought cell phone misbehavior to an international low. She couldn't have put on a tackier display if she had flossed her teeth and passed gas while she jabbered. I believe if someone had snatched the phone from her grubby little fist and stomped it into the carpet, that entire section of the airport would have erupted in spontaneous applause. And I'll guarantee we could have raised a pile of money for the stomper's defense fund with one pass of the hat.

George Patterson, who graduated from Knoxville's Bearden High School in 1996, has noticed that a lot of parents are shocked to discover "recipes for violence" on the Internet. George wants to know where these middle-aged cretins have been all along.

"There's nothing new, except the 'Net," he noted. "At fourteen, I got the recipe for nitroglycerin from Jules Verne. At sixteen, research for a school paper on the Hungarian revolution gave me all sorts of information about Molotov cocktails. And access to firearms was certainly easier back then. But even with all this information, I never thought about using any of these weapons."

I second George's motion. When I was growing up, just about every boy I knew mowed lawns and carried newspapers to buy his first shotgun—with full approval of his parents.

The difference between then and now? It's a quaint word called "responsibility." ⌒

I realize now there's a better avenue of corrective measure. I read about it in a news story out of Saudi Arabia. Seems there was this army captain who misused his cellular phone on an airplane. The court gave him seventy lashes. And we ain't talkin' no wet noodle, either.

True, the Saudi man's offense was more serious than that goof in Atlanta. He was using his cell phone during takeoff, despite orders from members of the crew to turn the bloomin' thing off. He could very well have caused the plane to crash. As it was, the flight was aborted and Cap'n Chatty was "escorted off," so the story said. Ouch. If they dole out seventy stripes for cell phone misuse, you can bet the "escortee" was treated to leg irons and billy clubs instead of red carpets and rose petals.

In the context of American justice, of course, this type of punishment seems grossly excessive. Even though we can get terribly peeved at unmannerly pinheads, we aren't as quick to apply the cat-o'-nine-tails.

Why, if that woman in the Atlanta airport had been brought up on cell phone misuse charges and I'd been sitting on the jury, I would only have recommended thirty lashes, tops.

The Never-ending Name Game

If you want to own a bit of Americana before it disappears, run out and buy a box of prunes. Better hurry. They won't be on the market shelves much longer. At least not as "prunes." They will be called "dried plums" instead.

As any third-grader can tell you, prunes are dried plums. But "prunes" is a terribly dated word. It conjures up mental images of sour-faced, constipated relics in high button shoes whose primary goal in life is a satisfactory experience in the little room down the hall. That's why the folks who produce this item have successfully lobbied the Food and Drug Administration for an official name change.

You can't blame 'em for trying. Even though prunes—dried plums, I mean—are nutritious and high in iron, calcium, potassium, and vitamin A, they have a less-than-pleasant image. As Howard Nager, vice-president of marketing for Sunsweet Growers, testified in Washington, "For many years, prunes were advertised for a very specific nutritional message—their strong association with laxation."

Nothing new here. Happens in all walks of life. It's how "janitors" became "sanitation engineers", "tax increases" became "revenue enhancements", and "churches" became "faith-based institutions." But this presto-changeo seems to occur most often with things we put into our mouths.

In 1973, I took part in a tour of Canadian wetlands, courtesy of the United States Fish and Wildlife Service and the Canadian Wildlife Service. One day as we were flying over the prairie farmlands of Saskatchewan, I saw vast expanses of yellow flowers. Seems like they went on for miles.

"What is that stuff?" I asked a Canadian.

"Rape," he replied.

"Never heard of it. Why do they grow it—for the yellow flowers?"

The guy looked at me like I'd just asked if peanuts were raised primarily as livestock feed.

"You never heard of rapeseed oil?" he exclaimed. "They must sell millions of gallons of it every year in the United States."

Indeed they do, I discovered upon my return. But we don't call it "rapeseed" oil because of the evil connotations. Down here, the socially acceptable name is "canola" oil.

The more I got to thinking about this spin, the more I realized there are a number of food items that could use a dose of it. "Yogurt," for example. Even though I now enjoy this dairy product, it took me forever to try a bite because the name sounds so utterly disgusting. Wouldn't something Madison Avenue–ish like "velvet cream" be more appealing? Same with "kidney" beans. Yuck. I don't care how they are shaped, how delicious they are, or how nutritious they may be. The very name makes me want to hurl. And there's the "butt" portion of a hog, which actually is the shoulder. Not to mention "anise" oil for licorice flavor.

Then again, certain foods are so vile no amount of nomenclative cosmetics will improve them. Brussels sprouts by any other name will forever be just as rotten.

She REALLY Took a Bite Out of Crime

I have spent the last few days asking myself the same question: "What the hell had that guy been drinking?!?!"

"That guy" is named Neil Hutchinson. He lives in Newcastle, England. He recently testified in a court hearing. He is, to the best of my determination, the latest victim of a crime related to "Bobbittism."

In this particular case, however, Hutchinson did not lose the same part of anatomy that John Bobbitt did when his irate wife, Lorena, attacked him with a knife. Instead, he lost something a bit farther to the south. Something that originally was part of a pair.

I hold before me a copy of the story about the court proceedings. In it, Denise Carr testified that she reduced Neil Hutchinson's personal southern inventory from two to one by—and here we ask all male readers to take a deep breath, lest they grow faint from sympathetic pain—*biting it off.*

According to the story, Denise Carr and her friend, Shelley Hutchinson (that's Neil's wife, if you're trying to keep score), had been out for the evening. An argument broke out when they came home, and Neil began striking Shelley. Denise allegedly leapt upon the man to assist her friend. There was a vast amount of punching, gouging, and biting.

These things, civilized or otherwise, do happen. Like it or not, men and women have been known to disagree violently with each other, both here and in England. Faces are cut. Bones are broken. Teeth get knocked out. But according to testimony, neither Denise Carr nor Neil Hutchinson realized the degree of southern inventory reduction until—take another deep breath, men—*they found it under a picture frame in the sitting room.*

Denise Carr originally was charged with "wounding with intent" but the charge was eventually reduced to "affray." (Oh, those dry-witted British.) For better or for worse, the case is slowly working its way through the British legal system. In the meantime, I have

How's this for a sign of the times: A reader contacted me about a produce stand here in Knoxville that operates on the honor system when the proprietor isn't around. The owner leaves out a set of scales, some plastic bags, slips of paper, a pen, and a Mason jar. Customers are asked to make their selections, jot down what they have purchased, and then deposit their money into the jar. The reader gave me directions, so I drove out to see for myself.

The situation was exactly as reported. The owner told me the system had worked perfectly for years. There's never been a theft, either of produce or cash. Just one itty-bitty hitch. I can't identify this vegetable seller or the location of her stand. Because—you guessed it—she's afraid all the publicity will bring in new customers who will steal her blind. The sad thing is, she's probably right.

a few suggestions for anyone out there in readership land who happens to be of the male persuasion and is stupid enough to fight with a woman.

First, pick your opponent carefully. I suspect that even tiny women can turn into a ball of fury when provoked.

Second, be exceedingly cautious about her choice of weapons. Sharp knives are scary enough. A set of choppers is downright deadly, not to mention potentially more painful.

Third, after the fighting has subsided, make a quick inventory of all body parts. Yes, especially those down yonder. If anything does turn up missing, don't forget to look under any and all picture frames before you leave the sitting room.

Dental Hygiene Has Gone to the Dogs

Any day now, I expect humane society officers to launch an investigation of me because I'm so cruel to my dog. This is a long-standing practice of mine. By today's standards, Goldie, my aging English setter, is the most deprived dog in the history of pet ownership.

I did not buy Goldie pasta doggie food when it came on the market. I did not buy her an eleven-thousand-dollar video camera headset so I could monitor her every move around our neighborhood. I did not buy her a bottle of designer doggie cologne, perfume, hair spray, or shampoo. Nor did I buy her a set of plastic Neuticles to replace the "thingies" she lost on that ill-fated trip to the vet's office. (Then again, being a she, Goldie didn't have external "thingies" in the first place. The ones she lost via spaying were of the internal variety. But it's the thought that counts—or, in this case, doesn't.) And now, I take computer keyboard in hand to announce that I am not going to buy Goldie any peanut butter–flavored toothpaste.

Perhaps you are a more caring dog owner than I am. In that case, I'm sure you'll want to run to your friendly neighborhood pet supply store and pluck twelve-fifty from your Levi's—six bucks for the toothpaste, six-fifty for a special brush.

A California company called Crazy Dog makes this stuff. I am reading one of Crazy Dog's news releases right now.

"Think it's hard to get your kids to brush their teeth after meals?" it says. "Then imagine how difficult it is to win your dog over to the idea of regular brushing! This is the problem that a growing number of pet owners face, now that more Americans are brushing their dogs' teeth."

The paper goes on to say that Crazy Dog peanut butter–flavored toothpaste is much less abrasive than the stuff for humans; that it has no foaming agents; that it can be swallowed, seeing as how dogs can't gargle and spit as we do; that the bristles in the special doggie toothbrush are of equal length, not "peaked" like the ones humans use.

Poor Goldie. She's going to have to get by with plain ol' ordinary bones for dental hygiene. Not only am I not going to brush her teeth, I'm also not going to buy her any dried pig ears, pig snouts, or cow noses. A Wisconsin vet supply house called Drs. Foster & Smith offers these slaughterhouse by-products via mail order. They are cooked, sterilized, then "hickory-smoked until light brown and delicious."

Call me callous. Call me insensitive. Call me cruel. But please tell me how an animal that rolls in dead fish, greets other dogs with The Sniff, drinks from the toilet, and spends hours at a time licking its privates could possibly tell—much less care—about how something tastes?

Guy Boos Day

There are two reasons why I hope the courts go easy on Guy Boos, the man who shot his washing machine.

First, his last name surely has been a source of immense personal suffering. How'd you like to go through life with people shouting your name every time they're mad? Let folks start hollering "Smiiith!" or "Joooones!" or "Thommmmpson!" whenever they're angry at umpires and referees, and you'll see what I mean.

The second reason I hope Boos doesn't get the book thrown at him too harshly is because he's apparently one of us—a frustrated, modern guy who's had enough of evil machinery.

Boos lives in Chippewa Falls, Wisconsin. He ran afoul of the law when he became angry at his washing machine. According to police, he pushed the offending appliance down one flight of stairs and onto his driveway. Then he whipped out a pistol and opened fire. The cops charged him with "endangering safety."

There is no excusing Boos's action with the pistol. Lord knows there's enough gun-slinging misery, intentional and accidental, in this country as it is. When I talked with Chippewa Falls police chief Joe Coughlin about the incident, he said Boos told the arresting officers that, in retrospect, firing his gun was "not a prudent thing to do." My sentiments exactly.

Nonetheless, I submit there are machines in our midst that deserve a sound thrashing, and no person should be punished for administering it.

I've been in Guy Boos's shoes. You've been in Guy Boos's shoes. All Gawd's chillen been in Guy Boos's shoes. (Which, now that I think about it, makes for an extremely tight fit.) We have the misfortune of owning a hateful, rotten, no-good, low-down, conniving machine that delights in toying with us—and nothing we do will remedy the problem.

Maybe it's a washing machine that eats clothes. Maybe it's a computer that shuts down inexplicably and purges itself of a detailed document we just entered. Maybe it's an outboard motor that fires up faithfully at the marina, then refuses to so much as cough when we're eighteen miles up the lake. Maybe it's a food processor that waits until we have filled it with cranberries, blueberries, or some other super-staining fruit before blowing its lid and spilling its guts on our new carpet.

Oh, sure. We take 'em to be repaired. Many times. But it doesn't do one whit of good. The no-count pieces of trash act like choir boys when Mr. Fixit is around. Then, like Eddie Haskell in the old *Leave It to Beaver* television series, they revert to their sneaky ways as soon as the coast is clear.

Perhaps there ought to be a designated day each year when evil machinery can be brought to a central location and summarily beaten with sticks, two-by-fours, rocks, shovels, hammers, baseball bats, horse whips, or any other tool of punishment deemed appropriate by the owner. We could call it Guy Boos Day in honor of the patron saint of righteous indignation.

Just thinking about it makes my heart skip a beat in delight.

Paying Proper Last Respects

Let's say Uncle Ferd—beloved relative, friendly neighbor, longtime Sunday school teacher, all-around good guy—kicks the bucket. Here are some immediate steps to take to properly pay your respects.

Step One. Fry a mess of chicken or bake a pie and take it to Uncle Ferd and Aunt Lida's house to help feed the family and friends.

Step Two. Call the florist, order a spray of flowers, and tell 'em to put everybody in the Sunday school class's name on the card.

Step Three. Make sure your marryin'-and-buryin' suit is cleaned and pressed, particularly if Aunt Lida has asked you to be a pallbearer.

Step Four. Go to the funeral home the night of receiving friends and make pertinent remarks like, "They, law! Don't he look nice!"

And finally, the newest and most important—

Step Five. Grab a felt-tipped marker and scribble some tender words on Uncle Ferd's casket. Mayhaps something on the order of:

I shore will miss the times we had, my dear ol' Uncle Ferd.

But now it's time to say goodbye, 'cause soon you'll be interred.

What's that? You've never heard of Step Five? Then obviously you don't keep up with the latest trends in undertaking.

A funeral supply company in Texas has just unveiled a casket that is designed to be written upon and comes complete with a special "gloss pearlescent" coating and a set of permanent markers for your convenience. Don't take my word for it. Hear it straight from the York Group of Houston, the nation's second-largest manufacturer of hardwood and metal caskets and casket components.

"While this product is new in our industry, for years we have received requests for caskets that could be written on, both from funeral directors and from families and friends who believed this was the most effective and appropriate expression of their grief," said George Foley Jr., executive vice president. "Until the York Expressions, no funeral service product invited family and friends to express their deepest feelings about their loved ones in a physical, tangible way. Ours does."

"Society's needs are changing," added Mark Kowalczyk, a funeral director from Utica, New York. "Today's grieving families are seeking to memorialize their loved ones in unique ways. I see this innovative product meeting that need."

"Active participation rather than passive observation is much healthier for the bereaved," added Bill Bates, president of Life Appreciation Training Seminars in North Bay Village, Florida, who has trained some four thousand funeral home employees to counsel mourners.

I know these learned people have a point. I know funerals are for the living. I know grief, if not addressed, can manifest itself in physical and emotional anguish for years—indeed, for the remainder of the life of the survivor. But scribbling on a casket as if it was a high school yearbook or a cast on a broken arm?

No thanks. Make mine plain pine, and hold the graffiti.

Cupid's Crazy Questions

Among the mounds of junk mail I received last week were letters from two dating services. I'm not sure what this means.

Is somebody trying to tell me something? My wife, perhaps? My mother-in-law? Or was this merely a coincidence, the by-product of a bulk-mail campaign for new customers? Whatever the case, I browsed through each envelope and came away with the distinct impression that these folks are barking up the wrong tree. Even if, heaven forbid, I ever entered the singles category again, dating services wouldn't work for me.

For one thing, they were seeking the wrong information. I looked over a compatibility quiz from both agencies and was amazed by the lack of important questions. Everything they wanted to know was insignificant. Such as, "What is your educational background? Are you working full time? Are you new to the area? Does smoking offend you? Would you prefer to meet someone who has children?"

Who cares? If I was in the market for a woman, I'd be a lot more interested in her vital statistics. Like, "Do you have your own pickup truck? Is it paid for? Do you prefer casting or fly fishing? How well can you call geese? How well can you cook geese? Do you know how to use a chainsaw? Can you drive a straight shift and drink coffee at the same time? Would you rather watch a football game on television or see it in the flesh from the fifty yard line?"

That's the kind of information inquiring minds really want to know.

One of the letters included an equally unimpressive personality profile. It contained a variety of statements and asked for my response: strongly agree, agree, depends, disagree, strongly disagree. I glanced up and down the list and had to check "depends" each time because virtually everything in life depends on the situation.

For instance, one sentence read, "People place too much emphasis on looks."

Maybe. Maybe not. I recently was hospitalized for abdominal surgery. On my initial trip to the surgeon's office, I was not the least bit concerned about what the guy looked like. I was much more interested in knowing his credentials and how he planned to rearrange my guts. But let me tell you this for an absolute fact: If he'd come into that examination room looking like Frankenstein's scar-faced, stilt-legged, grinning monster, I'd have jumped back into my britches and busted the door off its hinges.

Without a doubt, though, the most ridiculous question wanted to know, "How far are you willing to drive to meet that special someone? Twenty-five miles? Fifty miles?"

What? Me drive to meet her? If she's got her own truck, why can't she come over to my place?

A recent mailing from South Bend Sporting Goods in Northbrook, Illinois, left me scratching my head. The company was announcing a year-long promotion with its extensive line of fishing rods and reels. Buyers of this gear will receive a coupon for a free package of smoked salmon.

Excuse me? What does it say about a fishing tackle company's faith in its merchandise if they have to lure the buyer with a promise of ready-to-eat fish? ～

Camera-Shy

I just combed through a photography catalog and was relieved to discover those new "anti-lie" digital cameras are not yet on the market.

What a relief. The sport of fishing is safe for the time being.

Perhaps you've heard about these cameras. They're being tested by the Defense Department. The federal government wants to use them to weed out potential terrorists among airline passengers.

These new gizmos are packed with intricate heat sensors. They're able to pick up minute changes in facial tissue, particularly around the eyes, when a person tells a lie. Researchers at the Mayo Clinic in Rochester, Minnesota, said they out-performed traditional detection machines by a sizeable margin.

If these cameras can prevent hijackings, fine. If they can convict bank robbers, fine. If they can nab tax cheats, corporate crooks, fraud artists, and other societal scumbags, fine. But God forbid they would ever be used in the world of fishing. The very future of this noble sport hangs in the balance.

Lying is an integral part of fishing. It has been honed for tens of thousands of years. It is expected. Indeed, since the dawn of creation, fishermen have been proudly misleading each other. To break this cycle would be a travesty of social, not to mention sporting, justice.

There are as many types of fishing lies as there are fisher folk, but they more or less fall into one of two categories: (a) lies to embellish the truth and (b) lies to diminish the truth.

The first category is, by far, the more common. With only a smidgen of practice, rank beginners can quickly become seasoned experts. It works like this:

Gilbert Goober, who couldn't catch a fish at Captain D's, goes to a sporting goods store and maxes out four credit cards to purchase the latest rods, reels, lines, and lures. He's convinced all he has to do is wade into the nearest stream, wave his rod about, and vast schools of trout will swim up to the knees of his neoprene waders and surrender. Alas, when Gilbert does sally forth (often in the company of a fifth), the only thing he catches is the back of his head with a poorly cast fly. In a fit of rage and pain, he yanks at the imbedded hook and snaps his leader.

Excellent!

When Gilbert arrives at his office the next day, he gathers everyone around the coffee pot and gives 'em a blow-by-blow that is 99 percent fiction.

"Hooked the biggest critter in Stinky Creek yesterday morning!" he swears. "Fought him all over the place! Thought I had him worn down, but the dadburn thing made one final run and broke my line. Boy, what a hawg!"

Gilbert tells this lie with such passion his colleagues are convinced he tangled with the mother of all trout. They think he's a great fisherman. His ego is stroked. All because of a finely fashioned fib.

The second category is the opposite type of lie. Instead of taking a single strand of truth and weaving it into a rope, the teller unravels the facts to throw others off his trail. In this type of lie, the big one never gets away. In fact, the big one is never mentioned at all.

Let's say Zeb Zindingle has been annihilating the bass in Brewster's Pond for weeks. No matter what type of lure he throws, he cranks in four- and five-pounders on virtually every other cast. So he goes back to the office and spills his guts, right?

Are you nuts? Of course he doesn't. He wants to enjoy this secret honey hole all summer long. When the gang gathers around the coffee pot, and it's his turn to speak, Zeb only shakes his head sadly.

"Ain't no use tryin' Brewster's Pond," he sighs. "I been fishin' over there the last few weeks, and I don't think there's a thing in the place. Nothin' but a waste of time. If I's you fellows, I'd go up Stinky Creek. That big'un Gilbert Goober got hold of last week is still up there, I reckon."

Once again, everybody's happy, thanks to a well-crafted lie.

Now, are you starting to understand why it's so important that these new truth-detection devices stay under wraps? Good. So if you'll excuse me, I need to get back to work. Got a ton of things to do. Haven't got time for all this mindless chatter. I'm way behind schedule and—

Hey! Put that camera down!

The Perils of Holiday Junk Mail

T'was two months before Christmas, and all through my house, not a creature was stirring, not even a mouse. My wife and the kids—plus our fish, cats and dogs—had been buried alive by those dang catalogs.

"It happened so quickly," I sobbed to the cops. "I sent off five bucks for some blue argyle socks. Then mail-order houses from Baja to Maine put my name on their lists. Holy cow! It's insane!"

Every time that I walked to our box for the mail, I found tons of brochures with more gifts on sale. It was awful in August, but by mid-September, the Christmas load beat all that I can remember. It took seven trips daily to carry them in. In a matter of weeks, they had flooded our den. I burned them, recycled, and hauled 'em to dump, but the more I discarded the more that showed up. Gander Mountain, Norm Thompson, Lands' End—botheration! L.L. Bean, Bits and Pieces, Southwestern Foundation. Hershey's and Wireless and Spiegel—good grief! Oh, how I begged for some bulk-rate relief!

Yet still came more offers; each day was the same. They flowed out our mailbox like Iowa rain. From Frontgate, Cabela's, and Mack's Prairie Wings. How do they keep coming up with these things?

Housecoats and luggage and lamp shades and cheese; neckties and work boots and imported teas. Gift packs of apples and chocolate éclairs; slippers and sweaters and rugs for the stairs.

"Buy now for Christmas!" each catalog said. "Shop from your easy chair, sofa, or bed. Lots of selections, don't hassle with malls. Give us your money! Let us deck your halls!"

(Of course, by the time that you figure the bills, and add all the freight, handling charges, and frills, your money is gone and you're deep into hock. Then the company writes back, "It's no longer in stock.")

Still, hundreds and hundreds arrived by the hour: Mary Maxim and Penney's and King Arthur Flour. Williams-Sonoma and Coldwater Creek; these people must think I'm an Arab oil sheik. Hawking fruitcakes and candles and carvings and towels—I tell you, these jerks are a pain in the bowels! To buy eight percent of the items they sell would blow the national debt plumb to hell.

I thought of how nice it would be for a change to get rid of all of this seasonal pain. Just open the mailbox and pull out a letter. No catalogs! Wow! Does it get any better?

So I grabbed a machete and ran to the box, hoping to kill off this catalog pox. But the mail-order magnates had neutered my rages by sending a new batch of slick color pages. They hit me, and I was knocked clean off my feet. Pieces of catalogs littered the street. I staggered inside, badly wounded and reeling, and found dozens more catalogs piled to the ceiling.

"Help me! Please help me!" I begged to the cops. "Halt mail-order madness! Please yank out the stops!"

The officer told me he'd give it his all—if I'd order twelve tickets to his precinct's big ball.

Nobody has to buy return-address labels these days. That's because every non-profit outfit in the country will send you a couple of sheets for free—hoping, of course, you'll send them a few dollars in exchange for their generosity. This is one instance where it's better to receive than give. ~

There's Always Someone to Offend

I browsed through the Halloween section of a discount store the other day and came away with the impression that Knoxville is a very insensitive town. Why? Because many of the costumes and masks are not politically correct. And as anyone with half a brain knows, political correctness means everything in today's age of super sensitivity.

Oops. Let me correct my last statement. I shouldn't have used the term "half a brain," since it might be construed as a cruel remark about people who have undergone prefrontal lobotomies. What I meant to say was, "anyone with half a degree of common sense." No, wait. I don't mean to imply people who sometimes behave irrationally don't have a full measure of common sense. What I really should have said is, "anyone whose elevator goes almost to the top floor." Shucks, that's incorrect too. I wouldn't dare make fun of America's elevator industry and the good people who work in it. But I think you're starting to catch my drift.

I am enlightened about this matter because I have just finished reading Halloween guidelines from the Equity–Affirmative Action Advisory Committee in Iowa City, Iowa. It listed costumes that are no longer proper for kiddies to wear when they go trick-or-treating. Witches, devils, hobos, and many others are taboo because they reflect negative images.

I should say so. We don't want a bunch of fun-loving, candy-eating munchkins making people feel bad about themselves. That's why I was so dismayed at seeing so many insensitive costumes available in Knoxville stores.

A number of the masks depicted faces pocked by cuts and scars, with mouths full of jagged, yellow teeth. A lot of people have cuts and scars on their faces. And Lord only knows the need for dentistry. Surely masks like these will offend some people. I hope the store removes them from the shelf, pronto.

Same for cherry-flavored fake blood capsules. According to the directions, these are filled a harmless red liquid. Youngsters bite down on them to give the impression they are bleeding profusely from the mouth. Harmless, my foot! What kind of cruel message does this send to people who suffer from bleeding gums? Don't they feel bad enough about their condition?

Ditto for skull caps covered with skin-colored material. Put 'em on a ten-year-old's head, ha-ha-ha, and it gives the impression he's balder than an old man. Not that all old men are bald, of course. And not that being old, or bald, or a man, is bad. Forget I mentioned it. I apologize.

In fact, the more I pawed through the costumes, the more I realized there's no way not to offend someone. Thus, I suggest everyone immediately scrap their Halloween plans. No parties. No trick-or-treating. Nothing. Instead, let us spend the time in deep meditation about how we can be more friendly to one another.

And if some of the miserable little wretches—I mean, some of the cherubs in your neighborhood—react by burning a few tires in your back yard, I hope you are not offended by the smell.

Chapter 9

Home Is where the Heartburn Is

HOW'S SHE FEEL TO YOU, LARRY?

OH, MAN!

EXPOSED: LAWN SWAPPING.

R. DANIEL PROCTOR

Do not be confused by the title of this chapter. I love my home. I love my wife. I loved it when our children were still with us, and although I'm delighted they have lives and careers of their own, I can't help but grieve that they've flown the nest.

Mary Ann and I live in a log house on a wooded ridge on the distant outskirts of Knoxville. We're close enough to the interstate that I can drive to downtown if it is absolutely necessary, yet far enough removed from civilized people that I can recycle my coffee anytime I'm working outdoors—and don't have to worry about offending neighbors when I perform the rite. This is every male redneck Baby Boomer's dream.

The words "working outdoors" are crucial. I do not mind—indeed, I truly enjoy—building up a head of steam with a lawnmower, chainsaw, garden tiller, posthole digger, shovel, log splitting maul, wheelbarrow, or rake.

Well, maybe I could do without the rake. I liked to knocked myself silly with a rake once, and I've never trusted the evil things since. This occurred many years ago, back when we lived in a subdivision, and I felt duty-bound to rake leaves several times each fall. I never was one of those gentle, patient, pipe-smoking leaf rakers. I went at it with a vengeance, and I always got plenty of practice. We had a number of oaks, maples, dogwoods, poplars, and sweet gums, plus a row of giant white pines that shed brown needles like a waterfall every October.

White pine needles are a pain. They clog the tines of a rake worse than glue. You have to stop every few strokes and clean them out. One day I was rake-marching along the perimeter of the pines—*whoosh! whoosh! whoosh!*— creating an undulating mountain of brown needles. I'd reach one end of the line, clear the tines for the ten-thousandth time, advance two or three yards, and retrace my steps. It was slow progress. After perhaps half an hour, I had amassed a pine needle Matterhorn and had it positioned near our rhododendrons. With quick, hard, outward strokes of the rake, I began hurling great globs of needles atop the bushes for winter mulch.

That's when it happened.

It didn't take long. Looking back, I'd guess, oh, one-forty-seventh of a second. But in that instant, a series of events occurred. As one of my outstrokes began, the rake handle broke between my left and right hands. We are not taking a slow, *creeeeaaaak* type of break. We are talking *crack!* Like a rifle shot. The inertia carried the broken stub, in my left hand, into an arc above my head. Reaching the apex of the arc, it jerked downward violently, striking me across the left ear and temple like a club.

I saw not only stars but the complete Milky Way. I emitted as much of an oath as one can emit in what's left of one-forty-seventh of a second after being cold-cocked. I staggered like a drunkard until I finally came to my senses.

No permanent damage was done, thankfully. To me, that is. I wound up with a lump next to my ear, and that whole side of my head stayed tender for a good twenty-four hours. The rake handle fared worse. It was relegated to the kindling box. I immensely enjoyed watching it burn.

My appetite for chores drops off precipitously, however, once I come inside the house. I would rather drag my fingernails across a blackboard for two hours than run a vacuum cleaner for ten minutes. If this is male chauvinism, I stand guilty as charged. I think it has something to do with being a first-round Baby Boomer. Despite any political correctness I might've acquired about domestic duties down through the years, I am genetically linked to a generation that drew distinct lines between men's work and women's work. Fortunately, I have a very liberal wife in this regard. Mary Ann will work just as diligently outdoors as in.

I've got a sneaking suspicion this truism may apply to a number of Baby Boomer couples. I once read a magazine article about a poll of married men and women on the subject of household chores. In it, nearly half these people said they argued about who does what.

Nearly half of the women, that is. Forty-two percent of the women said they quarreled with their spouses over the division of labor regarding work details around the house. In contrast, only 35 percent of the men agreed. This is understandable because men rarely realize an argument has taken place. Consider this conversation in the Smiths' (not their real name) living room.

She: "It would be *very* (in this context, *very* indicates the presence of rigid neck muscles) helpful if you'd pick your smelly shoes and socks off the floor."

He: "Yeah, sure. Whatever you. . . .Wow! What a catch!"

She: "I'm going to the grocery store. Do you think it's possible to tear yourself away from *that TV* (see note above) long enough to run the vacuum cleaner while I'm gone?"

He: "Huh? Oh, yeah. I'll get to it as soon as . . . . Out? Aaaarrrgh! No way he was out!"

See what I mean? If a pollster telephoned at that precise moment and asked if the couple fussed about household chores, Mrs. Smith would reply, "Constantly." Mr. Smith, on the other hand, would say, "Hey, can you two hold it down for a minute? It's the top of the ninth!"

With that in mind, you will understand why I took the magazine article with a large measure of salt. Permit me to illustrate further.

One question asked, "Would you rather have OK sex in a clean house or great sex in a dirty house?"

What kind of a stupid question is that? Why didn't they offer the choice all men would select? Namely, "dirty sex in *any* house."

Here's another sample of this irrational quizzing: "Would you rather your son learn to change the oil in the car or do the ironing?"

Again—and I speak as an authority on the male mind in this regard—no correct option was offered. We'd rather our son take the car to have the oil changed and drop off the laundry at the same time.

Check out this gem: "How often should the toilet be cleaned?"

What? You mean those things are supposed to be cleaned? Isn't it enough that we learned to flush?

Oh, and I loved this one: "When was the last time you cleaned out the refrigerator?"

Could we choose, "When I was searching for the last beer in the twelve-pack"? Of course not. Nor, "Anytime my fishing worms get loose," either.

Clearly, these answers were not designed for Y-chromosome Baby Boomers. And I intend to write a strongly worded letter of protest to the editor of that magazine about it.

Just as soon as this ballgame is over.

One of us Has a Lot to Learn

Either I don't know how to cut grass or a lot of other people don't know about sex. It's that simple. There is no room for debate. One of us is enlightened and the other is dumber than a brick. Period.

That's the only conclusion I can reach after seeing the results of a survey of nearly four thousand Americans on the topic of "fun and enjoyment." The survey was made for the Home & Garden television network. When I perused the findings, I dang-near fainted.

According to the researchers, the majority of homeowners would rather cut the grass than frolic in it. When asked, "Which activities are you most likely to do in your spare time for fun and enjoyment?" 41 percent listed lawn mowing. Sex came in second (37 percent), followed by gardening (34 percent) and redecorating (23 percent).

Heaven help us.

I feel like the man who grew up in poverty during the Depression and then struck it big in the oil business. He made millions. His family threw a big bash for his seventy-fifth birthday. During the height of the festivities, someone called him to the podium and asked him to impart a bit of wisdom for the assembled masses. The ol' boy thought for a moment, then said, "I've been rich and I've been poor. Rich is better."

That's the way I feel about the vast differences in this matter.

I've cut a lot of grass in my lifetime. And I've—uh, well, er, that is—suffice to say I'm enough of a veteran of both campaigns to know lawn duty doesn't hold a flame to making whoopee. You tend to get sweaty during both exercises. Winded, too, if you happen to be pushing a mower across hilly terrain. But those are the only similarities, and the efforts expended to produce that sweat are *nowhere* near the same.

Oh, I suppose it is possible to see stars and feel the earth move during the height of lawn-mowing ecstasy. In fact, I can recall two personal instances along this line. In both situations, it occurred when I scraped across nests of ground-dwelling yellow jackets. By the time those hateful vermin had finished with my head, neck, legs, and ankles, I was seeing a veritable galaxy of stars. Then I finally got my feet churning fast enough to move across the earth at Olympic-sprinter speed. Not in a million years would I consider either of these a sexual experience—unless, perhaps, you include some of the specific cuss words I yelled.

Make no mistake. As your stereotypic pot-bellied, mortgage-paying, fertilizer-spreading Baby Boomer, I take pride in my yard. I work hard to keep it weed-free and Kelly green. But the key word here is "work." As in "labor" and "arduous task." There are chores that must be performed to make the yard look presentable. They offer the same recreational potential as a mound of raw, unpeeled potatoes does if you happen to be in the mood for fries.

And speaking of recreation, what other "fun and enjoyment" alternatives to sex did the research people have in mind besides lawn mowing, gardening, and—*aaaakkk!*—redecorating?

They never heard of fishing?

The Vetch Is Always Greener Department: For the better part of two years, I tried to establish a patch of crown vetch on an exposed piece of bare ground near a road cut. Liked to never got the stuff to grow. During the height of this vegetative frustration, I happened to be driving in another part of town and spotted a gorgeous stand of crown vetch, in full bloom, on the side yard of a residence. As I sat there in my car, oohing and aahing and coveting the bounty, I heard a noise. Looked up and saw a guy, no doubt the homeowner, astride a riding lawnmower. He attacked the vetch and took it to the ground. Indeed, one man's trash is another's treasure. ⌒

Mr. Preparedness

If aggravated stupidity was a criminal offense, I would be in jail for the next twenty years. I not only committed this heinous crime to begin with, I compounded the problem by repeating it several times. And the worst part is, I got into this mess by attempting to avert stupid mistakes.

I was trying to be Mr. Preparedness, just like they teach in Boy Scouts.

It all started when I was cleaning up my bass boat and getting it ready for the summer fishing season. While repacking the wheel bearings with grease, I happened to hit one of the tire valve stems with my hand. It hissed.

The valve stem, I mean. Very rarely does my hand hiss. Very rarely do valve stems hiss, either—unless they have dry-rotted and are about to snap off, resulting in an instant flat tire.

So I telephoned Tire Guy. He said it was no big deal. Just pop off the tire and bring it in, and he could fix it in minutes. Mr. Preparedness, of course, knows more than Tire Guy. Why waste time jacking up the boat trailer and removing the tire? Why not just tow the trailer to Tire Guy's shop?

Please note that Mr. Preparedness didn't merely slap the trailer onto the hitch of his pickup truck and roar off. Mr. Preparedness would never do something so stupid. He is prepared for problems, remember? That is why he tentatively rolled the trailer around in his driveway, just to make certain it would hold air. It did.

In point of fact, the tire held air all the way down Mr. Preparedness's driveway and all the way to the main road. And then—out where the traffic is heavy and fast and there's no shoulder to pull off onto—it went flatter than an interstate possum.

Backing up a convoy of cars and trucks, Mr. Preparedness managed to limp the rig half a mile or so until he could pull into a subdivision. There, he fell into the chore of changing to a spare tire. Yes, *of course* he had a spare. Mr. Preparedness is always ready for emergencies. What Mr. Preparedness was not ready for, however, was the fact that the #@%! lug nuts on the #@%! boat trailer were not the same size as the #@%! lug nut wrench behind the seat of his #@%! truck.

But once again, no problem. Mr. Preparedness reached for his cell phone to call Tire Guy and have him send help. Mr. Preparedness does not carry a cell phone so he can jabber aimlessly with friends while driving. No, indeed. Mr. Preparedness keeps a cell phone in his truck strictly for emergencies like this. What Mr. Preparedness does not do —*aarrgh!*—is routinely check his cell phone to make sure the batteries are charged.

I will spare you the rest of the ugly details. Suffice to say Mr. Preparedness knocked on enough doors to finally find someone who

Every garden needs a surprise. Mine in the summer of 1999 was a thirty-six-inch copperhead, coiled and cocked at the base of a tomato plant, scant inches away from my bare legs. I never consulted a record book about the matter, but I'll guarantee you I set a mark for the standing broad jump that will never be eclipsed.

In the summer of 2000, the surprise was far more benign. It was a gourd plant, strictly volunteer, that all but engulfed the place. Heaven only knows where the original seed came from. Maybe it was a stowaway in some of the pasture soil I had gathered earlier that year. Maybe it was recycled by a bird. Maybe it was brought in by a mouse. When you live in the woods like we do, anything's possible.

The thing grew throughout the summer at a rate that would put kudzu to shame. I had to be careful to stay away from the tentacles, lest I be pulled into the green mass and not seen until frost. It finally produced six "birdhouse" gourds. Not a bad output, I suppose, but it seemed quite inefficient given the huge volume of vines. Anybody who wants to grow these gourds on a commercial basis had better have four or five hundred spare acres available. And maybe a few goats to take care of the scraps. ⌒

would let him use a telephone to call Tire Guy. And Tire Guy came out and changed the tire. And then Mr. Preparedness and Tire Guy drove to Tire Guy's place and fixed everything. And Mr. Preparedness drove back home with his bass boat and parked it without further incident and then went out and bought the correct size lug nut wrench. Which he will likely never use in the next ten thousand years.

Mr. Preparedness assumes his pulse rate will return to normal in three or four more days.

Bugged by Beetles

I don't need to know everything there is about science. The moon and the stars got along fine for eons before me, for instance; they'll get along fine after I am gone. Same with distant elements in the periodic tables, exotic vegetation like lichens and mosses, tropical birds, saltwater fishes—in short, all manner of weirdisms I don't encounter on a routine basis.

Yet there is one burning scientific question that must be answered. Where do ladybugs come from? Specifically, the clouds of ladybugs that infest my home every fall and winter.

In ladybug fashion circles, the inside of my house has become *the* place to see and be seen. They gather on windowsills and windowpanes. They buzz around the mirrors. They hover around light fixtures until they drop—*ker-plink!*—from exhaustion and pile up in dainty little lady-bug mounds.

Apparently I am not alone. I recently spoke with Dr. Frank Hale, assistant professor of entomology and plant pathology at the University of Tennessee's Agricultural Extension Service in Nashville. He hears from bug-infested homeowners all the time. But in late winter, the calls increase.

"People see lady bugs more often in February and March because they're inside the homes, trying to get out," he told me.

You mean those beasties freeload off me all winter, and when it starts to turn spring, they want to go back to living off the land? Exactly.

"They come in the latter part of October," Hale said. "A lot of people call them 'Halloween beetles' because of the timing and because of their orange and black color."

Technically, these are "multi-colored Asian lady beetles." Hale says this particular species spread from an intentional release in Louisiana or Georgia in the early 1990s. The purpose of that program was to control pecan aphids. The beetles apparently will eat aphids besides those on pecan trees. They'll also gather in clusters.

"It's called 'aggregation behavior,'" he said.

Or aggravation behavior, as the case may be.

No, these ladybugs are not nearly as bad as, say, a swarm of termites or killer bees. But they're still a pain in the butt. Actually, they are a pain in other body parts. One of them bit me on the leg.

"Yes, they do have moving mouth parts," Hale said. "That one probably bit you because it was hungry or searching for water."

Meaning, I suppose, that I look like Jabba the Hutt of the aphid world.

Early on, I tried liberating the ladybugs I captured inside my place because I know they're good at destroying garden pests. But when they started showing up in platoons, I became less concerned about their welfare.

I have nubs for fingers, making it difficult to pick them off of a windowpane. So I have resorted to grabbing them with the sticky side of a piece of masking tape. Some of my bug missions have become indoor hunting trips as I stalk a windowpane and spring a surprise attack. My personal best is four bugs with a two-inch-long piece of tape. I debated having them mounted on a Popsicle stick and nailing it over the fireplace.

Hale says the very last thing folks should do is fumigate their houses in late winter. That's when there are lots of hibernating lady bugs behind walls and in cracks and crevices. Kill 'em then and all you're doing is laying a festive table for carpet beetles, which can also feed on woolens and silks.

A far less-destructive alternative is being tested by the United States Agriculture Department. It's an indoor bug trap that features a black light. Supposedly the black light attracts ladybugs the same way it did disco dancers back in the '80s.

"The early tests are very encouraging," Hale said. "I expect we'll see these products on the market one of these days. Homeowners should love them."

Maybe. Maybe not. If using a black light means my lady bugs will start wearing itty-bitty leisure suits, spinning around in slick-soled patent leather shoes, and singing, *stayin' aliiiiive!* in high-pitched choruses, I'm buying a large can of Raid.

Is there a symphony on this planet as soothing as the chorus created on summer nights by armies of crickets, katydids, jarflies, and other insects? True, when these critters get their communications cranked up to boom-box level, it sounds like mass confusion to human ears. I can't imagine how Bill Bug manages to attract Betty Bug in all that clatter. Then again, what do you suppose the roar of a football crowd sounds like to an insect? ∿

---

wallpaper woes

It took me nearly thirty years of marriage to discover the quickest route to divorce has nothing to do with finances, anniversary amnesia, child-rearing, quarrels with in-laws, or wet towels on the floor. It has to do with hanging wallpaper.

Take your basic Type-A man, who would rather be staked to an ant hill than hang wallpaper, and put him with his Type-B wife, who has hung hundreds of rolls of wallpaper through the years and thinks of it as recreational therapy. If they can start the day working together and are still living in the same state when the sun goes down, their bond is secure.

Mary Ann and I remain united. Happily, I might add. But during our wallpaper project from hell, I would have pegged our chances of marital survival somewhere between Elizabeth Taylor and Larry King.

It all started with a myth known as "pre-pasted" paper. To the uninitiated, this innocent term means "just add water." Wrong. "Pre-pasted" is derived from the ancient word "pre-plastered" and means you should consume massive amounts of intoxicating beverages before tackling the project. Even though hydrated according to the directions, our "pre-pasted" paper curled off the wall like Christmas ribbon.

I wanted to sue everybody from the manufacturer on down. Mary Ann wasn't fazed.

"This happens sometimes," she said nonchalantly. "It's not a problem. Just run to the store and buy some paste."

"You go to the store," I countered. "There'll probably be fifteen different brands. I won't know which one to get."

Against my better judgment, I went. And discovered, as usual, that I was wrong. There are *not* fifteen different brands of wallpaper paste on the market today. There are one hundred and fifteen. Per shelf.

I telephoned Mary Ann from the store. "Do you want the kind of paste that's pre-mixed or the kind you mix yourself?" I asked.

"Oh, just bring the powder," she replied. "It's a lot cheaper. All we have to do is stir it up with water."

"But the other stuff's all ready to go," I whined. "You just brush it on like mayonnaise."

The woman would not change her mind. So I bought something that appeared to be crystallized phlegm and took it home and mixed it with the recommended dosage of water. It turned into oatmeal with lumps the size of Rhode Island.

"Keep stirring," Mary Ann coached.

I did. The lumps turned into Vermont, New Hampshire, Connecticut, and Massachusetts. My fuse was already smoldering.

"Those lumps will go away eventually," she said in her ever-calm voice. "You're always in too much of a hurry."

The fuse was glowing like a blowtorch by now. "I'll show you how to hurry!" I exclaimed. "I'm gonna hurry back to the store with this (garbage) and buy some paste that's pre-mixed!"

Done. I even bought a brush to apply it with.

The paste was quite thick, like industrial-strength lotion. So thick, in fact, that it started pulling bristles out of my brush. By the third sheet of paper, it was shedding worse than a collie in summertime. By the tenth sheet, the brush looked like it had undergone several rounds of chemotherapy. Back to the store I went for more brushes. Many more.

Yes, through miracles and divine intervention, we did manage to get the wall papered. Mary Ann's Mother Teresa patience never wavered throughout the process. We are still speaking.

Oh, and by the way—shortly before we completed this little project, I established a Guinness record that will surely never be beaten: Longest Throw of a Wallpaper Paste Bucket and Wallpaper Paste Brush From Two-Story Window.

I doubt either has hit the ground yet.

Talking about Tools

May is National Tool Safety Month. The Hand Tool Institute says so.

Yes, there really is a Hand Tools Institute—or HTI, as we say back in the workshop. It is in Tarrytown, New York. And every May, these folks send out a scary warning about the dire consequences awaiting people who misuse hammers, saws, screwdrivers, wrenches, mallets, pliers, tin snips, and other implements found in hardware stores and Sears catalogs everywhere.

"Approximately seventy-six thousand persons receive emergency hospital treatment each year for serious injuries due to misusing hand tools," the latest advisory said.

I have no reason to doubt those figures. Actually, they may be quite conservative because people hate to admit they are goobers and don't know how to use a tool properly.

"Hmmmmm," says the emergency room doctor, as he inspects the handle of socket wrench protruding from a patient's leg. "How did this accident happen? Were you attempting to misuse this wrench, and it slipped out of your hands and stabbed your leg?"

"Uh, er, uh—gracious, no!" the goober replies. "I was, uh, let's see—oh yeah, I remember now. I was chasing the neighbor's dog out of my yard and slipped in wet grass and fell on this thing. Dadblamed kids probably got it out of my tool box and left it in the yard. You better believe I'm gonna have a stern talk with 'em when I get home, too."

But with full apologies to the HTI, I submit that it is every American's civic responsibility to misuse tools. We have built a proud nation by turning screws with dimes and pounding nails with screwdriver handles, and I say we keep it up.

Americans know how to use their time to the utmost efficiency, right? So why—if we are flat on our backs beneath the kitchen sink, trying to stop a leak—would we waste a full forty-two seconds squirming to our feet and traveling across the room to get the proper tool for the job when an old butter knife with a broken tip lies within easy reach?

Why—if we are cutting a piece of wood with a power saw and the electricity goes off—would we throw away the time and energy required to walk all the way to the basement and find a hand saw when there is a perfectly good hammer nearby and all it will take is a solid whack with the claw to finish cutting the board in the first place?

And why—if we are wrestling with a rusted-on nut—would we go to the expense of buying solvent, and then waiting for it to work, when we can pick up a hatchet and beat the hateful thing into submission?

Besides, you never can find a socket wrench when you need it. Sure as shooting, the kids will have left it out on the yard, just so you can fall on it while chasing the neighbor's dog.

wreck the Halls and Toss the Holly

Some people—and we know who we are—have no business attempting to decorate a Christmas tree. We have neither the patience nor the creativity required for this task. And we have no hope of acquiring either. We want the tree to be standing there in all its radiance, as beautiful as the catalog cover from Neiman-Marcus, approximately seven minutes after it is hauled in from the car (if freshly cut) or attic (artificial).

Little do we realize that decoration duties for the catalog tree took seven months and required the services of five interior designers, twelve-thousand dollars worth of ornaments, a work crew of fifteen, not to mention a hook-and-ladder unit from the local fire department. Still, we persist in this annual folly.

I made it further this year than ever before. I was well into the light-stringing stage before I blew a gasket and began slinging glass balls at random.

Ah, yes. The light strings. The colorful, twinkling light strings. The hateful, #$&*-ing light strings. I don't care what it says on the box about origin of manufacture. I am convinced every string of Christmas tree lights on the market today was produced at a torture prison deep in the outback of a Third World nation.

Be not deceived by the attractive packaging. These lights may look like they were lovingly tucked together with the care of a grandmother, but the moment you touch them, they snarl into more knots than can be tied on Eagle Scout demonstration day at summer camp. And that's the easy part.

Putting strings of lights *back* into the box when the holidays are over is a physical impossibility. They will never be successfully reinserted into the container whence they came, not even with the assistance of a physics professor, three shoehorns, and an econo-jar of Vaseline. It is better to throw away the whole mess—cords, plugs, bulbs, the works—and buy new each year.

Oops. Did I say "bulbs?" Bite my tongue. Surely the people who invented those itty-bitty bulbs were deprived of Christmas joy as children and decided to vent their frustrations and anger on the rest of humanity.

"Entire string works even if one bulb goes out," the box says.

True. But notice it doesn't say anything about what happens if one bulb isn't seated properly. Meaning you have to personally inspect all 4,932,748 bulbs in the string, jiggling and joggling right and left, until illumination is achieved. Trust me. You will not find this spiteful bulb on the first 4,932,747 attempts.

Even then, your stress level will only have been toyed with. Fiendish steps known as "ornament hanging" and "tinsel dangling" beckon menacingly, teasing you like a fickle lover, then mocking your sophomoric attempts.

Almost every Christmas I go to parties at homes in which every ornament on the tree looks like it was placed by computer. Once, I was tempted to ask for a tape measure just to satisfy my curiosity. I swear they covered the limbs as uniformly as scales on a fish, each precisely equidistant from its neighbor.

I am not so gifted. My idea of proportion is to hang seven hundred balls, do-dads, widgets, and related memorabilia on the nearest four branches and be done with it.

Same with tinsel. It's fine if Mother Nature wants to lovingly drip her real icicles, one-by-precious-one, off the tips of each individual limb. Mother Nature has plenty of time on her hands. I don't. I say grab a handful of glittery strands, step back five paces, and fling like Greg Maddux.

This is a preventative measure, the perfect antidote for post-Christmas blues. Forty-eight hours after the last refrain of "Silent Night" is sung, I'm usually so sick of looking at my haphazardously decorated tree, I can't *wait* to take it down.

Where'd That Hammer Go?

The world of anthropology is abuzz these days because of a startling discovery in Ethiopia. There, a team of scientists from Rutgers University has uncovered stone tools thought to be at least two and one-half million years old.

Researchers say if that estimate is correct, this would set the earliest record of tool making back about two hundred thousand years—or roughly how long you'd have to stand in line at Wal-Mart on December 26 to return the tool kit Uncle Luther gave you for Christmas when what you really wanted was Sega's Ultimate Mortal Kombat 3.

The Rutgers discovery was announced in the scientific journal *Nature.* It told how nearly three thousand implements had been located in the Gona region of northeastern Ethiopia. Based on dating of the dirt and volcanic ash surrounding the tools, the Rutgers scientists believe they are between 2.5 million and 2.6 million years old. Meaning, of course, that the warranty had long-since expired.

> **W**hy must a fifty-dollar shrub be lovingly planted and fertilized and watered for months if it is expected to live, when a discarded tuft of crabgrass can develop vibrant roots and send them into the core of the earth overnight? ⌣

Please understand that these tools were not of Black & Decker quality. They were crude stone "knives" made from flakes chipped off of larger rocks. Scientists theorize they were used to crack nuts, sharpen sticks for digging in the ground, or to cut up dead animals these prehistoric beings may have stumbled upon. But one thing is puzzling the team of researchers to no end. They can't figure out who made the tools because no fossils, bones, teeth, or any other evidence of life was found alongside them.

Duh. And these people are supposed to be educated?

I'll tell you why there is no sign of human activity around the tools. Any homeowner can tell you. It's because the hateful tools had been misplaced. Ig went lumbering out of his cave one morning to grub around for roots and larvae. He set aside his stone tools momentarily to scratch his back, gaze at the sun, or sidestep some wooly mammoth poop. In that instant, the miserable tools vanished into thin air, a phenomenon that has been repeated billions and billions of times over the millennia and will continue to do so until the last fire of civilization flickers out on this planet.

Or maybe Ig's kids were to blame. Ask any dad. You buy a new hammer to replace the one your children left in the woods last week when they were building a playhouse. But before you can drive the first nail with it, your hellions tote it to a friend's house to help with a school project. Poof! Gone again. Nary a trace.

I'm all for scientific research and wish the team from Rutgers all the best as they continue to sift through the mud and sand for more implements. But if they think the discovery of a few sharp stones will lead them to the shop of some prehistoric Bob Villa, they've got another think coming.

The Little Room down the Hall

Let's talk toilets.

October has been designated National Toilet Repair Month. I know this for a fact because I am holding a press kit from the Fluidmaster Company, which manufactures toilet parts.

(Boy, that oughta get you to first base when you're bar-cruising. You cut some good-looking gal out of the crowd, buy her a few drinks, and then, when she excuses herself for the powder room, you say something exceedingly cool like, "Check out the flapper and fill valve on the can back there. That's my company.")

I am not poking fun at the Fluidmaster people. Quite the contrary. I admire their moxie. Most of the time when companies want free publicity, they spend huge dollars to fund campaigns for their local Congresspersonage. Then they lobby His or Her Congresspersonage to introduce historically significant legislation, like designating National Toenail Fungus Awareness Month, in hopes it will boost sales of their toenail fungus ointment. The Fluidmaster people, who obviously work with plenty of bilgewater on the job, apparently didn't see the need for political formalities. According to the press kit I received, October is National Toilet Repair Month because, by gosh, Fluidmaster simply declared it so.

The press kit proved to be a veritable encyclopedia of plumbing history. In fact, I was so captivated by all the information, I took the entire package with me to my porcelain office, just down the hall, for further study.

Did you know, for instance, that the inventor of the modern flush toilet was a British plumber named Sir Thomas Crapper? He was the royal sanitary engineer for the monarchy. He patented his device in the late 1800s. During World War I, American Doughboys popularized his name when they began to use it interchangeably with his invention. Even today, this legend continues whenever someone says, "Excuse me, I gotta go to the Thomas."

There was also a plethora of amazing statistics, the kind of hard-hitting scientific data today's savvy consumers demand. Such as, "One leaky toilet can waste seventy-eight thousand gallons of water a year—enough to fill a backyard swimming pool."

(So *that's* how they fill swimming pools! Who would have ever imagined? But don't their arms get tired of flushing?)

Anyway, I was particularly intrigued by this information because we have just undergone major plumbing surgery at the Venable estate. We had been bothered by the same aggravating symptoms mentioned in the press release—specifically, "handle jiggling, wasted water, late-night noises, and leaks." We also had toilet problems. The press kit included dye tablets to put into the tank to detect if the flapper was leaking. Then it listed several easy-to-follow steps to make the necessary repairs.

I could have used the tablets and the information, but I didn't need them. Our toilets got fixed without help from either the press kit or a professional plumber. They got fixed because my wife did the job. She lifted the lids on the back of each toilet. She correctly identified the problems. She went to the hardware store and bought the proper whachamacallits and schjogmflagits to remedy the situation. Then she rolled up her sleeves and went to work.

I assisted by complaining loudly the entire time the water was turned off, making it dang-near impossible for me to brew a decent pot of coffee.

The Definitive word on words

When spring catalogs start arriving at my house, I know warm weather is just around the corner.

It's a *very long* corner, however. Considering the way the catalog people insist on rushing every season, ads for spring wares typically show up shortly after Halloween. One year during Thanksgiving week, I received four spring catalogs in the mail. Two were for fishing equipment, one for garden supplies, one for general merchandise.

I don't know why these companies continue to flirt with me, for I hardly ever buy from them. I'll bet I don't place one order for every two dozen catalogs that come to my house. But as a patriotic American, I try to do my part for tree-killing.

Most people browse through a spring seed catalog or a spring fishing catalog and start daydreaming of balmy mornings in May when, equipped with the latest tools or lures, they can attack the soil or the water with renewed passion. Not me. Even if I spent five thousand dollars on all that junk, the weeds would still flourish in my garden and I would still come home from the lake skunked.

Instead, I enjoy looking at catalogs through the eyes of a writer to see how a mundane item like a vegetable seed or a bass bait can be described over and over, page after page, year after year, and never sound the same. I am *soooo* envious of this skill.

Consider cucumbers. If I was writing a catalog, I would say something like, "These are elongated, green veggies that grow on a vine. They can be eaten fresh or pickled. Some people use them in sandwiches, but I don't recommend the practice because cucumber sandwiches taste yucky." Yet the Burpee catalog I received devoted eleven photographs and approximately six hundred words to describe fifteen varieties of the crazy things.

As far as I can tell, the Early Pride hybrid cucumber looks just like the Fanfare hybrid cucumber. But, according to the catalog writers, the Early Pride hybrid "bears huge crops of gorgeous cukes; harvest starts early and keeps on producing for many weeks; dark green fruits are eight and one-half inches by two inches with crisp, juicy flesh; plants are powdery mildew and mosaic tolerant," while the Fanfare Hybrid "has it all: great taste, compact plants, and excellent disease resistance to keep the harvest going; straight eight-to-nine-inch cukes are dark green and extremely uniform."

Same thing with plastic worms. With me at the keyboard, these would be "colored, flavored plastic strips that look like nothing you actually see in the water, but bass will bite them." But in the spring fishing catalog I got from Cabela's, there are more than fifty photos and Izaak-Walton-only-knows-how-many words devoted to plastic worms, eels, minnows, grubs, lizards, tadpoles, and leeches in a rainbow of colors.

According to the catalog, Zoom plastic worms "have been fooling bass for years. Fish will often literally fight just to hang onto one of the Zoom offerings because of the feel and taste." And just one column away, here's what the catalog says about Berkley Tournament Strength Power Worms: "Two times the power in the world's best bass worm! Twice the amount found in regular Power Worms! Tournament Strength Power Worms are guaranteed to give you that extra edge to catch big bass."

Remarkable. Where do these people find the verbiage to fill all this space? Is there a word mine somewhere, with thick, rich seams of nouns, verbs, adjectives, and adverbs that spew from the ground and tumble into railcars by the ton?

I hope so—and I'm anxiously waiting on the spring catalog that offers maps to it. Now, *there's* a product worth buying.

The Epitome of Good Health

I am, without question, the healthiest man in America. And my long-suffering wife is the healthiest woman. I base these bold statements on the facts that: (a) Americans need more germs and bacteria in their bodies and (b) Mary Ann and I have been up to our elbows in germs and bacteria.

My wife and I are so healthy, the funeral industry will probably start lobbying against us. At the current rate of our healthiness, she and I may live another hundred years—which is about how long it should take for the aroma in our garage to return to its former state.

A geneticist from Tufts University believes people are becoming too germ-conscious for their own good. Speaking at an infectious disease conference in Atlanta, Stuart Levy said manufacturers and advertisers have induced Americans to waste hundreds of millions of dollars on anti-bacterial soaps and detergents. Levy says we need a few cooties to keep our immune systems running at peak efficiency.

Worry not. If you are short a few bazillion germs, Mary Ann and I have plenty to spare. We received this bacterial windfall when I was walking through our garage and noticed that the upright freezer, which normally hums, was not humming. I opened the door and gazed upon the mother lode of good health.

Apparently a week earlier, while we were at the beach, a circuit breaker tripped in the garage. That's when the freezer quit humming and more than forty pounds of meat began to thaw. It was exceedingly thawed by the time I discovered it. Indeed, some of it was thawed to a stage they describe in the meat-processing business as "liquid."

I should have expected something like this would happen. We Venables—who vacation en masse with in-laws, out-laws, and other hangers-on—have a proud tradition of discovering household disasters when we get back from the beach. A few years ago, my brother Rick was greeted by an indoor waterfall when he came home. The supply line on his upstairs toilet had erupted while we were away. Given the nature of gravity, the resulting overflow soaked carpets and busted ceiling tiles through all three stories of his house. To the tune of thirty-two hundred buckazoids.

It was my turn this time around. This was my wild game freezer. The liquid stuff that went into plastic garbage bags had been deer, ducks, geese, wild turkey, bass, and crappie in their earlier lives. With the exception of the deer meat, which had been commercially processed, I had cleaned and packaged every item. Our up-to-the-elbows-in-good-health

---

Did you ever get that feeling that something, or somebody, was out to get you? A few years ago, Knoxvillians Clark and Ann Julius installed underground utilities. They developed a pretty lawn atop it. Naturally, the main power line under the street promptly went bananas, and in the course of repairs, their yard had to be ripped up. Just as that wound was healing—zappo!—a bolt of lightning fried their buried telephone and TV cable lines. Back came the heavy equipment.

Ann blamed a decorative troll, or "tomtar" in Swedish parlance, she had purchased several months earlier in Stockholm. According to Scandinavian legend, tomtars bring good luck to any household. Maybe this tomtar is not fluent in Scandinavian legend.

"I'll give him one more chance," she said to me. "Another lawn episode like these, and he's going back to Stockholm!" 〜

exercise gave Mary Ann an idea of how much fun meat-processing—or toxic waste disposal, as the case may be—truly is.

But to be perfectly Pollyannaish about it, things could have been worse. The meltdown had not reached the gag-a-maggot stage. The aroma in our garage right now is from blood—*muuuuch* blood—that pooled into the floor of the freezer and drained into the catch basin below. The two and one-half-hour cleanup required copious rolls of paper towels and plenty of ammonia washdowns, but at least the freezer is back in service.

In addition, if I've got to lose a freezer full of meat, summer is the best time of year for it to happen. Hunting season ended months earlier, meaning the larder was far more barren than it would have been in, say, November or December. Plus, I had taken a huge cooler of frozen meat to the beach for grilling, barbecuing, and fish fries. So the overall loss was minimal by comparison.

What's more, this wasn't a monetary loss per se—unless you calculate the hours, mileage, license fees, eats, and drinks spent in the process of acquiring the meat. But it does mean I need to increase my woods and waters activities. Immediately. There are hungry mouths to feed.

I'm sure the boss will understand the necessity for more "field research" on my part. Besides, it'll be good for my health.

Warning: These Words Might Strain your Eyes

I carried a box into the garage the other day, intending to put it on the top shelf. The box never reached its resting place, however. I left it on the garage floor, and it may wind up staying there for months. That's because I made the stupid mistake of reading the warning labels on my garage ladder, and now I'm almost afraid to use the thing.

Back when people had common sense, warning labels were limited to drain cleaner and rat poison. But these days, with liability lawyers poised at every turn, scary advisories have bloomed like mold in a petri dish.

Some of them are downright ludicrous. A few months ago, results of the "Wacky Warning Label Contest" were announced by the Michigan

Lawsuit Abuse Watch, a coalition of consumers and businesses. The winner was this gem on an iron: "Never iron clothes while they are being worn." Another was the sticker on a thirteen-inch wheelbarrow tire that read, "Not for highway use." But my personal favorite was this label on a bathroom heater: "This product is not to be used in bathrooms."

I wish I had known about the contest because I have a wacky label of my own to submit. I saw it on a box of shotgun shells used for duck hunting. It warns that handling the ammunition "may result in exposure to lead." Only trouble is, these aren't lead shells. They contain steel pellets, as required by federal law.

But the warnings on my garage ladder beat everything. Although I've owned this label-laden ladder more than two years, I'd never taken the time to read them until I was working with that box. I started counting. There were seven separate precautions—some etched into the surface, others merely glued on—plus a label from the Occupational Safety and Health Administration stating this product meets OSHA guidelines.

Two different stickers admonished me to be careful around wires because this is an aluminum ladder, capable of conducting electricity. That's reasonable enough, although the "WARNING!" headline and several red, jagged, ZZZZ icons made me start to think I maybe should have bought a wooden ladder—as if I, Mister Couldn't Fix It If His Life Depended On It, would even be fooling around with wires in the first place.

But then the messages began drifting toward the gray fringe of sanity.

One label said, "Do not use this product if you tire easily." Huh? What does that mean? That I should get eight full hours of sleep before putting the box on the shelves?

Another said, "Face the ladder when climbing up and down." Like I'm going to turn around and climb backward? Or maybe get real inventive and climb on my hands? Quite frankly, until I read the warning, it never dawned on me there was any way to go up and down a ladder besides facing it.

The more warnings I read—"do not walk or 'jog' the ladder to move it while standing on it" and "do not stand on top step," for instance—the more I got the feeling I was dealing with an eight-foot rattlesnake, not an eight-foot stepladder. So very carefully, I set it back in the corner where it belongs and tossed the box into a pile of junk at the base of the garage steps.

Aren't I afraid I might trip over it in the dark some day and maybe break a leg? Of course not. I checked the box thoroughly, and nowhere is there a label saying, "Do not leave this box in a pile of junk on the floor of a cluttered garage."

Hot Rocks

In the summer of 2001, it got hot enough to make rocks melt and dead wood bleed. This is not hearsay. I witnessed both phenomena with my own eyes.

You've probably seen sap running out of boards and pilings. Happens every now and then, especially around knots, when the heat really cranks up.

But the sap flow I saw was in my boat shed. The roof on this shed is supported by a row of six-by-sixes. These pine timbers have been in place four years. They are kiln-dried and sealed with several coats of stain. But the intense heat that summer caused one of them to bust out like it was crying. I should have tapped this rich vein and set up a turpentine mill.

The melting rock, however, was more unusual. I can't recall ever seeing anything like it—and I wouldn't have the opportunity had I not (a) gone jig fishing one day the winter before and (b) heisted the rock from TVA.

Jig fishing is a low-budget sport. All you need is a long (ten-to-twelve-foot) fiberglass pole, a length of heavy (thirty-to-forty-pound test) line, a big jig hook (6/0) with a plastic skirt, a cork the size of a golf ball, and a bucket of night crawlers. I have been jigging since the early '70s, and I doubt my investment in equipment for the duration has been over fifty bucks.

To practice this sport, you sit in the front of a boat and quietly scull along the bank, shaking the aforementioned jig and night crawlers in muddy water. When a bass strikes, you set the hook violently and engage in hand-to-fin combat. It is primitive fun and usually the only outdoor game in town during the cold, rainy days of late February and early March.

Jig fishing puts you quite close to the shore. You see rocks and stumps and, sadly, a lot of junk because the water is much lower than at any other time of year. One day on Fort Loudoun, something rather unusual caught my eye. It was a rock with a strange black streak across the top. Curious, I sculled closer and nudged it loose with the toe of my boot.

The rock was about eighteen inches long and three inches thick. The black streak turned out to be a chunk of tar that had settled, and solidified, in a shallow depression.

If you're a longtime Knoxvillian, you may remember the bad ol' days of the '40s, '50s, and '60s when tar was relatively common on Fort Loudoun—or "Fort Nasty" as it was sometimes called for obvious reasons. Environmental laws were nonexistent then. So, largely, was a societal conscience about such matters. Both industrial and residential effluent regularly flowed into the reservoir. I can remember old-timers like Claude Fox and Bob Burch describing Loudoun oil slicks that must have been the East Tennessee version of the *Exxon Valdez*.

Obviously, that was the source of this tar. The bank where I found the rock was in a curve of the channel, so I figured current and wind were responsible for the deposit. No doubt the slick had occurred in winter when the water was down. Thus, this tar had been sealed by water during the hot summer months ever since.

But not during the summer of 2001. You see, I snitched that rock off the shoreline and brought it home. Gave it to Mary Ann, who placed it atop a low wall in one of her flowerbeds. The following August, she was working in that corner of her flowers and happened to notice the rock, which had been baking in the relentless sunshine. It was dripping, like sweat running off an athlete. The forty- or fifty-year-old tar had come back to life.

Any other time, this would be classified a mess. Indeed, if some asphalt company or oil tanker had coated our entire garden with black goo, I'd be calling the law. But this smidgen of pollution began to pique my curiosity. I checked it almost daily to gauge the progress of the meltdown.

It was like the unusual situation in Copperhill and Ducktown, two Polk County, Tennessee, communities denuded by copper smelting operations a century ago. These cities became wastelands, one of the worst environmental nightmares in our state's history. It took seventy-five years of cleanup and reforestation to bring back the trees.

But the refurbishing was too good, too complete. Some of the townspeople began to wax nostalgic for the old wasted look—to the point that a portion of un-reclaimed land will be forever left permanently denuded, just to show folks the way things used to be.

Life is weird like that.

You Gotta Laugh to Keep from Cryin' was designed and typeset on a Macintosh computer system using QuarkXPress software. The body text is set in 10.5/15 Minion, and display type is set in Jinky. This book was designed and typeset by Cheryl Carrington and manufactured by Thomson-Shore, Inc.